SATHER CLASSICAL LECTURES

VOLUME FOUR

1928

EPOCHS OF GREEK AND ROMAN BIOGRAPHY

EPOCHS OF GREEK AND ROMAN BIOGRAPHY

BY

DUANE REED STUART

PROFESSOR OF CLASSICS IN PRINCETON UNIVERSITY

SATHER PROFESSOR OF CLASSICAL LITERATURE IN THE UNIVERSITY OF CALIFORNIA 1925

UNIVERSITY OF CALIFORNIA PRESS
BERKELEY, CALIFORNIA
1928

PREFACE

We have the word of Polybius that a comprehensive view of political history is not to be obtained by isolative study of events or epochs. Doubtless the principle is equally applicable to the ideal exposition of literary history. Nevertheless, decent consideration for the powers of endurance possessed by those genial auditors for whose ears the several chapters composing this book were originally set forth as the spoken word, precluded any attempt to survey completely the history of Greek and Roman biography. Hence it is that this volume is frankly episodic in structure. The reader will see that in most cases the topics chosen have been determined by the problems, or at least by some of them, that have emerged in connection with the subject to which these studies are devoted. Therefore, the author, again invoking the precedent of Polybius, would prefer that his work be judged more by what he says than by what he neglects to say.

It is also true that no small part of the pleasure that has been derived from the pursuit of an inveterate hobby has come from following the history of the biographical purpose among the Greeks and Romans as a phenomenon in the growth of human ideas. A thread of unity, however tenuous, is thus secured. I have sought to sketch through various stages the workings of the commemorative aim in so far as judicious limits suggested and a humane view necessitated. Biography is one of those genres of literature in connection with which it is refreshingly true that between ancient and modern practice there is no insurmountable barrier. Amatory poetry nowadays does not think back to classical elegy; Juvenal and Horace are no longer canons for the satirist. There are few Ibsens to respond in drama to the promptings of the Hellenic technique. But, as Plato still lives for the philosopher, among our psychoanalytic biographers and our biographical theorists there are some who are finding Plutarch's way as freshly authoritative as did James Boswell. I have therefore not tried to resist the temptation, by contrast and comparison, to show what is new and what is old in the ideals and methods of biographers.

The footnotes into which perhaps too many pages subside will, I hope, not be automatically dissuasive to certain readers who I should like to think may take this book in hand. The apparatus does not owe its presence to any gratuitous dread of writing a popular book on ancient biography. Neither have I been actuated by nervous eagerness to exhibit an impressive bibliography. The book is the fruit of specialized study in fields of which not too many scholars in this country have testified to the lure. It was therefore felt that a fairly plenteous armory of references, brought between two covers, might be of some value, not necessarily to the professional classicist, but to others who confess, as do many people nowadays, to an intelligent enthusiasm for biography in general. Furthermore, I have deemed it only just to render possible critical control of such matter as is controversial or the result of deduction.

The students in Princeton University and other institutions, whom through some years I have enjoyed initiating into this field of study, have always furnished stimulus. One of them, Mr. W. J. Oates, has been a zealous and accurate assistant in compiling the *Index*. Perhaps the book would never have been written if the generous scholars and administrators of the University of California had not rendered possible my sojourn among them, with its attendant duty and privilege of publication. Now that the book is done, *sit onus eis leve*.

Princeton, New Jersey,
April 10, 1928.

CONTENTS

CHAPTER I

THE COMMEMORATIVE SPIRIT AND ITS EARLY EXPRESSION AMONG THE GREEKS

They praised his earlship, his acts of prowess
worthily witnessed: and well it is
that men their master-friend mightily laud,
heartily love when hence he goes
from life in the body forlorn away.

—*Beowulf* xliii, Gummere's translation.

"I have remarked that a true delineation of the smallest man, and his scene of pilgrimage through life, is capable of interesting the greatest man; that all men are to an unspeakable degree brothers, each man's life a strange emblem of every man's." When, toward the close of the introductory chapter of his *Life of John Sterling*, Carlyle penned these words, he was responding to an instinct well-nigh generic among biographers. Biography is a branch of literary production that seems spontaneously to move its practitioners to unbosom themselves in deprecatory vein. Ever since the beginning of formal biographical writing among the Greeks, motivation and apology have tended to remain conventional features of its technique.

Often it is the significance of his subject that the biographer assumes he must undertake the responsibility of justifying. Not all characters or careers will seem at first sight to have strong claim on publisher's bounty and reader's attention. In such instances the burden of proof naturally rests on the author. Sterling's character was adjudged by Carlyle himself "not supremely original; neither was his fate in the world wonderful." Hence the disarming but justifiable assertion of the universal appeal of any faithful life-narrative, "the monitions and moralities" derivable from it. Sundry other topics on which biographers have been prone through the centuries to touch by way of confiding their intentions to the reader, are: ability of the writer; the propriety of suppressing or inserting this or that material; the method of presentation; rhetorical form. Perennial is the biographer's anxiety to forestall criticism.

Antecedent to all these considerations is the larger question: Should biographies be written at all? This query has been put and variously answered. "I do not hold," declared Sir Leslie Stephen with a candor admirable in one of the most prolific life-chroniclers of his day, "that the world has any claim for biographies upon the representatives of distinguished men."[1] In the very infancy of English biography Thomas Fuller, author of that inexhaustible mine of delight to the curious reader, *The History of the Worthies of England*, deemed it politic to anticipate the grumbling *cui bono* of that universal type of critic who regards the number of books

[1] *Studies of a Biographer* (New York, G. P. Putnam's Sons, 1898-1902), III, 220.

already in the world as a personal grievance. The excellent Fuller set forth by way of preface five ends which were to confer upon his work exemption from what he girds at in chapter 10 as "the numerosity of useless books." Hearken to his quaint blending of piety and canniness:

> Know then, I propound five ends to myself in this Book; first, to gain some glory to God; secondly, to preserve the memories of the dead; thirdly, to present examples to the living; fourthly, to entertain the reader with delight, and lastly (which I am not ashamed publicly to profess), to procure some honest profit to myself.

In the long series of apologetic prefaces written by biographers from Isocrates to Boswell, this is a veritable classic, presenting as it does a fairly adequate synopsis of the conceivable motives that through the centuries have affected the biographer's task.

That there would be in time to come grounds for plangent caviling at the "numerosity of needless" biographies, Thomas Fuller probably did not expect. Nevertheless, at present a cynical critic easily makes out a case along the lines of Sir James Barrie's outburst: "No one is so obscure nowadays but that he can have a book about him."[2] Biography long since has established itself as a literary kind. Witness the existence of such booklets as have come from the pens of Sidney Lee[3] and W. R. Thayer.[4] In publishers' lists and in weekly reviews biography has its caption along with the other categories of literature. Satirical comments on the reckless fecundity

[2] *Courage.* The Rectorial Address delivered at St. Andrews University, May 3, 1922 (London, Hodder and Stoughton), 27.

[3] *Principles of Biography* (Cambridge, The University Press, 1911).

[4] *The Art of Biography* (New York, Charles Scribner's Sons, 1920).

of the muse of biography (would she be named Mnemosyne?) meet one on every hand. Can one imagine a chance circle of bookish persons applying to our time Lord Bacon's expression of amazement that "the writing of lives should be no more frequent"?[5] Would Carlyle, if he were alive today, cling to his assertion that "there are many more men whose history deserves to be recorded than persons willing and able to record it"?[6]

It is true that biographers endowed with talent commensurate with the highest performance of their task have been rare birds always. But the "penury of English biography" of which Doctor Johnson complained in his *Life of Cowley* has long since given way to an embarrassment of riches. Willing chroniclers are found for Brigham Young and Jesse James, for persons prominent rather than eminent, notorious instead of noteworthy. It is as if the world had agreed to follow a procedure reprobated by Bishop Warburton in the case of a certain eighteenth-century biographer of Boileau—"lay it down as a principle that every life must be a book."[7] This is to make a biography as inevitable as a headstone unless the subject, with something of the foresight displayed by the Chinaman in respect to his coffin, has forestalled the necessity of a biography by writing an autobiography. Walter Scott's alarm at what he describes as a contemporary "rage for literary anecdote and private history,"[8] Stephen's phrase

[5] *De augmentis scientiarum* ii. 7; trans. by James Spedding in *The Works of Francis Bacon*, collected by James Spedding, R. L. Ellis, and D. D. Heath (London, Longmans and Co., 1870).

[6] *First Essay on Richter*, beginning.

[7] *In* the introductory chapter of Boswell's *Life of Samuel Johnson*.

[8] J. G. Lockhart, *The Life of Sir Walter Scott* (Edinburgh, Constable, 1902), I, 1.

"victim of a biography"[9] are intimate revelations of a point of view that the excesses of biographical composition engendered in an autobiographer and a biographer. In Stephen's case the pleasant irony of the situation is enhanced if we recall in passing that he did not escape the dreadful peril. Notwithstanding his deathbed admonition that "any sort of 'life' of me is impossible," Mr. Maitland[10] and other friends to the number of three score refused to take him at his word.

This deluge of biographies is a modern phenomenon. In antiquity, so far as I know, not even a satirist found provocation for our so trite railings against the redundancy of biographies. A Horace could jeer at overproduction in poetry with his

> Scribimus indocti doctique poemata passim.
> —*Epist.* ii. 1, 117.

Juvenal's detestation of the quantities of machine-made poetry of his day matched Keats's stricture on eighteenth-century poetasters:

> Easy was the task:
> A thousand handicraftsmen wore the mask
> Of Poesy.

But, to the ancient mind in general, the danger was rather that the path of glory might lead not merely to the grave but to oblivion. This was the string that antiquity was wont to pluck in poetry and in prose. Sir Thomas Browne's courtly language: "The iniquity of oblivion blindly scattereth her poppy, and deals with the memory of man without

[9] *Ibid.*

[10] F. W. Maitland, *The Life and Letters of Leslie Stephen* (New York, G. P. Putnam's Sons, 1908). See the preface and introduction, p. 2.

distinction to merit of perpetuity" (*Hydriot.* chap. 5), echoes the recurrent burden of the old-time threnody. "The valorous great, unsung, deep darkness holdeth" runs the melancholy commonplace in Pindar's words (*Nemean* vii. 12–13); Theocritus repeats the theme (*Idyll* xvi. 42 ff.). And Horace, for every schoolboy, sounds the pensive strain in his

> Paulum sepultae distat inertiae
> celata virtus,
>
> Unstoried manhood differs scarce from
> poltroonery entombed.
>
> —*Carm.* iv. 9, 29, 30.

In the pedestrian utterances of ancient biographers and historians of literature one meets the same obvious conceit. Thus Cicero points out in the *Brutus*, our portrait-gallery of Roman orators, that the poetry of Ennius alone preserved the memory of the eloquence of Cethegus; otherwise the world would have forgotten him "ut alios fortasse multos."—(*Brutus* xv. 60). The name of Agricola, Tacitus prophesies, will never be obliterated from the scrolls of fame, though many of the worthies of former time are as completely lost to memory as are their inglorious contemporaries.—(*Agricola* 46, 4).

To the modern consciousness it may well appear paradoxical that the jealous concern for posthumous fame voiced in these moralizings did not lead the classic peoples to an early recourse to the biographical form. However, not until the sun of Greek creative genius had passed its apogee did biography arise, in its normal aspect, as a separate history in prose of the whole life of a man. A partial validity may be granted to Sir Sidney Lee's remark that "biography exists to satisfy a natural instinct in man —the commemorative instinct."[11] Nevertheless, it is a fact of literary history that the genesis of formal biography among the Greeks and its revival since the Renaissance were not due merely to the possession by a nation of the commemorative impulse. The question of the origin of biography is not so simple. Formal biography has ever been a child late born in the family of literature.

At no period of their civilization did the inhabitants of the Hellenic world display that deep-seated passion for the perpetuation of self which, rooted in religious belief, moved the Egyptian kings and magnates to resort in the third millenium before Christ to their grandiose pictorial and monumental biographical records.[12] The Roman temperament, in this respect substantially in contrast with the Greek, was addicted to the composition of state and family chronicles designed to keep past generations in the memory of the living. Preservation of wax masks of dead ancestors and the exhibition of these dismal crudities of portraiture in the streets of Rome whenever a member of a patrician family was borne to the pyre, were customs alien to Hellenic folkway. Yet, if ever a race had a genius for commemoration, the Greeks had. They tended, however, toward idealistic rather than toward realistic and material methods.

Reverence for the great individuals of the past was part and parcel of the primitive religious con-

[11] *Op. cit.* 7.

[12] C. H. Breasted, *A History of Egypt from the Earliest Times to the Persian Conquest* (ed. 2; New York, Charles Scribner's Sons, 1916), 109, 133; A. Wiedemann, *Das alte Aegypten* (Heidelberg, Karl Winter, 1920), 388.

cepts of the Hellenic peoples. As students of Greek religion have prosecuted their labors, the commanding place occupied in religious belief by hero-worship and ancestor-worship has more and more clearly revealed itself. The books of Pfister[13] and Farnell,[14] two recent works in this field, give ample evidence of the wide dissemination and the hoary antiquity in Greek life of hero cults. Hero-worship and the ancestor-worship which might expand into hero-worship when the dead progenitor's deeds had lifted him above the common ruck and his virtues had impressed themselves on a public larger than the knot of clansmen gathered around the family hearth, are alike observances that found their origin in the will to commemorate isolated personalities. Besides pious veneration for the great departed, other motives, to be sure, contributed to the vitality of hero-worship in Greek life. There was the thought that the force of supermanhood could still make itself felt from beyond the grave. The tomb of the hero was a talisman, effective as a palladium in time of war. His beneficent activity, or *dynamis*, survived him in various departments of human life. However, these considerations do not alter the fact that religion itself made the Greek a devout celebrater of past and gone individual eminence.

Nor is this the whole story. Because the Greek was a Greek, he did not limit his devotion to the gestures of ritual, to libations and burnt offerings. As the sparks fly upward, he turned to poetry. The "Acts" of the heroes were set forth in song. In this

[13] Friedrich Pfister, *Der Reliquienkult im Altertum* (Giessen, A. Töpelmann, 1909–12).

[14] L. R. Farnell, *Greek Hero Cults and Ideas of Immortality* (Oxford, Clarendon Press, 1921).

sacred, commemorative poetry the biographical impulse was as truly operative as it was later to be in the composition of the several portrayals of the deeds and the sufferings of the Saints—the *Acta Sanctorum*, the *Passiones*, and the *Martyria*. Thus, while biography as a literary genre is of late development in the Greek world, some of the stimuli that ultimately impel to biography manifested themselves primevally.

More generations before Homer than we can estimate, in the lands bordering the Aegean, fancy had reached a stage of refinement at which it was realized that marble and bronze do not constitute the only memorials. The *Iliad* and the *Odyssey* form the treasuries into which the several nuggets were gathered, by how many hands, after what processes of refinement, do not here concern us. Certain it is that there was a common stratum of payrock, whether the delvers were one chiefly, or many. Taught by the Homeric minstrelsy, we can understand how it was that a race capable of embalming so imperishably the personalities of tribal heroes and their deeds of derring do, had no reason to erect pyramids or, until the days of decadence, to flaunt the bombast of long inscriptional records. Before the dawn of what we call Greek literature, there were bards who knew how to couch in artistic style the life-histories of warrior princes; there was a public ready to lend its ears to these works of commemoration.

Some ten years since, a German contributor[16] to our subject protested because the Homeric poems

[16] A. von Mess, "Die Anfänge der Biographie und der psychologischen Geschichtsschreibung in der griechischen Literatur, II," *R. M.* LXXI (1916), 79, 80.

had been left out of account as items in the history of ancient biography. The technical expositors of this branch of classical learning have, it is true, chosen to confine their studies to areas rather literally restricted. Ivo Bruns's classic work[16] assumes to deal with the evolution of the delineation of personality in the authors of the fifth and fourth centuries B.C. Friedrich Leo, whose book[17] on Graeco-Roman biography has stood through a quarter of a century as a *vade-mecum* for students of our subject, was concerned professedly with the development of biography as a prose form. Chronological and formal limitations tend in matters pertaining to the growth of human ideas to clip the wings of truth. To write the whole story of biographical evolution among the ancients, one must frame a definition broad enough to cover various artistic, verbal records of the deeds, personality, and character of the human unit—records that modern biography would not consent to house. Transmission of personality begins so long a time before Herodotus and Thucydides, Isocrates and Xenophon, that the literary historian, addressing himself to the theme, may well be moved to echo the preface of the harassed Odysseus and inquire: "What, then, shall I make the beginning of my tale? What its end?"

These meditations, will, it is hoped, make clear the reasons that commend entrance into the path that this discourse has taken and justify our pursuing farther the theme of biographical primitives.

[16] *Das literarische Porträt der Griechen im fünften und vierten Jahrhundert vor Christi Geburt* (Berlin, W. Hertz, 1896).

[17] *Die griechisch-römische Biographie nach ihrer litterarischen Form* (Leipzig, Teubner, 1901).

It is a far cry from heroic saga to formal biography. Yet the impulse that fostered saga has remained one of the incentives to biography throughout the centuries. *One* of the incentives, I say, because that happy formula "The commemorative instinct" has long since ceased fully to cover the case. Even among the ancients the time came when the informative and the monitory purposes became primarily influential in the production of annals of the individual life. The way in which a man had lived became an object of inquiry desirable for the sake of knowledge and as a model for human conduct rather than for the sake merely of handing down his memory to posterity. Nowadays, the commemorative desire is indubitably the chief pretext in the making of many a biography. For example, Lady Jebb's[18] life of her husband, Professor George Herbert Palmer's[19] tribute to his wife, are items in a countless series of biographical works primarily expressive of the memorial spirit.

But, while we have not denied ourselves the luxury of pious tribute and family biography, we, as a matter of course, respond to the promptings of historical interest and intellectual curiosity. We have discovered, far more poignantly than the ancients ever experienced it, an enthusiasm for reliving with those who have strutted the stage of life every scene of their drama, grand or petty, inspiring or pitiable. The modern delectation for realism stirs the wish to press behind the scene and to feast inquisitive eyes on the sight of the player,

[18] *Life and Letters of Sir Richard Claverhouse Jebb* (Cambridge, The University Press, 1907).

[19] *The Life of Alice Freeman Palmer* (Boston, Houghton Mifflin, 1908).

when, presumably free from prying gaze, he has doffed mask, wig, and buskins. Ponder on such revelations of twentieth-century biography as Wordsworth's French love-child, O. Henry's prison cell. Add Lytton Strachey's *Queen Victoria*, Gamaliel Bradford's *Damaged Souls*, Maurois' *Ariel*, Lucas-Dubreton's *Samuel Pepys*. In these cases it would be absurd to conjure with talk of the commemorative instinct. Not its spur impels us to snatch away the veil from imperfect mortality, to bare, as the up-to-date life-narrator each day is trying to expose, the actual man's or woman's play of mentality, pulsations of emotion, experiences of the soul.

Our German contributor is right. The *Iliad* and the *Odyssey* are replete with the life-histories of personages. The Greeks themselves believed that these figures had once walked beneath the sun and, as corporeal men and women, breathed the breath of life. In the case of many of the Homeric heroes, present-day scholarship is tending to turn far back on the path that leads to the Greek point of view and to admit the presence of rich stores of actuality in Hellenic saga. Every fresh misgiving expressed concerning the universal validity of the theory that the epic heroes and heroines are mere degradations of old deities, 'faded divinities' as the term is, serves to enhance the biographical quality of great tracts of epic material.[20] The poems as we have them argue for the early existence of a literary finesse capable of something beyond the narrative ballad celebrating the adventures of the tribal hero. The primitive craftsman possessed no mean powers of characterization.

[20] *See* Farnell, *op. cit.* 280 ff.

To be sure, the fashion was once upon a time to deny this element of artistry to the Homeric poems. The poet, we were told, dealt in types, not in individual figures.[21] It may be admitted that the emotional reactions of the Homeric worthies and their moral standards exhibit a certain sameness. But to aver that power of characterization is foreign to the art of the Homeric poems is to shut one's eyes to the pragmatic test. The several figures take shape before us as clearly limned personalities of flesh and blood. The gargoyle physiognomy of Thersites does not merely symbolize the shameless effrontery embodied in his name. Even he, individualized as a king's son, has become one of the claimants to a historicity apart from the poet's inventiveness.[22] If in the grotesque ensemble sketched by the poet there be more caricature than portraiture, back of it is the seeing eye. Caricature itself is dependent on discriminative capacity. What is caricature but the wilful perversion of naturalism?

The most doughty champion of Vergil's merit would shrink from taking the floor against Addison's[23] contention that Homer surpasses the Roman in exactness and versatility of characterization, product of a sophisticated age though the *Aeneid* is. Much can be said for the skill with which the Mantuan made the tragic femininity of Dido convincing. In her case a master refurbished the strokes with which

[21] "Its [the *Iliad's*] value does not consist in an excellent sustaining of characters. . . . . There is simply the cunning man, the great-headed, coarse, stupid man, the proud man."—Thomas Carlyle, *Lectures on the History of Literature* (New York, Charles Scribner's Sons, 1892), 19.

[22] Gilbert Murray, *The Rise of the Greek Epic* (ed. 3; Oxford, Clarendon Press, 1924), 213.

[23] "Criticism on Milton's *The Paradise Lost*," *The Spectator*, no. cclxxiii.

Euripides and the Alexandrians delineated their love-lorn heroines, and he created a personage that, *pace* my friend Professor J. A. Scott, does "live."[24] The Roman dipped into the ink-well of his time when he made loyal adherence to a single marriage vow a high point in the conflict of desires raging in the heart of the widowed queen. In many a Latin inscription the epithet *univira*, "one-husbanded," bears witness how conspicuous continent fidelity was in the Roman matron's ideal code of conduct. This and other artful touches that make for verisimilitude in the *Aeneid*, however, pale before the colorful realism of the Homeric galaxy. As an article in the aesthetic appreciation of Homer, his art in characterization has come to be independent of dissentient views as to authorship. Scott,[25] with his well-known predilections for the unity of Homer, states the case for Homeric power of individualization with no less heartiness than do some of the middle-of-the-road scholars,[26] who admit the existence of an *Ur-Ilias* but hold that the epic in its present form consists of a series of superimposed strata.

When a legend dealing with the prowess and the personality of an individual is taken over by epic, that which arose as a segregated work of commemoration is merged on the greater canvas with the depiction of collective destinies. We pass from the incidents of a single career to the march of events in which a plurality of persons participates. The Homeric poems serve as indices to such pre-

[24] *The Unity of Homer* (Berkeley, University of California Press, 1921), 180.

[25] *Op. cit.*

[26] E.g., R. Wagner, *Die hellenische Kultur* (Leipzig, Teubner, 1905) 162–65.

Homeric literary sensibilities, narrative stores, and ethnic usages as properly concern the investigator of biographical origins. The literary dimensions of the *Iliad* and the *Odyssey*, the latter a tale which, comparatively speaking, concentrates on individual action and shifts .with facility into the autobiographical method, transfer these works to the domain of history. The literary legatees of Homer are, in one aspect, Herodotus and the logographers. Greek history, primarily the record of the diffused life of peoples, came in later times to focus its narratives on an especial city or community. The local histories of Attica, the so-called *Atthides*, and the *Ktiseis*, accounts of the foundation of cities, so numerous in the Alexandrian period, were resultants of the operation of the isolative principle working at the same time to produce the history of the single life.

It is self-evident that among the forerunners of prose biography belong, besides heroic saga, many lyric forms that concentrate on the treatment of a personality, and—to return to our previous metaphor—make it the sole picture on the canvas. Hymn and dithyramb, the threnody or dirge, the encomium and its cognate, the epinician ode, centered always or primarily around the deeds and the destinies of individuals. Uniting these forms and biography there is thus a connecting link. Elegy also is reducible to this same common denominator, even if we resist the temptation to invoke the traditional account of its origin in the lament for a dead hero and cleave to one of the modern theories of a ritualistic origin. The use of elegy in the grave epigram conferred upon it a scope commensurate with the lyric forms just enumerated, to say nothing of the fact that this pliant instrument of poetic expression commended itself readily throughout its history for such utterances of personal grief as the *Lyde* of Antimachus, for example.

What dare we say of tragedy? An ancient lexicographer defined tragedy as "the representation of the lives and the discourses of the heroes."[27] Much of Greek drama forms a corpus narrating the life-experiences of heroic personages whose historicity the average Greek mind was not given to questioning. Tragedy drew abundantly from epic, the repository of the *Acta Heroum*. As the story of Christ's life and other annals of the Gospels furnished the material for the liturgical drama of the Middle Ages, Greek audiences were in the normal instance witnessing sacred biography cast in dramatic form. The dramatization of the occasions on which the Athenian national hero, Theseus, stood forth, a Mr. Greatheart, to champion the oppressed and comfort the afflicted, must have aroused in the breast of the Athenian spectator emotions comparable to those with which we answered a few years ago to the appeal of John Drinkwater's *Lincoln*. Blending together epic material with lyric, Greek tragedy made constant use, as a structural member, of the dirge; the dirge was in origin a tribute to the individual dead. Thus far we may safely go in discussing the commemorative elements of tragedy.

Acceptance of one of the newer theories as to the origin of tragedy would immensely enhance its

[27] *Etymologicon magnum* 763. 58.

standing among poetic devices fashioned by the commemorative desire. It is well known that the pens of the *cognoscenti* have vigorously challenged in recent years the traditional literary account of the growth of tragedy from the rude choral dithyramb performed in honor of Dionysus. One of the directions that modern research has taken under the hands of critics such as Crusius, Ridgeway, Nilsson, Dieterich, Pfister,[28] and others has sought the genesis in rites involving the commemoration of individual personalities—mimetic celebrations held at the tombs of heroes, dirges, the practices of ancestor-worship as the case may be. It would be rash here to embark on the troubled waters of this controversy which so many have tried to chart. Furthermore, it is unnecessary for our purpose to descend to special pleading in order more clearly to illustrate how instinctively the Greek mind paid homage to the fame of a great personality by poetic record. We need not say 'mimetic record,' although my own prejudices tend in that direction. Whether tragedy was an outgrowth from primitive mimicry of the vicissitudes of a heroic career, was the result of a blending with hero-worship of laments connected with the Dionysiac cult, or, as Professor Gilbert

[28] Crusius, art. "Dithyrambos," Pauly-Wissowa. *R-E.* V, 1203 ff.; also a résumé of his views by M. Maas, *Woch. f. klass. Phil.*, XXI (1904), 779 ff.; W. Ridgeway, *The Origin of Tragedy* (Cambridge, The University Press, 1910); *The Dramas and Dramatic Dances of Non-European Races* (Cambridge, The University Press, 1915), esp. the Introduction; M. P. Nilsson, "Der Ursprung der Tragödie," *Neue Jahrb. f. d. klass. Alt.*, XXVII (1911), 609 ff., 673 ff.; A. Dieterich, "Die Entstehung der Tragödie," *Archiv. f. Religionswissenschaft*, XI (1908), 163ff. =*Kleine Schriften*, 414 ff.; Pfister, *op. cit.* II, 557. *See also* D. C. Stuart, "The Origin of Greek Tragedy," *Am. Phil. Assoc. Trans. and Proc.*, XLVII (1916), 173–204; R. C. Flickinger, *The Greek Theater and Its Drama* (ed. 3; University of Chicago Press, 1926), 1–35.

Murray[29] believes, beginning with the ritual of a vegetation spirit, was extended to embrace representations of the events of any heroic life, daemonic or mortal, observances involving literary commemoration of a hero and celebrated at his tomb were an authentic folk-way. There is the passage of Herodotus[30]—bulking so large in the apparatus of students of dramatic origins—in which it is related that the inhabitants of Sicyon celebrated the sufferings of Adrastus with tragic choruses. At Megalopolis encomia and hymns were sung each year around the grave of Philopoemen. In such cult usages[31] the Greeks ordinarily put worthies of saga and worthies of history on the same footing.

Between biography and the chief forms of Greek poetry commemorative of personality we have been tracing a spiritual kinship. The ligature may seem too self-evident to justify so many words. At all events, realization of this tie is prerequisite to a philosophical understanding of the rise of classical biography. To the Greek of the literary ages preceding the use of prose, his bards were his biographers. With ages of this literary tradition behind, during which the commemorative spirit had found such complete utterance in forms of poetry already perfected, it was natural that these should continue their sway long after philosophers, historians, and other chroniclers had capitulated to the more elastic prose medium. Some of the pioneer works of portraiture in prose simply carried on the purpose of

[29] *Euripides and His Age* (New York, Henry Holt, 1913), 59 ff.; "The Ritual Forms Preserved in Greek Tragedy," *in* Jane Harrison, *Themis* (Cambridge, The University Press, 1912), 341 ff.

[30] v. 67.

[31] Other examples in Pfister, *op. cit.* II, 497; Nilsson, *op. cit.* 631, 632.

the poetic tradition. Greek literary theory was fully aware of this connection, which was visualized now as an affinity, now in terms of lineal descent. To elucidate: Two of the early specimens of *quasi* biography with which we shall have to reckon, are Isocrates' eulogy of Evagoras, tyrant of Cyprian Salamis, which was written at the beginning of the second quarter of the fourth century B.C., and the similar tribute paid by Xenophon to Agesilaus sometime after the death of the great Spartan king, an event probably to be assigned to the winter of 361–360. Isocrates describes his work as a direct descendant of the poetical encomium, and the first-born, besides. Of this question of primogeniture, much more in a future chapter. Xenophon expresses his sense of the family likeness between the prose encomium and the poetic *threnos* by warning his readers that the *Agesilaus* is to be regarded as an utterance of praise, not of lamentation.

Dirge and encomium have, as it were, the common denominator, praise. The range of the encomium, however, was intrinsically much wider than that of the *threnos*, which had for its sole theme glorification of the dead. But when the prose encomium came, as it did, to be the vehicle for extolling a great personality that had passed away, the kinship of the two forms naturally made itself felt. Hence Xenophon's words of caution directed to his readers: "Nor because Agesilaus is praised now that he is dead, let any one for this reason deem this discourse a dirge, but rather an encomium."[32] Only a too literal interpretation of this passage could suggest that there were known to Xenophon dirges

[32] *Ages.* x. 3.

that could vie in biographical detail and in directness of personal delineation with the *Agesilaus*. Analogy of subject and common laudatory aim must have been the points of contact that he had in mind between dirge and encomium. He desired, as the context following shows, to point the moral that a life such as that of Agesilaus, rich in glory and ended in the fulness of time, should evoke the major chord of eulogy, not the minor chord of grief.

The dirge had an origin as natural to human experience as are bereavement and grief. So long as it remained on the levels of folk-poetry, it doubtless preserved an artless biographical realism which it afterwards lost. As Nilsson[33] was the first to point out, preliterary dirges contained both epic and lyric elements. Along with emotional outbursts in which a body of mourners might give vent in chorus to their personal grief, there was specific recitative by an arch-cantor, or arch-cantrix. The tribute paid by the leader was eulogistic and narrative, the deeds and the virtues of the deceased were rehearsed in ballad fashion. A suggestive analogy to what the content of the primitive dirge must have been, is furnished by the epic threnody chanted by the twelve henchmen of Beowulf as they rode around the barrow. Besides lauding him as ruler and warrior, they

> Quoth that of all the kings of earth,
> of men he was mildest and most belovéd,
> to his kin the kindest, keenest for praise.
>
> —*Beowulf* xliii. 3180–82.[34]

[33] *Op. cit.* 618 ff. On the dirge as a universal folk-usage, *see* E. Schmidt, "Die Anfänge der Literatur und die Literatur der primitiven Völker," *Die Kultur der Gegenwart*, I, vii (Leipzig, Teubner, 1906), 18, 19.

[34] F. B. Gummere, *The Oldest English Epic* (New York, Macmillan 1909), 158.

This résumé of career and character is biography in swaddling-clothes, to be sure, but none the less biography.

Our earliest specimens of Greek threnody, those incorporated in the *Iliad*, are not literal reproductions of the folk-dirge. The ennobling hand of the literary artist has already wrought its transformation. The *locus classicus* (*Iliad* xxiv. 720 ff.), presenting the ceremonial laments of Andromache, Hekabe, and Helen over the dead body of Hector, reveals the selective process and the illustrative aim. Thus each of the chief mourners is made to set forth a theme—Hector's valor, his piety and its reward, his gentleness. These traits have a biographical value; the first two, formulated as *andreia* and *eusebeia*, became stock features of characterization in the later prose encomium. But if we grieve for Hector, it is not because an image of him, complete in every detail, is set before us by direct portrayal. We are enabled to see him through the eyes of the women who best loved him and so to realize what his life meant to them, what his death cost them. The delineative effectiveness of the passage lies in the impression exerted on the reader and in the atmosphere created. Not long ago Mr. S. M. Crothers contended rightly in one of his charming essays[35] that the ideal biography must always take cognizance of the impact of a personality upon contemporary consciousness. The ancients discovered this principle and invoked it both in history and biography. As Bruns[36] has shown on many a page, Herodotus,

[35] "Satan among the Biographers," *Atlantic Month.* CXXXI (1923), 289–97.

[36] *Op. cit.* The following passages in the *Evagoras* are illustrative: 22; 24; 29; 43; 58–59.

Thucydides, and Xenophon utilized this method of vicarious characterization under which a delineator of personality conceals his subjective estimate in the effect wrought by a man on his fellows. The natural aesthetics of Homer anticipated in this regard ancient biographer and modern critic alike.

The Homeric poet's consciousness of the effectiveness imparted to art by the typical and the selective gives premonitions of what the dirge afterwards became as a branch of formal lyricism. The Greek genius in its higher flights was perfectly aware that truth is not conditioned on complete summary of facts, on minute chronicling of externalities, or on diffuse rhapsody. Hence no Greek poet of the sixth or the fifth century B.C. would have thought that, to be effective, his tribute to the memory of a dead man or to the glory of a living victor must include analytic recital of his subject's exploits and virtues. Greek poetry in its workings had discovered the truth that its concern was with the universal and the crucial in life and nature long before Aristotle became dryly articulate concerning this principle. Hence in the dirges of Simonides of Ceos and Pindar, under whose hands the lyric germ in threnody attained fruition, the individual's fate was merged with the cosmic scheme of things. For both bards the composition of a dirge spelled the liberation of pensive reveries on the transitoriness of life, the mutability of fortune, death's certainty, and the destiny of the soul in the world beyond. The consolatory strain naturally found a place. The world of myth was drawn on for illustrative precedent.[37]

[37] *See* Pindar *frg.* 139, Bergk, *Poetae lyrici Graeci* (ed. 5; rec. O. Schroeder, Leipzig, Teubner, 1900); Simonides *frg.* 36, and, if the

However, to relate fully "What Alcibiades did or underwent" would have been an unthinkable breach of artistic canons.

The threnody is the forerunner of the *logos epitaphios*, the funeral eulogy in prose. Each served to release the same emotions, kindled by the same cause. To the modern consciousness a prose tribute seems so natural an outlet for appreciation of the individual life that has passed the universal bourn as to suggest the query: Could the practice ever have been circumscribed by the limits of time or space? Must not the instinct, to which modern humanity responds as a matter of course, have governed all ancient humanity, given the attainment of a certain elevation of culture?

Generalization of this sort has its perils. It is precisely in relation to the hard facts of workaday life that ethnic prejudices may differentiate themselves most sharply. Nevertheless, set prose eulogy of the dead formed a regular feature of the funeral ceremonies of the ancient Egyptians than whom no people has ever exhibited a more fervent devotion to the pageantry of sepulture. A passage of Diodorus Siculus (i. 92) recounts how the kinsmen of a dead person extolled him publicly. Upbringing and education were rehearsed, also the virtues exhibited after the subject had attained man's estate, namely, piety, justness, and self-control. The source of Diodorus made the Egyptian eulogist follow a schematology closely resembling that sanctioned by

broodings of the wave-tossed Danae over the infant Perseus are rightly assigned to the *threnoi*, *frg*. 37 (*PLG* ed. 4; Leipzig, Teubner, 1914). Blass, *Hermes* XXX (1895), 314 ff. classed this fragment among the dithyrambs, and is followed by Pfister, *op. cit.* II, 552. E. Diehl, *Anthologia Lyrica*, II. i (Leipzig, Teubner, 1924), accepts Bergk's classification.

Greek rhetorical theory. Organization of the subject-matter of prose eulogy according to chronological stages was one of the conventional methods of Greek and Roman encomiasts.[38] This is also true of the itemization of the stock virtues of manhood. However, we are not to dismiss the passage in Diodorus as an uncritical trajection of the rules of the Greek encomium to another people. The reporter of the usage, whoever he was, naturally tended to formulate his account of the Egyptian obituary encomium in terms of its likenesses to and—we must not forget—its differences[39] from the Greek encomium as he knew it. Egyptian sources themselves substantiate the account of Diodorus, with a variation in detail that brings these eulogies closer to the domain of literary biography. In certain instances, at least, they were committed beforehand to a tablet or to a papyrus roll and read at some stage of the funeral rites by an officiating priest or a sacred scribe.[40]

Among the Romans formal prose eulogy of the individual dead was an ethnic usage which *malgré lui* put the Roman, at least from the early days of the Republic, far along on the road to biography. The original Greek attitude toward the custom of obituary harangues is unfortunately not so clearly documented as are the Egyptian and the Roman. Sometime after the Persian Wars the Athenians enacted a law providing that at the public funeral of

[38] M. Pohlenz, *Aus Platos Werdezeit* (Berlin, Weidmann, 1913), 268, 269 and notes, gives a full résumé of the ancient practice, with examples.

[39] E.g., the comment that the Egyptians, unlike the Greeks, deemed it superfluous to extol the ancestry of the dead.

[40] I. G. Wilkinson, *The Manners and Customs of the Ancient Egyptians* (edition revised by Samuel Birch, New York, Scribner and Welford, 1879), III, 446, 450.

those citizens who had fallen in battle some chosen speaker should deliver a eulogy of the dead patriots. Those who had fallen on the field of honor are eulogized collectively in most of our extant examples[41] of this kind of eloquence. There is absence of personal allusion; the glories of the individual hero are fused in those of the whole band.

An *epitaphios* written by Hyperides, and the sole specimen that has come down to us from Greek classical times as actually delivered, departs in this respect from its fellows. The eulogy was composed in honor of those Athenians who lost their lives in the Lamian War, an offensive undertaken in 323 B.C. by Athens and her allies against the Macedonians after the news of the death of Alexander had reached Greece. Leosthenes, commander of the expedition, had fallen before the walls of Lamia. In the speech the dead general, a friend of the orator, be it observed, is so singled out for praise that the tribute to his patriotic vision and his valor forms the focal point. However, the speech was delivered at a time when encomia and *epitaphioi* in honor of an individual had had ample precedent, not only in the *Evagoras* and the *Agesilaus*, but also in a flood of such treatises loosed by the death of Xenophon's son, Gryllus, on the field of Mantinea in 362 B.C.[42] Thus Hyperides' departure from the impersonal

[41] I.e., Pericles' speech in honor of the citizens of Athens who fell in the early years of the Peloponnesian War (Thucydides ii. 35 ff.); the *epitaphios* by Gorgias, of which we have only one fragment of any length, Baiter-Sauppe, *Oratores Attici* (Zürich, Hoehr, 1839–50), Pars Post. 129, 130; E. Drerup, "Die Anfänge der rhetorischen Kunstprosa," *Jahrb. f. class. Phil.* XXVII, Supplbd. (1902), 256; the example incorporated in the *Menexenus* of Plato; those attributed to Lysias and Demosthenes.

[42] Aristotle *in* Diog. Laert. ii. 55.

methods of eulogy that had previously obtained in this kind of eloquence mirrors the way of the times in which he lived. As freedom crumbled and communal spirit faded, the individual citizen was accredited with an insular fame to a degree impossible in the palmy days of the Greek city-state. Hyperides, evidently conscious that thus to stress the especial fame of Leosthenes might be censured as an offensive innovation, takes pains to justify himself. He urges that the deserts of leader and soldiers are so inextricably linked that praise of the one is praise of them all.

Therefore, Hyperides' procedure in this instance is an index of temporal significance only. What we should like to know is whether in the fifth century and before, when a great Athenian died, any speaker arose to pronounce, if not in public, then in the presence of mourning friends and relatives, a formal eulogy of the dead man's character and career. No Roman of a prominence comparable with that of a Solon, an Aeschylus, or an Aristides went unpraised to the tomb except in very exceptional circumstances. Are we to assume that Greek sensitiveness was less acute or Greek notions otherwise?

It has seemed worth while to assemble the scattered shreds of evidence from the treatises, mostly technical, in which they lie enmeshed.[43] Characteristic of the early social legislation of both Greece and Rome was the effort to curb extravagance both in financial outlay and in the display of grief at funerals. Solon's repressive measures are well authenticated. According to Cicero (*De legibus* ii.

[43] *See especially* Elsa Gossmann, *Quaestiones ad Graecorum orationum funebrium formam pertinentes* (Jena, G. Nevenhahn, 1908), 14–16.

26. 65), one of these restrictions prohibited eulogy of the dead except at public funerals. Cicero's informant was his admired Demetrius of Phaleron, a legislator and reformer who had both reasons and facilities for acquainting himself with Solonian legislation. It would thus appear that in early Athenian custom prose eulogy of the dead had once had a place, else why the restriction?

With this passage have been connected the lines (1541 ff.) of the *Agamemnon* of Aeschylus, in which the chorus after the murder of the king vents its horrified perplexity in four interrogatories. The gist of the questions runs as follows: (1) Who will bury him? (2) Who will sing his coronach? (3) Shall his murderess have heart to wail him, a thankless compensation? (4) Who, o'er the man divine, venting with tears at the tomb a *tale of praise*,[44] with sincerity of heart shall sorrow? Pfister[45] in my opinion is mistaken in his assumption that the only literary tribute referred to in the passage is a lyric dirge. The chorus has ceased to think about a poetic lament when the second query, "Who will sing his coronach?" has been answered by the third, the sense of which is, Will Clytemnestra be capable of such effrontery? This suggested possibility is natural and is inspired by ritualistic usage. The dirge was a function in which male as well as female intimates of the dead might participate, but in which canonically women, those on whom bereavement rested

[44] The Greek word is αἶνος in the MSS. Most editors accept the almost certain emendation of Voss, αἶνον. N. Wecklein, *Aeschylos Orestie* (Leipzig, Teubner, 1888), 158 Anh., taking umbrage at the notion that an *epitaphios* in honor of an individual could have figured in the thought of Aeschylus, expelled the word αἶνος by emendation. Such a remedy is superannuated and gratuitous.

[45] *Op. cit.* II, 554.

most gravely, were protagonists.[46] Just as in the twenty-fourth book of the *Iliad* the widowed Andromache has first say, so here Agamemnon's wife would at first thought occur to the chorus as the appointed leader of the dirge. The question asks itself and once asked, normal possibilities, so far as the contemplated dirge is concerned, are fulfilled. Hence in the fourth query—introduced, let us note, by a separative δέ—the thought has progressed to another observance marking a great man's funeral. With the tradition preserved by Cicero pointing the way, it is hard to escape the conclusion that this further ceremonial was a laudatory speech. Aeschylus was thus writing in terms of a traditional practice that may not have been perpetuated to his own times in case Solon's sumptuary laws were more effective than legislation directed against the ingrained preferences of human habit often is.

We may well reckon, then, among our precursors of formal biography a verbal, prose tribute to the dead which arose under family auspices precisely as did the dirge, the funeral eulogy of the Egyptians, and the *laudatio funebris* of the Romans.[47] How far back the usage reached in point of time, how widely it was distributed among the several classes of society in the same state or among the different peoples of

[46] In the *Iliad* xviii. 314 ff., Achilles leads the lament over Patroclus, but this does not obviate the performance of a ceremonial dirge sung by women, viz., the Trojan captives, 339, 340. In *Beowulf* the widow's dirge, sung while the body is being burned on the pyre, precedes the henchmen's encomium.

[47] In this conclusion I am in agreement with Paley, note *ad loc.*; Fr. Vollmer, "Laudationum funebrium historia et reliquiarum editio," *Jahrb. f. class. Phil.* XVIII, Supplbd. (1892), 451; E. Gossmann, *loc. cit.*; W. Seyffert, *De Xenophontis Agesilao quaestiones* (Göttingen, Dieterich, 1909), 41; A. Dieterich, *Nekyia* (ed. 2; Leipzig, Teubner, 1913), 88, 89, n. 2.

Greece, we have no means of knowing. There is no mention in Homer of such a feature of obsequies; there its analogue, the dirge, alone holds the field. We have no evidence to show, unless the allusion in Aeschylus is so counted, that the custom survived down to fifth-century Athens when, following the usual law of religious evolution, from family to communal rite, that is, the public *epitaphios* reached its heyday. We are equally in the dark as to whether the private *epitaphios* was committed to writing and took on that documentary permanence that was as breath to Roman nostrils. In Alexandrian times we encounter a type of treatise entitled *perideipnon* or "funeral feast." Such a work, for example, was devoted to Plato by his successor Speusippus,[48] and contained biographical material, to wit, the stock legend of Plato's divine paternity. Clearly, a description of the funeral feast served as the setting for a laudatory recapitulation of Plato's life. These works, it has been suggested, may have been a literary recostuming of the facts of ancient folk-usage. However this may be, the prerhetorical funeral eulogy, as its existence has been postulated, had a unique standing in that it was the primitive outcropping in prose soil of the commemorative vein developed by the Greeks earlier and more richly in poetry.

[48] Diog. Laert. iii. 2.

CHAPTER II

THE FIFTH CENTURY

"With the world of intellectual production, as with that of organic generation, nature makes no sudden starts. *Natura facit nihil per saltum.*"—Walter Pater, *Plato and Platonism.*

Ever since scholarly curiosity began among the Greeks, the mind of man has experienced a naïve satisfaction in mechanically defining the stages of human progress. The names of inventors and innovators, the facts of dates and cycles: By these we strive to calculate our dead reckoning as we voyage over "the sea of knowledge." In the days when man the thinker was young upon the earth, imaginations that could not grasp the wondrous laws of natural origin and organic evolution took refuge in making Daedalus the "inventor" of the lifelike statue, Cadmus of the alphabet, Homer of the epic, Callinus or someone else of elegy. Books on discoverers and discoveries—εὑρεταί and εὑρήματα as the Greek has it—came to have an established place in erudition. The modern man even, supposedly educated to the truth inherent in that sapient formula of Topsy, "I 'spect I growed," deep in his heart is prone to yearn for the graphic charms of name and date.

In studying the growth of a literary form, to satisfy this amiable weakness is often as difficult as the effort to satisfy it is unscientific. One reads of Oriental conjurers whose sleight of hand makes or seems to make a seed mature into a flowering plant before the eyes. The history of literary creativity, especially when viewed from afar, apparently records many analogous feats. Some instantaneous efflorescence seems to follow upon the wave of a gifted generator's wand. Nevertheless, the seed, it will be found, was at hand, a *multum in parvo*, relic of past fruitages and essential to new growth. What says Cicero? "Nihil est enim simul et inventum et perfectum; nec dubitari debet quin fuerint ante Homerum poetae." (*Brutus* 71.)

The *Memorabilia* and the *Agesilaus* of Xenophon and the *Encomium on Evagoras* by Isocrates happen to be in Greek literature the earliest extant prose treatises devoted exclusively to the transmission of historical lives and personalities. They have thus a visual significance. Another deep blaze on the trail is marked by sundry chapters in the first and the second books of Xenophon's *Anabasis*. In his story of the Expedition of the Ten Thousand, Xenophon appends to the accounts of the deaths of Cyrus the Younger and some of the Greek generals who supported the Persian Young Pretender in his ill-starred campaign, biographical epilogues, sketching the lives and the characters of the dead leaders. Even the plodding schoolboy who struggles through these epilogues in the original—a phenomenon too infrequent in these degenerate days—is aware that he is reading incipient biography. These interludes in the *Anabasis*, and the separate works of personal portraiture just mentioned belong in time to the first half of the fourth century B.C. Nevertheless, all alike strike their roots into intellectual strata sunk more or less beneath the level of that age.

Evagoras, ruler of Cyprian Salamis, died in 374 B.C. The average lettered reader is more familiar with the name of the realm than with that of its ruler. The course of literary empire has decreed that the writings of Isocrates seldom fall within the ken of multitudes that have thrilled to Horace's picture of the dauntless Teucer, heartening his comrades "to-morrow to sail again the vasty ocean plain and found in a new land a Salamis of confusing name." Nicocles, the son and the successor of Evagoras, placed with Isocrates, the popular Athenian artist in prose, an order for a fitting eulogy. The piece was duly composed, not many years after the death of Evagoras, we surmise, and doubtless was well paid for.[1]

For Graeco-Roman rhetoric the encomium on Evagoras attained the standing of a model influential on the technique of encomiastic biography. In this capacity, it merits a not inconspicuous place in European literary tradition. Modern literary estimates, however, have not perpetuated the valuation assigned to the treatise on the assessment-roll of antiquity. It has been edited twice only in English.[2] Its significance as one of the earliest products of the

[1] R. Volkmann, *Die Rhetorik der Griechen und Römer* (ed. 2; Leipzig, Teubner, 1885), 327, with insufficient reasons dates the treatise *circa* 360 B.C. A date previous to 370 B.C. is probable; *see* Ed. Meyer, *Geschichte des Altertums* V (Stuttgart and Berlin, Cotta, 1902), 199; E. Drerup, *Isocratis opera omnia* (Leipzig, Dieterich, 1906), I, p. cxlii; Münscher in Pauly-Wissowa, *R-E* IX, 2, 2192, who protests against the view that the *Evagoras* was a shop product, written for pay.

[2] E. S. Forster, *Isocrates' Cyprian Orations* (Oxford, Clarendon Press, 1912), who refers to an edition by H. Clarke (London, Swan, Sonnenschein, 1885).

will to present in prose an isolated portrayal of a historical character, has been completely smothered in the learned pages of professional scholarship. I cannot find that the work has ever been so much as mentioned by those writers who in encyclopedia and handbook have treated the subject of biography for the benefit of the general reader. The wider appeal of Xenophon and the greater fame of the personalities delineated by him in the *Memorabilia* and the *Agesilaus* have conferred on these books a prestige well-nigh exclusive in the popular rating as pioneer steps in biographical writing.

This appraisal of the *Memorabilia*, if left unmodified, might well convey to one unfamiliar with its content and its literary precedents an erroneous impression both as to Xenophon's inventiveness and the character of the work itself. The *Memorabilia* is one of a literary group called forth by the controversy concerning Socrates and his mission in which his friends and foes sought, after his execution, to canonize or to defame him. In this strife, destined to be prolonged for centuries after his death, Plato, Xenophon, the sophist Polycrates, and the orator Lysias were early combatants. All these men undertook to assess, in one literary form or another, the character and the mission of Socrates. Where Plato, Polycrates, and Lysias chose the speech form, Xenophon declared for that of the narrative memoir. He conceived the work in its original plan as a rejoinder to the onslaught made on Socrates by Polycrates not later than 393 B.C. In chapters one and two of the first book Xenophon's presentation is controlled merely by the various counts in the current accusations of Socrates, namely, impiety and corruption of the youth. The spirit is that of retort, not of portraiture.

As the work grew in Xenophon's hands through various stages of composition, his aim shifted gradually from refutation of indictments to positive exposition of his subject's principles and behavior. The typical method is to develop some tenet of the Socratic views as to what most becomes a man in his attitude toward the gods and toward his fellowmen, by illustrative dialogue between the philosopher and another, by anecdote, incident, and the like. This is biography in the sense in which the corpus of Plato is biography. Incidentally, as the enumeration of the doctrines of Socrates proceeds, we meet various photographic touches that call up the human figure of the man, his frugal life and simple tastes, his typical activities from day to day. Xenophon did not essay to present the life of Socrates in a sustained, systematic manner from birth to death. The work gives a congeries of loosely associated glimpses into Socrates' thought on the several ideals of human life, illustrated by examples of his intercourse with his fellows when he was at the height of his maturity. Hence, if we are to honor the assertion, made by Edmund Gosse in his perspicuous account of biography in the *Encyclopedia Britannica*, "We meet first with deliberate biography in Xenophon's memoirs of Socrates, a work of epoch-making value," we can do so only with large reservations. W. H. Dunn[3] in his excellent history of English

[3] *English Biography* (New York, E. P. Dutton, 1916), 237. Owing to loose definition we hear of divers 'earliest specimens of biography.' According to B. Perrin, *Plutarch's Themistocles and Aristides* (New York,

biography repeats Gosse's estimate and calls the *Memorabilia* "the first specimen of deliberate biography." However, unlike Mr. Gosse, he does not leave his readers with the mere statement, misleading as it is in isolation, but modifies it adequately.

In the decade after the death of Socrates it was not a new thought to write down the sayings of a great man and to sketch the *mise en scène.* About the middle of the fifth century the tragic poet, Ion of Chios, played the part of "a chield takin' notes" on the doings and sayings of prominent persons with whom he came in contact, in Athens and elsewhere. The extant fragments[4] of his work (Ἐπιδημίαι or "Sojournings" is the picturesque title) reveal a vivid interest in the personal idiosyncracies of Ion's great contemporaries and—what is rare until a later age of biographical literature—even physical traits.[5] Such worthies as Cimon, Pericles, and Sophocles are depicted, in a charming gossipy vein, as they comported themselves when they were not on dress parade. Memoirs thus have a history prior to Xenophon. His *Memorabilia* was merely focused on one dominant figure, whereas Ion's book resembled the 'Recollections' of persons who discourse nowadays on 'Famous Men That I Have Met.'

Scribner's 1901), 64, Thucydides in his excursus on Pausanias and Themistocles "gave us our earliest specimen of Greek biography—portions of *Lives* with distinct character-sketching." Says J. B. Bury, *The Ancient Greek Historians* (New York, Macmillan, 1909), 153: "The earliest biography we possess is the *Evagoras* of Isocrates." The statement of pioneership thus varies according to whether one means by 'biography' biographical content, or a detached literary product. It is also affected by one's estimate of the literary character of the *Memorabilia.* The point is not of reverberating significance, after all.

[4] Müller, *Fragmenta historicorum Graecorum* (Paris, Firmin Didot, 1848), II, 46.

[5] See *frg.* 6, the personal appearance of Cimon.

The significance of the biographical epilogues in the *Anabasis* as milestones in the progress of biography is a commonplace of modern learned criticism but by no means its discovery. We have the assurance of Boswell that one day in the year 1780 Doctor Johnson let fall the following comment:

> He apprehended that the delineation of *characters* in the end of the first Book of the *Retreat of the Ten Thousand* was the first instance of the kind that was known.[6]

One who has the hardihood to set right Johnson in a matter of petty detail is now safer from the thunders of challenged omniscience than was a contemporary caviler. Hence, with the true Johnsonian relish for another's slips, we may venture to observe that the memory of the sage, if we can trust the accuracy of Boswell's report, was slightly at fault. There is but *one* "delineation of character in the end" of the *first* book of the *Anabasis*, namely, the biographical encomium of Cyrus. A plurality of sketches does not occur until the close of the second book, where the lives and the characters of Clearchus and others of the Greek generals are epitomized. Nevertheless, twentieth-century scholarship must cheerfully admit that Doctor Johnson's observation is substantially correct and did credit to his intellectual acumen. In this *obiter dictum* he laid his finger not on absolutely the first, but on the first conspicuous and extensive instance in Greek literature of the incorporation of biographical material in a historical narrative.[7]

Punctilious criticism can merely observe that Thucydides furnished Xenophon the precedent for

[6] *Boswell's Life of Johnson*, edited by G. B. Hill (Oxford, Clarendon Press, 1887), IV, 31, 32.

[7] Leo, *op. cit.* 87.

the insertion of the biographical résumé, in spite of the restraint with which this kind of data was admitted to his work by the former historian. The classic instance is Thucydides i. 138, where, prefixed to the historian's account of the death of Themistocles, is a brilliant analysis of the intellectual gifts of that expatriated statesman. Elsewhere, in connection with the treatment of a salient moment in the careers of such men as Antiphon and Theramenes, Thucydides summed up in a terse phrase or two their political ability and intellectual qualities.[8] The historian's appreciation of Nicias (vii. 86), like the sketches in the *Anabasis*, is *post mortem*. It would seem that, since the reputation of Nicias for uprightness of character was so high, Thucydides intended in this case to stress ethical valuation.[9] This is exceptional as compared with the other instances; there mentality alone is signalized.

Therefore, Xenophon, strictly estimated, no more introduced the biographical résumé into literature than he did the memoir. As compared with Thucydides, he had a larger recourse to the device; he gave freer entry to moral estimates and to the more intimate attributes that go to make up personality. One can think of various agencies that would contribute to this extension; the simpler, more personal nature of the *Anabasis*, a narrative memoir instead of the history of an epoch in the life of a state;

[8] viii. 68. It is a commonplace of criticism that in praising Antiphon as second to none in ἀρετῇ, Thucydides had in mind not moral worth but the qualities displayed by the orator as a partisan and a political leader; *see* Jowett's note *ad loc.*; H. C. Goodhart, *The Eighth Book of Thucydides' History* (London, Macmillan, 1893), *ad. loc.*

[9] Bruns, *op. cit.* 18, regards the appraisal of Nicias as expressing the general estimate of contemporaries instead of merely the subjective view of the historian. Why?

Xenophon's schooling in the Socratic methods of evaluating human behavior according to the ideals of right and wrong living; his bourgeois but keen interest in the surface realities of everyday life.

As has been remarked, all these specimens of portraiture in prose that loom so large in the literary history of the subject deserve the place in the sunshine traditionally assigned to them mostly because they are palpable steps in the progress of biographical production. There was no sudden, magical flowering. Germination was a gradual process and was stimulated by various forces. The action of these forces in Greek intellectual life is traceable through epochs of different duration back to beginnings more or less distant from the culmination in the fourth-century exemplars already enumerated. In trying to follow the course of these influences and to compute the periods in which they were operative, it is possible to a certain degree to make play with the stock chronological divisions of Greek history. Thus, such a temporal approximation as the Age of Pericles, say, is a sensible cover-term for mental prejudices, literary and philosophical movements that fostered the estimate and delineation of personality. On the other hand, we have seen that anything approaching a complete cognizance of the workings of the commemorative impulse is conditioned on peering back through the mists of centuries to times antedating literary remains. It is also true that retrospection far back of the fifth century is necessary for the study of another basic factor in the evolution of biography, namely, consciousness of individuality.

The conviction on the part of the human intellect that the life of an individual has in itself a value, an interest, or both is a *sine qua non* of biographical writing. The concept of personality must have impinged on man's brain-pan. The Greek has long since been elevated to his pedestal as the discoverer and the liberator of human individuality. Against the dun background of Oriental mass-life, permeated by caste and hierarchy, so despot-ridden that in political theory noble and commoner alike were *douloi*, slaves of the monarch, rises the free individualism of the Greek genius. Collectively this new freedom was incarnated in the small city-state, personally in the life and thought of the Hellenic citizen himself, "with his self-knowledge and self-control," as Mr. Butcher[10] has phrased it.

Modern philosophy, to be sure, expresses its doubts whether the idea of personality as this has developed in modern ken since the Renaissance ever entered into the calculations of the Greeks and the Romans. With the niceties of such speculation the student of biography need not profoundly concern himself. Suffice it to say that, during the centuries lying between the life depicted in the Homeric poems and the meridian of Attic life, individual self-consciousness waxes more and more vocal. Hesiod had constituted himself the spokesman of his own kind, the poor man, to whom "mallow and asphodel were gain enow." Recipient of the olive wand of poesy bestowed by the Muses, the bard segregated himself from the gluttonous clods about him.[11] The notes of self-expression are, of course, vibrant in Alcaeus, Sappho, Archilochus, Hipponax. The poems of Solon exhale the aroma of a vivid personality. As

[10] *Harvard Lectures on Greek Subjects* (London, 1904), 8.

[11] *Theogony* 26 ff.

some one has said, he is one of the oldest Greeks whom we feel that we really know. Empedocles, assuming a hieratic pose, voiced thus the pretensions of his proud ego: "I fare before you a deathless god, a mortal man no more."[12] The autobiographical note ringing in the utterances of these and other writers is matched in works of art, where from the seventh century on more and more frequently we find that the maker has inscribed his name, sometimes with designation of father and nationality. The impulse to these revelations of identity lies, of course, in the individual's realization that he is a being apart from others. The fact has dawned upon him that the *meum* has a claim to distinction as against the *tuum*. Concomitant with the recognition of personality in one's self goes the power to visualize it in others. This is the sound law formulated by Jacob Burckhardt.[13]

Increasing power to analyze the traits of humanity, its ideals and achievements, was bound to keep pace with the advance of individual consciousness and the contrastive ability therein implicit. A thought that was bound to find spokesmen in the age of enlightenment was that a man should be assessed on the basis of his worth as a psychical unit, that the character of an individual must be sundered from the qualities postulated for his class. As everybody knows, in the Homeric poems and in Theognis the man of noble birth and of riches is the 'good' man.

[12] H. Diels, *Die Fragmente der Vorsokratiker* (Berlin, Weidmann, 1903), 215, *frg.* 112, 4–5.

[13] *Die Cultur der Renaissance in Italien* (ed. 9; Leipzig, E. U. Seemann, 1904), II, 25. I owe this reference as well as other matter in this context to G. Misch, *Geschichte der Autobiographie* (I, Leipzig, Teubner, 1907; II, 1926), I, 54 ff.

The Roman's *boni*, *optimi*, and *optimates* furnish a trite analogy in conception.[14] Like the knights of the age of chivalry, the early Greek aristocrat was assumed to hold a monopoly of all things that made life worth living. Graces of mind and body were his only; the churlish commoner incarnated all baseness and ugliness. The letter of the ancient dogma survived to the days of ethical enlightenment in the inclusive formula for ideal gentility καλοκἀγαθία. But to Euripides "a man" was "a man for a' that." Before the philosopher-dramatist had made, in such utterances as *Ion* 854, "A slave, if he be good, is no worse than a freedman," the iconoclastic suggestion that inner worth instead of rank was the ultimate test of character, Heraclitus, himself a great individuality, had proclaimed: "One is worth a multitude to me if he be the best."[15] That same isolative intelligence, ever intent on separating the rare gold from the common dross, had declared that "Man's character is the artificer of his fortunes."[16]

Of course, we are not to assume that such yeast instantaneously leavened the loaf. Intellectual pioneers proverbially raise lonely voices from the wilderness. Euripides, poetic mouthpiece of the age of enlightenment, Anaxagoras and Socrates, his two great heterodox mentors, were men ahead of their time. None the less is it true that in the latter half

[14] Fr. Welcker, *Theognidis reliquiae* (Frankfort-on-Main, Broenner, 1826), p. xxvi.

[15] Diels, *op. cit. frg.* 49; I. Bywater, *Heracliti Ephesii reliquiae* (Oxford, Clarendon Press, 1877), *frg.* 113.

[16] I accept this as the correct interpretation; *see* A. Fairbanks, *The First Philosophers of Greece* (London, K. Paul *et al.*, 1898), 53; R. von Pöhlmann, "Das Sokratesproblem," in *Aus Altertum und Gegenwart* (N. F., Munich, C. H. Beck, 1911), 93. Diels, *op. cit. frg.*, 119 translates ἦθος "*Sinn.*"

of the fifth century the potentiality of the individual in the scheme of things came to be the central fact of intellectual and civic life. Methods making for the individual's success in life formed the lessons which the Sophists professed to inculcate. The conditions of right living for the individual were the quest of the Socratic interrogatory. In this search the human example, with its weaknesses and its pretensions, alike the fruit of ignorance or half-knowledge, was the object of the master's analysis.

Across the stage was moving, in greater numbers than ever before in Athenian life, a brilliant series of figures calculated to arrest men's gaze. Protagoras and Gorgias, Pericles and Cimon, Anaxagoras and Socrates, Alcibiades, Cleon, Critias, Theramenes, Phidias, Euripides, and Sophocles—all were shining marks. Ignored they could not be. Eulogy or condemnation were the alternatives in which that candid directness of the Greek genius, so instructively discussed by R. W. Livingstone,[17] could vent itself. Comic poets, partisan orators, political pamphleteers, memoirists who were unhampered by the reticent principles of formal historiography, found in the human subject their scope of activity. Whether they set up the pillory of caricature, shot the poisoned dart of scandal, essayed rehabilitation and eulogy, they were, in a broad sense, presenting their interpretation of personalities. They were sifting the traits of their fellow-men.

Hence it is that the more one reflects upon these tendencies that display themselves in the intellectual life of Athens during the Peloponnesian War and the

[17] *The Greek Genius and Its Meaning to Us* (Oxford, Clarendon Press, 1912), 74 ff.

two decades preceding the combat, the more injudicious it seems to detach the manifestations of the biographical impulse in the first half of the fourth century from those pertaining to the last half of the fifth, except by the external criterion of surviving performance. The danger is that, by overstressing formal distinctions, we may obscure the fact that the fourth-century examples of literary portraiture mark further advances in directions in which steps had been taken, not alone in the fifth century, but in periods more remote. The prose encomium of a historical personage had had a long history of poetic precedent. The biographical epilogue is present in incipient form in Thucydides, to say nothing of its genetic affinity to the spirit that prompted the dirge and the private *epitaphios* for the existence of which we have argued.

The few fragments of Ion's memoirs show a ripeness of technique and a taste for the anecdotal and the realistic that may well point to a richer development and a wider vogue of this kind of literature than the relics themselves indicate. If we shrink from resorting to this method of inference (rather overworked in literary criticism), we have at least Ion. His comings and goings between Athens and the island of Chios are typical of the circulation from city to city of the gifted and inquisitive souls who were finding "the world so full of a number of things." Athens was the rallying point, the intellectual clearing house for these itinerant *littérateurs* and philosophers. It is an interesting fact that those men whose names are attached to such biographical initiatives as are discernible at this time, were, like Ion, outlanders from Magna Graecia and the islands.

Besides the poet-memoirist, another man recorded in prose the impression made on him by certain figures dominant in the Athenian civic life of his time. His name is Stesimbrotus; he was born in Thasos; the title of his work is (translated) "Concerning Themistocles, Thucydides [son of Melesias], and Pericles." The old-time view characterized this book as a political broadside, conceived in the intellectual levity of the sophists with whom Stesimbrotus is undoubtedly to be numbered.[18] To describe this treatise as a political pamphlet rather than a memoir is a literary distinction that, to my way of thinking, does not carry far. Ion, no less than Stesimbrotus, wrote with a bias for Cimon, representative of conservatism, and against Pericles, viewed by his opponents as a dangerous radical in government and thought. Plutarch, who at times shows a modern awareness of the fashion in which personal animus might distort or satirize truth, waves both Ion and Stesimbrotus aside as unjudicial appraisers of Pericles' temper and morals.[19] For us the important point is not the defects of Stesimbrotus in historicity,[20] but the extent to which he devoted himself to personal delineation and to the private

[18] Müller, *FHG* II, 53; K. F. Hermann, *Ind. lect. aest.* (Marburg, 1836), p. viii; later critics, e.g., Christ, *Griechische Litteraturgeschichte* I, ed. 6, 458, and Bruns, *op. cit.*, 48–50, classed the work as a memoir, although the former describes it as "tatsächlich eine bösartige Parteischrift." B. Perrin's estimate, *Plutarch's Cimon and Pericles* (New York, Scribner's Sons, 1910) 36, a "political pamphlet" that "made no pretence of being legitimate history or biography," rates the work on the basis of modern biographical desiderata rather than by the standards of ancient biography.

[19] *Pericles* 5; 13.

[20] Plutarch seems to have been unduly severe on a source to which he probably had recourse more frequently than surface references reveal; *see* Ed. Heuer, *De Stesimbroto Thasio eiusque reliquiis* (Münster, Coppenrath, 1863), 31 ff.

life of his subjects. The ulterior motive, grounded in political, philosophical, or personal partisanship, the propagandist appeal for or against, were always likely to shape the ends of ancient biography. (Need we insist too strictly on the limiting adjective "ancient" when the talk is on this topic?) The control exercised by such aims over a tractate in which personality is isolated for study and appraisal cannot be set up as a shibboleth against its right, if not to enter the camp of biography, at least to be enrolled among the outposts.

In the first place, a restricted scope is suggested by the title. In the case of men of affairs this form of title is a more reliable indication of biographical content than is true when the name of a man of letters appears in a like caption. A book "On Alcaeus," for example, a frequent type of title,[21] may have been a work of appreciation and exegesis; the poetry, not the poet, may have been the chief theme. In the nature of the case a treatise inscribed "Concerning Pericles" is removed from that ambiguity.

The actual facts of content, when we can get an inkling of them, furnish, it is clear, the most competent index of literary character. The fragments of this work of Stesimbrotus that have come down to us—Plutarch's *Lives* is the all but exclusive repository—deal in the main with topics that throughout ancient biography recur with schematic regularity. The teachers of Themistocles (*frg.* 1); the education of Cimon (*frg.* 3); Cimon's temperamental cast or *tropos* (*frg.* 3); civic ideals, in his case tinctured with admiration for Sparta (*frgs.* 4, 5); his

[21] *See* Leo, *op. cit.*, 105. However, as will later appear, one must not be too sweeping in the application of this principle.

children (*frg.* 5). In his treatment of Pericles, Stesimbrotus broached the topic of personal morals (*frgs.* 9, 10), and also, it would appear, in his account of Cimon (*frg.* 3).[22] This is a canonical rubric in the *chroniques scandaleuses* dear to the hearts of most ancient and many modern biographers. It cannot be due merely to the accidents of survival that in our extant fragments of Stesimbrotus persons and their acts occupy the center of the narrative, that history is introduced as a background from which stand out the deeds, sentiments, and, significantly enough, the utterances of the individual participant. For Stesimbrotus had space for direct quotation and for anecdotal byplay.[23] In this respect also he is a true predecessor not only of Xenophon, but also of the fourth-century scholars under whose tutelage criticism has agreed to see conscious biography making its formal début in the society of literature. In sum, this treatise of Stesimbrotus was the admixture of public and private life that we find in Nepos and Plutarch. It is difficult to see just where this work falls short of deserving the rating "deliberate biography," even if it were not deliberative. Stesimbrotus was a biographer in the same sense and to the same extent that Xenophon in the *Memorabilia* and the *Agesilaus*, Isocrates in the *Evagoras* were biographers—and not biographers.

In a future chapter we shall see how under the hands of the pupils of Aristotle the spirit of inquiry into the lives of men became fervently active.

[22] Stesimbrotus would have been forced to take cognizance of contemporary gossip concerning the relations of Cimon and Elpinice, Cimon's half-sister, and was doubtless among those alluded to by Plutarch in his refutation of the sinister version of the story; *see* Müller, *FHG frg.* 3; Heuer, *op. cit.*, 38.

[23] E.g., *frgs.* 4, 6, 8.

Biographical composition waxed catholic in its range. The lives of men of light and leading in the various domains of literature and wisdom were placed on a parity with the lives of statesmen and generals. However, until the fourth century traces of interest in literary biography are by no means entirely lacking. In the latter half of the fifth century some steps had been taken in that direction, faintly outlined though they are for us. They centered about the poetry of Homer which, notwithstanding the railings of a Xenophanes, was to the average Greek mind of the fifth century as much "Il mar di tutto il senno" as Dante found Vergil. The pages of Homer claimed homage not only as consummate achievements of genius. They were the final court of appeal in many affairs of life. To such a careful parent as the father of the young Niceratus in Xenophon's *Symposium*, the books of Homer were what the *Catechism* and the *Bible* were to stricter generations of Americans.

No wonder, then, that study and exegesis of the contents were tasks that engaged some of the eager intellects of the period of enlightenment. Thus arose a sort of preliminary Alexandrinism which, expending itself chiefly on the Homeric poems, included also a wider range of poetic and musical studies. Stesimbrotus of Thasos joined this to his other literary interests. The names of other non-Athenians, Metrodorus of Lampsacus, Glaucus[24] of Rhegium, and

[24] Heuer, *op. cit.*, 16, calls him Glaucon and identifies him with the Teian mentioned by Aristotle *Rhet.* iii. 1 as a writer on dramatic literature. The nationality of Glaucus is not certain. However, that he was a contemporary of Antiphon, the orator, is shown by the fact that the book on poets was assigned to the latter. His *floruit* is therefore to be assigned to the time of the Peloponnesian War rather than with E. Hiller, "Die Fragmente des Glaukos von Rhegion," *R. M.* XLI (1886), 402 ff., to the first quarter of the fourth century.

Damastes of Sigeum, all of whom flourished in the last decades of the fifth century, have come down to us as authorities in this field of scholarly endeavor which can be traced back as far as Theagenes of Rhegium who lived in the sixth century in the time of King Cambyses of Persia, and was traditionally regarded as the first Homeric critic.[25] The school to which Stesimbrotus, Metrodorus, and others belonged was given to disengaging hidden metaphysical and ethical meanings from the poetry of Homer. But together with the inanities of allegorical interpretation cognizance was taken in the study of the poets of such topics as chronology, descent, literary originality, teachers, and innovations. All these stock items of literary biography actually appear in our few fragments of a work by Glaucus, the title of which is "Concerning Ancient Poets and Musicians."[26] We have to resign ourselves to all but complete ignorance as to what Stesimbrotus may have recorded concerning the man Homer in his work on that poet save the assertion that Smyrna was the birthplace.[27] The titles of the works of Damastes show a bent toward genealogical compilation and the cataloguer's activity. He is quoted as one of the dissentient authorities on the subject of Homer's birthplace and descent.[28] This would indicate that Damastes put into his work "On Poets and Sophists" material of the sort that we know Glaucus handled in the book above referred to.

[25] Schol. B ad Il. Υ. 67, IV, p. 231, 27 Dind.; Tatian, *Adv. Graecos*, 31.

[26] Müller *FHG* II, 23.

[27] A. Westermann, *Vitarum scriptores Graeci minores* (Braunschweig, G. Westermann, 1845), 31.

[28] Westermann, *op. cit.* 30.

The emblematic force of such manifestations of biographical activity as have come down to us from the fifth century should not be too much disparaged. They may well be indicative of a scope of interest surpassing the few relics. I incline to a somewhat heretical view: It is not a foregone conclusion that the expositors of literary history were so engrossed with questions of chronology, technical progress, and the like, that they would eschew incorporating illustrative anecdotes, apothegms, incidents, mythical or otherwise. Matter of this sort certainly had become attached to the personalities whose works were being treated. Biographical legends concerning Homer, Hesiod, Arion, and the Seven Wise Men had crystallized before the time of Herodotus; lore of this kind can be traced back to the early fifth century, and in the case of Homer to an earlier period.[29] Both Ion and Stesimbrotus show that from the middle of the century on there was a public appetite for the episodic and the sensational in the private life of contemporary figures. Why should not this curiosity have extended to include great men of the past? These matters, to be sure, are speculative. I wish, however, to utter a word of warning against the prevalent assumption that the little we can learn about the biographical conditions of the latter part of the fifth century gives a picture actually photographic.

The view has been advanced that in fifth-century Greece there were inhibitions making against a hearty surrender to the biographical desire. A generation ago, the comfortable theory was pro-

[29] O. Crusius, "Zur Kritik der antiken Ansichten über die Echtheit homerischer Dichtungen," *Philol.* LIV (1895), 713; 728.

mulgated that the workings of jealousy, prone in the Greek city-states to assail any man who had raised himself above his fellows, exerted a repressive effect on both plastic and literary portraiture in the fifth century. In an utterance typical of this point of view Constant Martha[30] characterized Athens as the jealous republic which had invented ostracism and refrained from glorifying her great citizens for fear of exalting family pride and raising up a new Pisistratus. In 1889 Eric Lippelt[31] developed this theme in a dissertation to which Leo[32] accorded rightly the credit of laying the foundations for the study of Xenophon's part in the genesis of Greek biography. Lippelt averred that the epinicia and the encomia of Pindar furnish ocular demonstration that the poet felt compelled to avoid the baleful machinations of envy. Hence it is that the poet, instead of extolling directly the individual victor, prefers to make him shine by the light reflected by the achievements of heroes and ancestors who have won similar triumphs. Nor is it by chance, alleged Lippelt, that the extant fragments of the encomia celebrate tyrants and not the citizens of free states. To the same cause is due the absence of realistic portraiture in the fifth century. In this connection Lippelt recalls the popular resentment stirred by Phidias when he carved his own likeness and that of Pericles on the shield of Athena Parthenos, and by the Spartan Pausanias when, after the battle of Plataea, he dedicated in his own name a tripod to Delphian Apollo.[33]

[30] "L'oraison funèbre chez les Romains," *Revue des deux mondes*, XXI (1877), 655.

[31] *Quaestiones biographicae* (Bonn, K. Georg, 1889).

[32] *Op. cit.*, 87, n. 2.

[33] Lippelt, *op. cit.*, 5, 6.

Explanation of the contrasts that may exist between the facts of biographical activity as we meet them in the fifth and the fourth centuries do not lie in such facile generalizations. It would be hardly worth while to combat Lippelt's view, were it not that some discussion of the points at issue will help more lucidly to reproduce certain aspects of Greek feeling and practice that pertain to the delineation of personality.

The epinician odes of Pindar were not consciously organized as we find them because of the poet's desire to forestall envy of the victor's fame. Artistic feeling, rhetorical convention, traditional values furnished him his prescription. The Greek poet practiced in his praise of a living victor the restraint that, as we have seen, characterized his poems of mourning, and for the same reason. In his unerring taste he was aware that the ends of eulogy could be attained with greater aesthetic effectiveness by other methods than by the direct, restricted, personal tribute. Thus it was that the praise of the victorious chariot or athlete was subtly blended with magnification of the triumphant contestant's ancestry, with praise of his city and its tutelary gods, of the games at which he had earned his plaudits. The whole fabric was the while shot through with the bright threads of mythology and tinted with the more somber hues of worldly wisdom and prudent monition. The present is, as the Greek poet realized, often most opulently honored when it is linked to a glorious past. Modern canons of artistry have clearly discerned that it was Vergil's inspired devotion to this same principle that imparts to the *Aeneid* one of its chief merits as a work of genius. A nice perspicacity led him to set in the center of his tale not Augustus, not the lordly Rome of his own day, but the divine founders of the Julian House, their toilsome beginnings, the work that the great end had crowned. This method is the quintessence of effectiveness. It is truly Pindaric, truly Greek.

That the enemies of Phidias accused him of having introduced among the male figures battling with the Amazons apparent semblances of himself and Pericles, does not, of course, prove that he actually did so.[34] But even if the story be authentic and not the fanciful embroidering of later historiography, even if it be true that the bald-headed old man on the Strangford Shield is a likeness of Phidias, as most critics[35] have been tempted by the romantic glamor of the identification to believe, envy of the prominence that such advertisement of self had conferred would not be the sole or the chief cause of a popular outcry. The general umbrage on which legal impeachment could count in fifth-century Athens—and this is the point that concerns us—would rest on a basis more substantial than unworthy emotional reaction. The element of religion would enter in. A decent piety would be outraged by the unauthorized aggrandizement of an individual that involved taking liberties with votive offerings.[36] The sense

[34] Plutarch, *Pericles* 31.

[35] A. Furtwängler, *Masterpieces of Greek Sculpture* (New York, Scribner's Sons, 1895), 48, following one or two previous skeptics, dismissed the story as a legendary fabrication. For the vulgate view *see* E. Gardner, *A Handbook of Greek Sculpture* (ed. 2; London, Macmillan, 1920), 289; J. G. Frazer, *Pausanias's Description of Greece* (London, Macmillan, 1898), II, 312; B. Perrin, *Plutarch's Cimon and Pericles* (New York, Scribner's Sons, 1910), 264.

[36] Perrin's suggestion, *loc. cit.*, that the presence of the figures did not seem impious to the Athenians because the alleged images were never altered, should preferably be utilized as proof that they were not intended as likenesses.

of the fitness of things is no less than spleen one of the eternal verities of communal life. It was not envy that was chiefly instrumental in giving tongue to the protests against the presence of the designer's initials on the Lincoln penny a few years ago—to compare small things with great.

A more trustworthy picture of Greek civic feeling on these matters is forthcoming from Thucydides' account of the downfall of Sparta's Benedict Arnold, King Pausanias. The couplet that Pausanias on his own authority had inscribed on the tripod read:

> Pausanias, captain of the Hellenes, having destroyed the Persian host,
> Made this offering to Phoebus for a memorial.

The historian's account continues:

> The Lacedaemonians at once effaced the lines and inscribed on the tripod the names of the cities which had taken part in the overthrow of the Barbarian and in the dedication of the offering.[37]

Here spoke the cardinal principle of the normal Greek theory. Its central idea was exaltation of the state over the individual citizen. Persons were deputies, functioning merely for the welfare of the community. So victories were won by the state and by the aid of the gods of the state. Gilbert Murray[38] once suggested that the leading rôles played in the Trojan War by the Homeric Pantheon and tribal heroes are an earlier reflection of this national attitude of mind. Against this thought may be urged the objection that a free commingling of gods and

[37] *Thucy.* i. 132, Jowett's translation; *see* B. Jowett, *Thucydides Translated into English* (ed. 2; Oxford, Clarendon Press, 1900), I, 82.

[38] *The Rise of the Greek Epic* (ed. 2; Oxford, Clarendon Press, 1911), 240; in the third edition, apparently, the suggestion is relinquished—*see* 229, ed. 3.

men in all relations of life is characteristic of saga; celestial powers and lordly mortals are invariably to the fore in folk-tale and annals of the brave days of old. However this may be, the well-known inscription[39] from Selinus, quoted by Professor Murray to illustrate his point, is at least one of the most lucid expressions of the fifth-century view. The inscription belongs to the middle of the century and reads: "Thanks to the following gods the men of Selinus conquered: We conquered because of Zeus, Phobos, Heracles, Apollo, Poseidon, the Tyndaridae, Athene, Malophoros [Demeter], Pasicrateia [Proserpina], and the others, but especially thanks to Zeus."

The inscriptions placed on the *Hermae* which Cimon was allowed to set up in commemoration of the victories won by him over the Persians glorified Athenian valor without mentioning the general's name. Notwithstanding this omission, Plutarch comments that Cimon's contemporaries thought that their general had won the highest honor that could be bestowed.[40] Demosthenes outspokenly resents the custom of his time according to which the honors for a victory were conferred upon the generals instead of on the people as a whole.[41] The bronze portrait statue of Conon and the inscription lauding him as liberator of the allies of Athens are pronounced by the same orator honors all but unique.[42] Aeschines also asserts that a triumphant general should find his reward not in special enactments in his honor but in the memory of his grateful fellow-citizens.[43]

[39] *IGA*, 515; Kaibel, *IG* XIV, 268; Dittenberger, *Sylloge*, ed. 3, 1122.

[40] *Cimon* 7; 8.

[41] *Contra Aristoc.* 198; *see* E. C. W. Weber's note *ad loc.* in *Oratio in Aristocratem* (Jena, Croeker, 1845), 504.

[42] *Contra Lept.* 69.

[43] *Contra Ctes.* 182–84.

These are the standards by which to judge the offense given by Pausanias and used as a handle, truly or falsely, in the case against Phidias. These men were accused of having reprehensibly defied the solid ideals on which rested Greek notions as to the relations of the individual to the state. The profanation attributed to Phidias would appear the more heinous because it involved magnification of the contemporary figures of himself and Pericles in a combat waged and won by the deified Theseus.

> Fame and her less fair followers, envy, strife,
> Stupid detraction, jealousy, cabal:

Matthew Arnold's lines repeat a *cliché* omnipresent in ancient literature. It is self-evident that the motive would be found applicable by any writer who was setting himself to record a human life as a biographer or an encomiast. I imagine, if the truth were known, that the concept of envy as a check to biography took its rise in the complaint of Isocrates, uttered in the preface of the *Evagoras*[44] to the effect that, whereas the worthies of antiquity did not lack their due meed of praise in epic, dithyramb, and tragedy, envy had hitherto prevented eulogy of illustrious contemporaries. Tacitus, in the introduction of the *Agricola*,[45] takes a similar line. But the thought of each author is directed toward the kind of treatise he is planning to write, namely, the encomiastic. Each writer is intent on dignifying his work as a departure from contemporary tendencies. To apply such generalizations too literally is perilous criticism.

[44] *Evagoras* 6. [45] *Agricola* 1. 1.

Furthermore, with a potential biographer in the fifth century, the alternative was not an encomium or nothing. The encomiastic was merely one of two paths to follow in giving verbal expression to one's estimate of any given subject, animate or inanimate, person or thing. The obverse mood, the censorious and destructive, occupied just as definite a place in Greek rhetorical theory and practice. In the technical terminology, a *psogos* or a *loidoria*, treatises dedicated to censure and abuse, were the foils to *epainos*, a laudation, and encomium. Both these categories were recognized as vehicles equally at the disposal of any *littérateur* who might feel minded to record his estimate of the acts and the traits of a personage. These forms could be and were utilized in freakish displays of rhetorical dexterity. Witness the encomia on cruets,[46] salt, reckoning-pebbles, mice, and a motley array of unpromising themes[47] that engaged the sophistry of these ancient scholastics. The two leading exponents of these stylistic flourishes, Alcidamas and Polycrates, began their careers in the fifth century. That literary *tour de force*, the rehabilitation of Helen of Troy that has come down to us under the name of Gorgias[48] and which, most scholars hold, is the very treatise that stimulated

[46] The correct interpretation of βομβυλιοί Isocrates, *Helen* 12; *see* U. von Wilamowitz-Moellendorff, *Plato* (ed. 2; Berlin, Weidmann, 1920), II, 119, n. 1.

[47] *See* Fr. Blass, *Die attische Beredsamkeit* (ed. 2; Leipzig, Teubner, 1892), II, 370; T. C. Burgess, "Epideictic Literature," in *Chicago Studies in Classical Philology* III (1902), 157 ff.; Ed. Stemplinger, *Das Plagiat in der griechischen Literatur* (Leipzig, Teubner, 1912), 146; A. S. Pease, "Things without Honor," *Class. Phil.* XXI (1926), 27–42, esp. 29.

[48] By predominance of opinion now accepted as an authentic work of Gorgias; *see* Münscher in *P-W* IX, 2183. Wilamowitz is still unconvinced but believes that the treatise is that which Isocrates had in mind, *op. cit.*, 117. This is a much vexed question concerning which views diverge; *P-W* Halbbd. XVIII, 2181–83.

Isocrates to his later corrective effort on the same theme, is disqualified from consideration as serious biography by the sportive spirit in which it is written. On the other hand, when personages of recent or contemporary history came, as they did come, to be subjects of formal eulogy or censure, who shall say that the resulting treatises were not to all intents and purposes as much biographical documents as are the encomia on Evagoras and Agesilaus? Already in the fifth century we hear of the play and counterplay of these weapons of appreciation or depreciation in the political combats waged about such figures as Alcibiades and Theramenes. Antiphon's *loidoriai* of[49] Alcibiades is a surviving title.

As the story is told, it would appear that the prose encomium and its counterpart, the vilification, came as conscious literary modes to Athens in the ship that brought Gorgias of Leontini in the year 427 B.C. He it is whom ancient critical opinion regarded as the exponent *par excellence* of these methods.[50] Not that he can be credited with having invented the weapons; they had been forged, at least rudely, along with other forensic arms, in the fires of litigation kindled in Sicily by the expulsion of the tyrants from the several cities. Disparagement of an adversary, praise of a friend were bound to be the spontaneous issue of actual conflicts in the ancient court of law. In the *Phaedrus* of Plato (p. 267 A), Tisias, who together with Corax was a pioneer in the systemization of Greek rhetoric, is put on a parity with Gorgias as a practitioner of the pretty art "of

[49] Dated *circa* 418 B.C. by Blass, *op. cit.* I, 106.

[50] The tradition is preserved in Cicero, *Brutus* 47, and undoubtedly reverts to Aristotle.

making the little appear great and the great little." Praising and blaming were the means by which these ends were attained, and so they remained in Cicero's day two of the cardinal desiderata of oratorical ability. Witness Cicero's inclusion of them in his characterization of Cato's oratory (*Brutus* 65).

We do not need Plutarch's report[51] that Solon forbade the abuse of the living in a court of justice to assure us that Sicilian rhetoric needed only to codify the rules of a game that had long been played in Athens. Furthermore, for twenty years before the arrival of Gorgias, the forward-looking minds of the Aegean world had been schooled in the processes of inquiry and negation by other sophists. For the aim of our study it is unnecessary to consider the several phases of the sophistic movement or to take cognizance of the formal methods by which Protagoras and his *confrères* carried on. Virtue *vs.* Vice; Wealth *vs.* Poverty; Tyranny *vs.* Subjection; Is life a misery or a blessing: Such were the commodities that were weighed in the sophists' scales before the eyes of the politically and the intellectually aspiring youths. These discussions of abstract themes were vivified by the use of allegory and of examples drawn from mythology. Back of it all lay the realization that every point of view has its possible negative, every concept its possible alternative. The tenet of Protagoras that it is feasible to maintain two contradictory opinions concerning every subject[52] is typical of the creed that many Athenian intellectuals were following from the year 450 on. Sicilian rhetoric, with its formal use of praise and censure, merely

[51] *Solon* 21. [52] Diog. Laert. ix. 51.

made more explicit use of methods and postulates that were already familiar to the Athenians.

These regions into which the drift of our polemic has gradually carried us form, as I take it, an essential part of our itinerary. To follow the development of Greek biography into the fourth century and beyond, account must be taken not only of the place occupied in Greek intellectual life by the commemorative impulse, of the traditional forms that helped to mould the extant specimens of Greek biography and quasi biography, but also of the rhetorical and philosophical modes and manners antecedent to these specimens. Both Xenophon and Isocrates were heirs of the Gorgian methods and principles. This tradition put a premium, not on truth but on the fulfilment of a purpose arbitrarily preconceived, on making out a case, *pro* or *con*, with literary effectiveness. What though a Socrates, as we shall later see, threw the great weight of his influence on the other pan of the scale? Through the agency of rhetoric, especially as exemplified by Isocrates and his followers, the ideals of eloquent make-believe spread far their hegemony in history and biography. Personal bias is the standing menace to biography. From the beginning the ancient practitioner was exposed to a worse peril, namely, an attitude of mind that legitimated or even dictated personal bias.

CHAPTER III

THE PROSE ENCOMIUM OF HISTORICAL PERSONAGES

Encomium in old times was poets' work
But poets, having lavishly long since
Exhausted all materials of the art,
The task now falls into the public hand.
—Cowper, *The Task*, vi. 715–18.

The task of any biographer is one of interpretation. He fashions in his book the conduit through which is conducted to his receptive audience knowledge of a personality. The image which he holds up to view must necessarily be cast in the mould of his own brain; his words alone form the material in which the effigy is bodied forth. For, effigy it must be after all. However glibly we may apply to the work of the able modern biographer the conventional epithets of approval, "impartial" and "objective," the fact remains that what comes to us is a symbol, a figment of the man that was. So an uncompromising idealist might conceivably insist that the most capable of biographers is doomed to a kind of failure, that the best of biographies must be a deceptive, foreshortened semblance, a mere wraith of reality. What of biography if there were literal adherence to such utterances as Emerson's:

> Do not foolishly ask of the inscrutable, obliterated past what it cannot tell—the details of that nature, of that day, called Byron, or Burke.[1]

[1] "Literary Ethics," in *Works* (Centenary edition; Cambridge, Riverside Press, 1903), I, 163.

or again:

> But there are no such men as we fable; no Jesus, nor Pericles, nor Caesar, nor Angelo, nor Washington, such as we have made.[2]

If transcendental niceties gave no pause to the ancient prose encomiast of personages, he nevertheless felt or pretended to feel a certain sense of impotence.[3] However, his misgivings were not lest he might find himself unable to reconstruct in his mind his subject in the completeness of reality, but lest his own talents might prove inadequate to the greatness of his theme. His craftsmanship, he feared, might play him false. No ancient biographer could ever have cried with Walt Whitman:

> As if any man really knew aught of my life;
> As if you, O cunning soul, did not keep your
> secret well,[4]

or dismissed the possibility that a written record can preserve a vital likeness; no ancient biographer was haunted by that sense of the untranslatableness of a human life by which another modern poet was moved to depreciate biography as:

> Words so truly dead
> They raise no image of the heart and head,
> The life, the man alive, the friend we knew,
> The mind ours argued with or listened to,
> None; but are dead and all life's keenness, all,
> Is dead as print before the funeral.
> Even deader after, when the dates are sought,
> And cold minds disagree with what we thought.[5]

[2] "Nominalist and Realist," *op. cit.* III, 227.

[3] Isocrates *Evag.* 73; Xenophon *Ages.* 1. 1.

[4] In the oft-quoted "When I read the book, the biography famous." The lines here quoted belong to the original version and do not appear in later imprints of *Leaves of Grass*.

[5] John Masefield, "Biography."

Intent on the perfection of the written word, the ancient encomiast went straight to his task and agonized not at all in efforts to pick up the thread that would lead hither and yon through the labyrinth of personality to a lucid goal of psychical verisimilitude.

His business was to magnify, not to dissect. Such analysis of character as he indulged in was shaped to this end. The events of his subject's life were presented with no eye on complete and authentic historicity but in order to achieve idealization. Emphasis on incidents that most redounded to the credit of the man, exaggeration, even, of praiseworthy acts, suppression of failures and defects were legitimate devices. In short, the statue was to be gilded and endowed with the luster of perfection. Agesilaus was lame in one leg. Diopithes, supporter of the claims of Leotychides to the succession after the death of King Agis, urged this disability in an attempt to disqualify Agesilaus and cited in support of the contention the famous oracle[6] warning Sparta to beware of a lame sovereignty. In the *Hellenica*[7] Xenophon recounted how this stiff knee of his hero might have altered the course of history. In the encomium at the most the reader's knowledge of the defect is taken for granted; no specific reference to the lameness was permitted to introduce a false note in the paean of praise. Xenophon the historian thus takes one path; Xenophon the encomiast another, a type of divergence between the two forms sanctioned throughout ancient literature. Again, in the *Agesilaus*[8] the hero's elevation to the throne is attributed

[6] Plutarch *Ages.* 3. [7] iii. 3. [8] 1, 5.

to the sheer deserts of lineage and virtue. There is no hint that Lysander's influence was decisive in bringing to pass the preferment of Agesilaus.

The veneer applied by Isocrates is still more transforming. Evagoras, according to credible history, was assassinated under romantic but disgraceful circumstances. An affair of gallantry and a eunuch's plot figure in the account, the details of which are not quite certain.[9] Isocrates, silent as to the manner of his admiration's death, is content to say that Evagoras lived to old age and escaped its infirmities.[10] The murder is banished from the encomiast's narrative as classical tragedy removed gory deeds from the spectator's view.

Deeds and excellencies are the basic ingredients, of course, of all our surviving specimens of Greek prose encomium of historical personages. How noble the man was, how glorious his exploits are the warp and the woof of composition. The texture of eulogy, however, could be diversified within these limits according to the pattern after which the two sets of threads were intermingled and according to the frequency with which the craftsman drew from one bobbin or the other. Such eclecticism in arrangement as we find is the result less of inventiveness on the part of the individual encomiast than it is due to the exercise of option among established schemes. Taken by and large, the ancient biographer was addicted to formal patterns of presentation. Hence it is, as Leo has shown, that the extant lives of Greek

[9] Theopompus *frg.* 101 in *Hellenica Oxyrhynchia* (Oxford text edition); Aristotle, *Politics* vii (V). 1311 B; Diod. Sic. xv. 47, 8; *see* Beloch, *Griechische Geschichte* (ed. 2; Berlin and Leipzig, Vereinig. wissenschft. Verleger, 1923), III, 2, 99; *P-W* VI, 1, 827.

[10] *Evag.* 71.

men of letters, the *Lives* of Nepos, and the biographies of emperors and literary men written by Suetonius are so susceptible to diagrammatic analysis. Even Plutarch's *Lives*, the high-water mark of ancient biographical aptitude, are built over calculated frameworks, however casually the narrative seems to flow. So the fourth-century encomiast, dealing with a form that in its main outlines had been fashioned by poetry before it was codified by rhetoric, was bound to follow certain grooves.

In one of his essays[11] William Hazlitt speaks of a species of portrait painting once prevalent, in which each face was cast in a regular, preconceived mould. The eyebrows were arched mathematically as if with a pair of compasses; the distances between nose and mouth, forehead and chin were determined according to a foregone conclusion, and the features of the individual subject were afterwards accommodated as best they could be to this plotted design. The figures turned out by the prose encomiast were to a certain extent products of a similar Procrustean technique. Modern biography, whatever an author's prejudices may be for or against his subject, tries to work outward from the man. The ancient encomiast, on the contrary, started with certain presumptions as to the constituents of goodness and greatness, and strove to make the human subject measure up to these tests. The facts of character and career were utilized to exemplify and to demonstrate these presupposed qualities. Thus Isocrates formed in his mind the picture of an ideal monarch to which the figure of Evagoras was made to conform.

[11] "On the Prose Style of Poets."

Further to illustrate our contrast let us consider the topic of ancestry, sometimes prolonged through tediously annalistic pages by present-day biographers. In devoting a space greater or less to his subject's ancestors the author will count on at least a theoretical interest on the part of his readers in the historical facts of origin and descent. Alive to the formative potentialities of heredity, as no ancient biographer could realize them, we feel that we cannot know a man unless we know something of what lies behind his arrival on this terrestrial sphere. We search in the qualities of his ancestors, in the accidents and the designs of their careers for the key with which to unlock the chambers of his personality. In the eyes of the ancient encomiast exalted lineage was a postulate of greatness inevitable as the very fact of birth. In ancestry he sought one of the assets of distinction; he subscribed to the words of the proverb: "The glory of children are their fathers."

The encomiast approached his work with the hypothesis that there were foreordained excellencies without which lofty character could not be imagined as existing. The four cardinal virtues, valor, wisdom, temperance, and justness, which, evolving naturally in the moral consciousness of Greece, were systematized into criteria of ethical valuation, furnished measuring rods. Taking these in hand, the encomiast would seek to show that his hero lived up to this standard of all that did become a man. The virtues were used as receptacles into which the purveyor would gather the appropriate material forthcoming from his study of the subject's life. The cardinal virtues could be and were augmented by subdivision and addition. For example piety, more strictly to be defined as righteousness in dealing with the gods, was not infrequently counted as a fifth.[12] In Aristotle's[13] analysis of epaenetic discourse the number of these pigeonholes is markedly increased.

With all the prepossessions that dictated the attitude of the encomiast and affected the presentation of his material some variety in structure was attainable. But having said this, we must also bear in mind for future reference that, because of the common background furnished by poetry and rhetoric, parallelism both in method of arrangement and range of ideas is likely to exist between encomia that have no atavistic connection. The most patent variation in respect to framework is achieved in proportion as the encomiast adheres to a severe classification of his data under the virtues as captions, or declares for a freer method. If I wish to prove, as our old schoolboy formula phrases it, that King Agesilaus was the flower of manly and royal excellence, I may set down as theorems his virtues, one after another, and utilize his behavior during his career to demonstrate that he was pious, just, temperate, wise, and brave. This method, as wooden as it is lucid, especially commended itself to Xenophon, and was followed in certain instances by Isocrates, not, however, in his most ambitious effort, the *Evagoras*. The scheme, as we shall see, was older than both the *Evagoras* and the *Agesilaus*. Again: If I deem it incumbent on me to show that Evagoras was the acme of human and princely perfections, I may unfold the narrative of his life as it was lived, and, as the story wends its way from

[12] Cf. Plato *Protagoras* 330 B; 349 B. [13] *Rhetoric* i. 9.

event to event, by admonitory nudges I may direct the reader's attention to the virtues as they are illustrated *gradatim* by his deeds.

In the former method the chronicler preëngages the reader's estimate by setting down as a caption an adjective of description, a noun denoting quality, or the like. Hence we might call this the 'anticipatory' scheme. At all events it has a history that extends from the rise of Greek encomiastic biography down within the bounds of modern biography. Something analogous to it still marks the typical journalistic obituary. "Author, educator, soldier, philologist, philosopher": thus read the epithetic characterization with which began in the Associated Press the life-sketch devoted to a great American scholar. So Xenophon in (so far as we know) the first encomium that came from his pen, starts with a foreword, epitomizing as follows the character of the dead Cyrus: "Thus died Cyrus, the Persian that of all the Persians who lived after Cyrus the Elder, was the most kingly and the most worthy of sovereignty."[14] The keynote of the sketch is thus sounded at the beginning. Having set forth the theorem, Xenophon proceeds to demonstrate it with mathematical precision. Through the three stages of boyhood, youth, and manhood, the attributes that befit a man born to rule are analytically expounded. The different categories are plainly mapped for the reader by means of captions and resumptive formulas.

In phrasing the various rubrics and their subdivisions, superlatives,[15] indigenous always to the

[14] *Anab.* i. 9. 1.

[15] Note the succession in less than ten lines of αἰδημονέστατος, φιλιππότατος, φιλομαθέστατον, μελετηρότατον, φιλοθηρότατος, φιλοκινδυνότατος.

mood of panegyric, do yeoman service. Frequent illustration and amplification impart animation and color to what otherwise would be a catalogue jejune enough. For in this scheme the normal materials of biography, such as events and features of conduct in various relations of life, are interwoven as illustration and proof. Anecdote is testimony: Witness the picturesque story (i. 9. 6) of Cyrus' hand-to-hand encounter with a bear. The narration is given as an example sequent upon the caption, "the dauntlessness of Cyrus in the chase." The campaign against the Pisidians and the Mysians is treated not for its value as a historical event but to develop another topic, namely, "the honor bestowed by him on those brave in war" (i. 9. 14).

This methodical system of marshaling his data Xenophon called into requisition also in a life-sketch that is not conceived as an encomium, namely, his account[16] of the career and personality of Clearchus, commander-in-chief of the Greek forces in the expedition of Cyrus. Here the same method of articulation was invoked successfully to bring about insertion of concrete biographical details, such as the lowering visage of Clearchus and his raucous voice (ii. 6. 9). These physical traits, however, are not introduced primarily as touches of realistic description. They merely account for the results achieved by Clearchus as a disciplinarian. Xenophon was not directly concerned with catering to the human curiosity harbored by modern readers of biography as to the looks of a historical personage. Otherwise, if not in his sketches of the other Greek generals, certainly in

[16] *Anab.* ii. 6. 1–15.

his portrayal of his hero Cyrus he would have paid some attention to this item of literary portraiture.

This stiff and tabular scheme of delineation is that which one might well expect would commend itself to a mind like Xenophon's, methodical and forthright to a degree. Nevertheless, a structural regularity that gave satisfaction to a precisian's temperament is not incompatible with realistic touches that impart flesh and blood to biographical embodiments. This fact is incidentally evident in the biographical contexts of the *Anabasis;* in the *Agesilaus* it is more copiously illustrated, as we shall see.

Xenophon was in the autumn of life when he composed the encomium on the Spartan king. Then it is that a craftsman's attitude toward the rigid prescriptions of his art tends to become less strait-laced. In younger days the *ipse dixit* of school theories exacts homage; to mellowed experience formulas and recipes appeal no longer as sacrosanct. Nevertheless the structural plan of the *Agesilaus* shows a compartment-like exactness characteristic of the rhetorical patterns emanating from Gorgias and his kind.

The treatise is transparently reducible to Divisions A, B, and C, each with subheads. After a brief prologue—two sentences animadverting upon the difficulty of composing a fitting tribute to Agesilaus but asserting the necessity of the attempt—comes a joint glorification, also condensed, of the king's ancestry and of the realm over which he held sway. No effort is made to trace the growth of Agesilaus in character and parts through the formative periods of boyhood and youth. This procedure departs from a widely recognized practice of ancient encomium,[17] which, though prone to concentrate upon the finished character, did sanction the ascending approach through childhood and early youth to manhood. We have seen that in the encomium on Cyrus Xenophon's discourse passed through these three stages. Similarly, Isocrates asserts (*Evag.* 22–23) that the personal beauty, the strength, and the self-control characterizing his hero in childhood anticipated the fruition of these qualities in the adult man, as well as the addition of others, to wit, valor, wisdom, and justness. In principle the ancient encomiast might thus be alive to the truth of the platitude, often invoked in modern biography, that the child is father to the man, even if Xenophon's narrative in the *Agesilaus* leaps from glory of race and state to the topic of Agesilaus' elevation to the throne.

Next, having orientated his readers with an introductory sentence, as is his punctilious way, our author launches into one of the main sections of his discourse, an account of the deeds of Agesilaus, separated in lucid fashion into (1) Campaigns in Asia; (2) Events after his recall to Greece. The dictum laid down (1, 6) to the effect that the deeds of a man best disclose the stamp of his nature, is a conventional tenet of ancient biography, later to be as influential on Plutarch's method as it was axiomatic of prose encomium. Xenophon's narrative has the easy flow of historical chronicle. Large tracts of it,

[17] E.g., this is the scheme commended by such theorists as Anaximenes, P. Wendland, *Anaximenes von Lampsakos* (Berlin, Weidmann, 1905), 56, 57, and Quintilian, *Inst. Or.* iii. 7. 15.

as we know,[18] utilize, with such reworking as the demands of encomium necessitated, material found also in the *Hellenica*.

Xenophon was not content to trust to the undirected vision of the reader to discern the light thrown on the merits of his hero by the bare recital of achievements. Instead of allowing events alone to tell the story our author has a way of engaging the reader's appreciation by punctuating the narrative ever and anon by sentences of appraisal. Now he utters a formal declaration like: "This it would seem he did admirably" (1, 24), or "As a general should" (1, 17); or "Verily it is meet to marvel at this in Agesilaus" (1, 36). Another favorite device is the rhetorical question introduced by Πῶς οὐ or some similar interrogative formula, like: "Is there any way in which Agesilaus failed to cover himself with glory in this act or in that?" (e.g., 1, 27; 1, 37; 2, 25). These sentences ring out at intervals like alarm clocks set to wake some drowsy reader to consciousness of the true value of the deeds of Agesilaus as indices to his greatness. They are as monotonous in their effect as they are instructive of the author's aim and downright methods. The encomiast's function was that of advocate, a rôle that many who call themselves biographers too blithely assume. These devices of interpretation and amplification are Xenophon's individual way of meeting a responsibility acknowledged throughout ancient encomiastic biography but, as the art of Tacitus in the *Agricola* attests, susceptible of being discharged by more subtle methods.

[18] A detailed comparison is given by W. Seyffert, *De Xenophontis Agesilao quaestiones* (Göttingen, Dieterich, 1909), 1–18.

Having in this chronologically ordered division used the deeds of his hero as a vast background against which to display virtues, Xenophon next proceeds to hang up virtues as frames for deeds. In other words the various components of the *aretê* of Agesilaus are used in succession as rubrics under which to group illustrative material—*tekmêria* or "proofs" is the technical term. The appreciation develops through the cardinal virtues, holiness (3, 2–5), justness (4), temperance (5), courage (6, 1–3), wisdom (6, 4–8). Succeeding captions deal with other laudable qualities, such as patriotism (7), including not only love of Sparta but devotion to the common weal of Greece; personal graciousness and charm, English words which ill translate the Greek adjective *eucharis* (8, 1–2); greatness of soul, an unsatisfactory rendition of *megalognōmosynê* (8, 3–4). Every one of these topics is amplified, now by citation of specific incidents, now by unillustrated, generalizing assertions. This descriptive cataloguing of virtues occupies roughly a third of the whole treatise, and concludes with an elaborate *syncrisis* or "comparison" of the simple ideals expressed in Agesilaus' mode of life with the self-indulgent luxury of the Persian king (9). This comparison is couched in a long series of antitheses. The scheme of presentation, it is important to remember, is essentially a replica of that followed by Xenophon some years previously when he paid his tribute to Cyrus.

There follows an epilogue (10) in which Agesilaus is commended as an example in ideal manhood and his life is formally assessed as beatific. Our artist might well here have laid down his palette. He was, however, still fain not so much to paint the rose as to reduce the portrait to an easily portable miniature. In order to enhance the edificatory power of the lesson taught by the life of Agesilaus, Xenophon appends a handy syllabus of sundry virtues treated before *in extenso*. Piety and the rest have their word but neither in order of arrangement nor in phraseology is there slavish repetition. In style this recapitulation is a perfect fanfaronade of antithetical eloquence. Evidently there was active in this context, besides the practical aim of summing up the case in order to drive home his valuation of Agesilaus, the deliberate effort on Xenophon's part to qualify as an artist in words.

With the rest of his generation Xenophon in youth had learned how to be "literary." We cannot be sure that like his friend Proxenus he had sat as a pupil at the feet of Gorgias. But in any case he had imbibed a working knowledge of the stylistic devices of which Gorgias was the leading exponent and which are traditionally connected with the great sophist's name. The casual reader of Xenophon carries away the impression of a self-contained pen. Nevertheless, various works besides the *Agesilaus* show the author's familiarity with the modes of rhetorical adornment and his lasting relish for them.[19] The stylistic features of the *Agesilaus* that seem to set it apart from the Xenophontic manner and which formerly inspired ill-considered attacks upon its authenticity result in large measure from the honest but not too gifted author's conscientious effort to

[19] *See* H. Schacht, *De Xenophontis studiis rhetoricis* (Berlin, G. Schade, 1890), 24 ff.; 35; Seyffert, *op. cit.*, 43–52.

dress his language to suit the occasion.[20] It was the great day of the biographical encomium. The admirers of Xenophon's son Gryllus, killed at Mantinea a year or so before the death of King Agesilaus, had, it will be recalled,[21] written many such honorific pieces. Xenophon was not the only one to pay the tribute to Agesilaus.[22] When the year 361/360 B.C. brought the end of that Spartan king under whom Xenophon had served, whom he had known as man to man, and unfeignedly admired, he "let himself go." Eager to pay the highest honor to the subject of his portraiture, perhaps wishful to emulate the literary graces of other tributes to Agesilaus and those in honor of his son, seeking—we may easily imagine—also to beguile his paternal sense of loss, Xenophon in his old age drew from the rhetorical herbarium constructed in his youth the set flowers of eloquence.

Mechanical schematology and a striving for "fine writing" in biographical tribute might seem to interpose hopeless obstacles to vivid and truly representative delineation. Xenophon's *Agesilaus*, it must be confessed, does not stand out in all its dimensions so convincingly as do some of Plutarch's best drawn figures. Nevertheless, after reading Xenophon's eulogy, one is somehow aware that one has come near to meeting a man. Xenophon made rhetoric and realism bedfellows with a success that Isocrates in the *Evagoras* could not or did not attain. Some of the causes making for Xenophon's closer approach to

[20] H. Richards, *Notes on Xenophon and Others* (London, E. Grant Richards, 1907), 82.

[21] Diog. Laert. ii. 55, previously quoted.

[22] Isocrates *Epist.* 9. 1.

naturalism have been referred to already in passing: his sincere enthusiasm for his subject; the personal contacts to which this enthusiasm was due; the unquenchable interest of an old soldier in the military life. *Con amore* he inserted such bits of colorful word-painting as the picture of the activities in the training-camp at Ephesus (1, 25–26)—the competing spearsmen and archers, the crowded race-course, the busy armorers. The passage is a close replica of *Hellenica* iii. 4. 16 ff.; verbal changes were introduced evidently with a view to stylistic effect.[23] One feels that this description as well as the descriptions of alignments and combats Xenophon simply could not bring himself to omit from the *Agesilaus*, notwithstanding its more specialized aim. Since the primacy of Agesilaus as moving spirit and responsible agent in these events is never lost sight of, these descriptive contexts are legitimate and effective as background.

Unfavorable criticism is an ingredient rare enough in encomiastic biography. Still Xenophon, viewing a maneuver of Agesilaus at Coronea (2, 12) with the eye of a tactician primarily, can pronounce it, in the objective language of the historian used in the *Hellenica* (iv. 3. 19),[24] more valiant than safe. Moreover, Xenophon had a Boswellian appreciation of the value of an anecdote, the scenic effectiveness of narrated incident and conversation. The chapters devoted to the exposition of virtues are especially rich in this, the essential stuff of biography. When it is a question of throwing into high relief the cardinal virtue, temperance, he tells a story about

[23] Seyffert, *op. cit.* 5.

[24] The adverb ἀναμφιλόγως is substituted for the ἀναμφισβητήτως of the *Hellenica*.

Agesilaus' resistance of the seductiveness of a beautiful youth and the embarrassment of the languishing tempter at the rebuff encountered (5, 4–6). We read the stout Doric oath[25] rapped out by the continent Spartan as he vows that not even if he were to be made the fairest, strongest, and most fleet of men would he recall the kiss his self-control had once refused. What adds piquancy to the asseveration is Agesilaus' signal lack of these personal advantages.

Work of idealization though it is, the *Agesilaus* was receptive even to those details of private life that help to conjure up the figure of a man. Xenophon would have had no sympathy with the kind of "prudery" which Coleridge complains actuated Spratt "in refusing to let his friend Cowley appear in his slippers and dressing-gown."[26] There is, however, a difference in intention between Xenophon and the genuine biographer in respect to the introduction of these intimate data. Whereas Suetonius and Plutarch use material of this sort in response to what Theophilus Cibber calls "curiosity to know the little stories and particularities"[27] of men who have played a conspicuous rôle—and very human such inquisitiveness is—Xenophon was actuated by the desire to point a moral or illustrate a quality. Thus, when he speaks of the frugality of Agesilaus and the simple ménage of the king, it is not for the purpose of devoting, in Suetonian fashion, a rubric to personal habits, but in order to bring out the contrast between the acquisitive luxuriousness of the Persian monarch and the Spartan's contempt for soft living. So mention is made, for example, of the house of Agesilaus

[25] *οὐ τὼ σιώ.* [26] *Biographia Literaria* I, chap. 3.

[27] *Lives of the Poets* (London, R. Griffiths, 1753), I, 124.

and its simple gear, of its doors so rudely antique that one might imagine that they dated back to the time of his ancestors, the sons of Hercules (8, 7). It is recorded that the chaise in which his daughter[28] went to participate in the festival of the *Hyacinthia* at Amyclae was no more pretentious than the equipages of the ordinary citizens. The democratic king did not countenance a carriage superior to the common lot of "gigmanity."

Until we come to biography proper, touches of intimate delineation such as these are exceptional. The *Evagoras* shows a conspicuous lack of them. Both Xenophon and Isocrates, if we judge them by the desiderata of modern biography, neglect essential topics. What, for example, should we think of an account of a human life that, as is true of both encomia, is silent about the mother's name, says nothing concerning marriage and wife? Marriage alliance is a topic that can be adapted to the technique of encomium without great expenditure of finesse. In the encomium of Alcibiades included by Isocrates in his speech "On the Chariot-Span," the marriage of Alcibiades with the daughter of a father so rich and eminent as Hipponicus is cited as a deserved badge of distinction (31). If the physical disabilities of Agesilaus excluded a sketch of his personal appearance, Evagoras did not suffer under such handicaps. Yet Isocrates, having assured his readers that Evagoras as a boy was endowed with beauty and bodily strength and that these increased as the boy became a man (22–23), deemed that the exigencies of

[28] Adopting Casaubon's insertion *ἡ θυγάτηρ αὐτοῦ*. It is clear from Plutarch *Ages.* 19 that in the text of Xenophon known to him the daughter, not the king, was the passenger. Plutarch also understood *ἐπὶ πολιτικοῦ καννάθρου* as the phrase is taken above.

physical portraiture had been satisfied. The learned Dicaearchus of Messene, one of Aristotle's pupils belonging, as we shall see in a future chapter, to the history of biography, complained that Xenophon nowhere mentioned the name of the daughter of Agesilaus.[29] Xenophon (9, 6) does refer by name to Cynisca, the sister of Agesilaus. Nicocles, one of the children of Evagoras, and his father's successor, is mentioned, of course, as the recipient of the treatise, in the prooemium (1) and in the epilogue (73). A younger son, Pnytagoras, is named in section sixty-two of the *Evagoras*. Aside from these instances neither encomiast regarded record of the kin or descendants of his subject as germane to his purpose.

Nowhere in the encomium of Evagoras is there any excursion into genre detail, graphic incident, everyday life. It speaks volumes for the difference between the two encomiasts' methods and attitudes that Isocrates does not once quote a speech or an apothegm. All his color is laid on with the broad strokes of a dripping brush. The correlative sequences *οὕτως, τοιοῦτος, τοσοῦτος . . . ὥστε* are pet formulas of the Isocratean rhapsody comparable with the rhetorical questions with which Xenophon touches the reader's ear: "So far was Evagoras superior in the excellencies of body and soul that . . ." (23); "Evagoras rose to such a pitch of greatheartedness that . . ." (27); "Evagoras governed the state with so scrupulous a regard for gods and men that . . ." (43). And so it goes. No summit of

[29] With the emended text in the passage just referred to, her name could easily have been mentioned; *see* Dicaearchus *frg.* 17, Müller, *FHG* II, 240.

laudation towers so high as to discommode with its rarefied atmosphere this superhero. The spirit of the whole treatise is reproduced in a nutshell by a context of which this is the gist: "All the hyperboles applied by the poets to men of yore are most appropriate to his nature. If anyone was ever a god among men, Evagoras deserves that title." (72). This paragon of human beings, generals, and administrators does not ring true. Xenophon, himself no enemy to superlatives, could show Agesilaus tempted by the devil of the flesh and point to an occasion on the field of battle where bravery degenerated into rashness. The positively inhuman perfection of Evagoras removes him from the liability to mortal frailty and error.

Criticism has in general taken hearty umbrage at the faulty verisimilitude of this would-be portrait, at its rococo style and sumptuousness of adulation, veritably oriental, as Bruns[30] described it. Münscher, to be sure, dissenting from such extreme condemnation, attributes the fulsomeness of the eulogist in part to the precedents of Gorgian rhetoric, in the manipulation of which Isocrates is not to be taken too seriously.[31] Isocrates, this critic holds, frankly admired Evagoras. But the trouble is, Isocrates doth protest too much. His very exuberance arouses in the reader suspicions as to his sincerity and as to the facts of his acquaintance with his hero. Isocrates might have written as he does from hearsay and have sought to conceal his lack of intimate knowledge beneath purple folds of rhetoric. There is nothing to betoken the existence of the personal association

[30] *Op. cit.*, 115.

[31] *P-W* IX, Halbbd. 18, 2192.

that imparts to the *Agesilaus* so much of its fresh vitality.

Now, while the critics have been given to complaints that the fumes of the incense burned by Isocrates at the shrine of Evagoras are overpowering and have been not unappreciative of the superior realism of Xenophon's tribute, at the same time the idea has been cherished generally that the *Evagoras* served as the literary model for the *Agesilaus*. Bruns,[32] discerning in the antithetical structure of the character sketches of Proxenus and Menon in the *Anabasis* (ii. 6. 16 ff.) resemblance to the serried ranks of antitheses ranged in sections forty-three to forty-six of the *Evagoras*, assumed an even earlier influence of Isocrates on his contemporary craftsman. Discussion of these theories will take us into arid stretches of erudition. Nevertheless we must suffer and be strong if we are to set right grossly distorted views as to the history of prose encomium and do full justice to Xenophon's deserts as a biographical encomiast.

Nothing could be farther from the truth than the doctrine espoused by Kaibel[33] in 1890 and Bruns[34] in 1896, repeated wholeheartedly, though with some

[32] *Op. cit.*, 138. M. Pohlenz, *Aus Platons Werdezeit* (Berlin, Weidmann, 1913), 269, n. 1 cites verbal parallels between Isocrates *Ad Nicoclem* 24 and the characterization of Clearchus, *Anab.* ii. 6. 7–8, and, assuming that Isocrates was the imitator, proposes to date the *Anabasis* prior to the year 374 B.C. The contrast between the views of Bruns and Pohlenz is a vivid reminder of the slippery character of inferences based on verbal resemblances. A recent writer, A. Kappelmacher, *Anz. d. Akad. der Wiss. i. Wien, Philos.-hist. Kl.* 1923 (April 11), nevertheless sees in the *Panegyric* of Isocrates 145 ff. the influence of the *Anabasis*, and dates the latter book between 390 and 387/6. Against this early dating of the *Anabasis* see J. Mesk, *Wiener Studien* XLIII (1922–1923), 136 ff. and Bursian's *Jahresbericht* LI (1925), 11–13.

[33] *Hermes* XXV (1890), 595 ff.

[34] *Op. cit.*, 126 ff.

modification by Leo[35] in 1901, and advanced with further reservation by Fraustadt[36] in 1909, to the effect that Xenophon would not have constructed the *Agesilaus* as he did—throughout, according to Kaibel and Bruns, in certain parts, according to Leo and Fraustadt—had he not been under the spell of the *Evagoras*. The relation between Isocrates and Xenophon is not that of mentor and imitator respectively. Both should be ranged side by side as co-heirs of an older tradition, starting from which each traveled his own road.

Kaibel and Bruns wrote at a day when the dazzling parallel, followed more blindly than it is now, too often acted as an *ignis fatuus* leading to a *terra infirma* of conclusion. If the *Agesilaus* showed similarities in structure, style, and conceits with the *Evagoras*, then, forsooth, Xenophon must be an imitator, since Isocrates wrote his encomium first. This method of research is old-fashioned. We are now chary about using such indications as evidence of direct relationship between two exponents of a literary genre which has, as had the encomium at this time, a long history of varied production behind it. How nebulous is the evidence making for the belief that the *Evagoras* stimulated Xenophon to imitation is shown by the shifting view of the critics as to the tracts of the *Agesilaus* in which copying is supposedly discernible. The movement has been a steady diminuendo which we need follow in outline only.

[35] *Op. cit.*, 91, 92.

[36] G. Fraustadt, *Encomiorum in litteris Graecis usque ad Romanam aetatem historia* (Leipzig, Noske, 1909), 67–70.

After Leo's ax had lopped off about one-third of the Isocratean overgrowth, in that this scholar accredited to Xenophon's own impulse the second main division of the *Agesilaus*, namely, the illustrated catalogue of virtues (chaps. 3–9), Fraustadt continued the process of subtraction. He confined the vestiges of Xenophon's imitation to chapters ten and eleven, the epilogue and the recapitulation, a matter of about four pages out of thirty-one of Teubner text. Quantitatively reckoned this is a great shrinkage from the generous calculations of Kaibel and Bruns. This brief context at the end of the *Agesilaus* has remained the stronghold for champions of the traditional view. In the antithetical characterization of chapter eleven Münscher[37] in 1916 saw especially the traces of imitation on Xenophon's part, although this scholar showed a reactionary tendency to cling to the older theories which assumed that Xenophon also gleaned from Isocrates suggestions as to structural arrangement in other parts of the *Agesilaus*.[38]

Reactionary, I say, because in the meantime the more rational tendencies that we have touched on as befitting the modern scholar's attitude toward such parallelism as exists between the two encomia had been exemplified by Seyffert, a pupil of Leo.[39] Seyffert adduced cogent reasons for denying *in toto* that Xenophon was indebted to the *Evagoras* as an imitator is beholden to a model. Xenophon, Seyffert assumed, had doubtless read the *Evagoras* (an

[37] *P.-W* IX, Halbbd. 18, 2193.

[38] Leo's view that the narrative of deeds forming the first part of the *Agesilaus* is modeled on the *Evagoras* is repeated in the latest edition of Christ's *Gesch. der Griech. Litt.* (ed. 6; Munich, Beck, 1912–13), I, 505, n. 6.

[39] *Op. cit.*, 27 ff.; 42; 51, 52.

assumption for a priori reasons plausible),[40] but its effect upon him was as a revelation how not to compose an encomium. Seyffert stretched the evidence far in order to prove the existence of literary antagonism between Xenophon and Isocrates. To his credit, however, be it said that he was the first to refuse to be cozened into the belief that the antithetical appreciation of Agesilaus (11) was necessarily modeled on the resumptive estimate, also antithetically arranged, of the merits of Evagoras as a ruler (43ff). Contrastive balancing of ideas is one of those features of the written and the spoken word that no mind needs the suggestion of another to adopt. Such devices arise spontaneously when any human brain is intent on giving colorful and effective expression to thought. We may agree with Mr. Chesterton[41] that the world of existence itself is replete with antithetical poles—night, day; good, bad; courage, fear—hence that it is small wonder that the world of thought merely acknowledges and expresses the contrasting principles of the world of reality.

[40] Seyffert erred, however, in seeking proof in the parallelism between Xenophon's opening remark that he is aware that it is not an easy thing to write an encomium adequate to the ἀρετή and the δόξα of his subject and the words of Isocrates of similar import (*Evag.* 8): Οἶδα μὲν οὖν, ὅτι χαλεπόν ἐστιν, ὃ μέλλω ποιεῖν, ἀνδρὸς ἀρετὴν διὰ λόγων ἐγκωμιάζειν. No weight can be attached correctly to a likeness resident in so veritable an apologetic commonplace. In this vein Pericles opened his funeral oration (Thucy. ii. 35. 2) and Gorgias prefaced his Olympian oration by asserting the difficulty of keeping proper proportions in eulogy. Doxopater, summing up the standing features of encomia, said (Walz, *Rhetores Graeci*, II, 449, 33): "It is the law of encomiasts to agree always that the subject is greater than words can match." Furthermore, Xenophon found his obstacle in the indescribable perfection of his subject, Isocrates in the medium he is purposing to use.

[41] "Pope and the Art of Satire," *Varied Types* (New York, Dodd, Mead and Co., 1903), 46; also in *Five Types* (New York, Henry Holt, 1911), 19.

How groundless, then, is the view that Xenophon caught the notion of antithetical characterization from Isocrates when back of them both was Gorgias, hailed in antiquity[42] as the original and the intemperate exponent of contrastive utterance. The resemblance of Xenophon's antitheses to specimens of the device surviving from the writings of Gorgias as well as found in compositions fashioned after his manner, is patent.[43] Furthermore, thanks to Blass and Norden,[44] it is now a commonplace of knowledge that in respect to antitheses and others of the so-called "Gorgian figures" he of Leontini merely formally exploited stylistic devices which the unassisted light of nature had suggested to poets as early as Homer and Hesiod, which had become integral features of the manner of Heraclitus and Empedocles, were favored by Sophoclean art,[45] and, in sum, had entered into the texture of the language before the coming of Gorgias to Athens.

Analogies in idea and literary conceit that attract the attention of the reader of the two epilogues may be explained by a similar course of reasoning. The didactic appeal found in both finales and the commendation of each man as an ethical example are to be valued merely as echoes of themes that natural emotion and mental custom had established as the conventional components of dirge, encomiastic poetry, and prose *epitaphios*. Seyffert[46] animadverted upon a few

[42] Cicero *Orator* 175; Diod. Sic. xii. 53.

[43] Seyffert, *op. cit.*, 40.

[44] *Die Attische Beredsamkeit* (ed. 2; Leipzig, Teubner, 1887), I, 66 ff.; *Die antike Kunstprosa* (ed. 3; Leipzig, Teubner, 1915), I, 15–29.

[45] O. Navarre, *Essai sur la rhétorique grecque avant Aristote* (Paris, Hachette, 1900), 106–11; G. Thiele, *Hermes* XXXVI (1901), 224; 233.

[46] *Op. cit.*, 36, 37.

of these instances, but by no means exhausted them. Especially in connection with a parallelism in motive on which Kaibel,[47] Bruns,[48] and Fraustadt[49] laid great stress as proof that the *Evagoras* was Xenophon's inspiration, the progress of literary research has shed new light. In similar veins both encomiasts proclaim in their epilogues the blessedness of their heroes' lives. "What did the felicity of Evagoras lack?" is the declamatory query of Isocrates (71). The items of felicity are: lineage, noble beyond compare; unequaled physical and mental gifts; sovereignty gloriously achieved and coextensive with life; immortal fame; a life prolonged to old age but immune from the ills that afflict old age; and lastly, that rare combination, offspring both numerous and goodly, blessings phrased by the Greek as *polypedia* and *eupedia.* Xenophon (10, 4), more briefly, and for once less concretely than Isocrates, calls Agesilaus blessed because he had realized most completely of men of his time his youthful passion for renown; secondly, because never throughout his reign was he balked in his high ambitions; finally, because, having attained the farthest limit of human life, he died without having incurred offense either as regards those whom he led or those against whom he made war.

Now this analytic appraising of blessings which is made by some person assessing in poetry or in prose the happiness of a mortal lot, which may or may not have terminated, was a traditional device of Greek commemorative literature.[50] The Greeks had for

[47] *Loc. cit.* [48] *Op. cit.*, 132. [49] *Op. cit.*, 69.

[50] The topic has been exhaustively treated by G. L. Dirichlet, "De veterum macarismis," *Religionsgeschichtliche Versuche und Vorarbeiten* XIV (1913–1914), Heft 4.

such summarizing of temporal felicity an especial word, namely, μακαρισμός or "a calling blessed," a term first occurring in Plato's *Republic* 591 D. The practice had a spontaneous origin in the meditations of mourners, eulogists, of anyone who, stirred to contemplate the life of another, would be led to inventory the happiness that had attended that life and that perhaps compensated for its close. The germ of the *macarismus* lies in the words with which Odysseus apostrophized the Greeks who had fallen before the walls of Troy, "thrice and fourfold blessed" because they had died and had escaped the hardships of the wanderer. Gratulatory plaudits also naturally greet the fortunate at the moment at which they are deemed to have attained the pinnacle of happiness and are living to enjoy their lot. Thus from the folk-custom of felicitating by acclamation the bride and the bridegroom at weddings, the formula passed into the epithalamia.[61] Similarly, as the epinician odes of Pindar and Bacchylides testify, the motive was sometimes invoked in the praise of victorious athletes.[62] It passed into prose *epitaphios* and encomium as a traditional element, introduced especially at the close of the tribute, where the consolatory mood, indigenous to literature of this kind, naturally held sway and the thought would turn to summing up the blessings that had attended a human life.

In view of the conventional character of the contexts in our two eulogists, only superficial methods of criticism could regard the parallelism as due to the fact that Xenophon here had his eye upon the

[61] Dirichlet, *op. cit.*, 32–34.

[62] E.g., Pindar *Pyth.* 5. 20; 10. 22; *Nem.* 11. 11.

Evagoras. A literary device of so long a history and of such inevitable pertinence to biographical eulogy was by the fourth century common literary heritage. It must have been at home in the *epitaphioi* of the fifth century, as it was in the fourth;[53] certainly it is in harmony with the spirit of the fragment of the *epitaphios* of Gorgias that has come down to us.[54]

Exposition of the subjects' acts and their mental and moral qualities forms, as has been said, the body of both encomia. Herein "By their [deeds] ye shall know them" is the text that each author makes his own.[55] However, while Xenophon and Isocrates are at one in accepting the doctrine that the traits of personality are best interpreted and illumined by deeds, they differ widely in their respective applications of the principle. There is nothing in the *Evagoras* comparable with the bipartite division into narrative of deeds and descriptive catalogue of virtues that marks the *Agesilaus.* The way of Isocrates was to commingle throughout his discourse these two elements, so that we find him now characterizing and describing, anon narrating and citing.

This essential contrast in method is so plain that it never should have escaped the thoughtful reader. Where Xenophon, with occasional parenthetical comment, unfolds his chronicle from the wars in Asia to the ill-starred interposition of Agesilaus in the affairs of Egypt, Isocrates fastens in succession on one of the two or three outstanding exploits of Evagoras—his seizure of the throne from which his line had been ejected, his cooperation with Conon,

[53] Dirichlet, *op. cit.*, 44–46.
[54] Baiter-Sauppe, *Oratores Attici*, Pars post. 129, 130.
[55] *Evag.* 30; 33; 46; 65; *Ages.* 1. 6.

the ten years' war between Cyprus and Persia. He amplifies the exploit for what it reveals of the virtues of his hero's mind and heart, or rather for what it can be made to reveal. The facts of history are a perfectly malleable substance. In treating the coup d'état of Evagoras and his fifty companions, he dilates from every angle on the magnitude of the feat. Passion is torn to tatters. No throne was ever more gloriously won (34, 39). Heaven itself ordained that the reigning usurper should be murdered by other hands than those of Evagoras, whose piety was thus preserved immaculate (25, 26). "Happy warrior" indeed! In formal comparison the achievement of Evagoras in winning his rightful sovereignty, the virtues displayed are exalted above all other examples of like exploits. And it was for no petty prize that Evagoras was contending, cries Isocrates, but for the greatest of all blessings, supreme power.

In all this rant, which may serve further to illustrate both temper and method, Isocrates does not assemble deeds under specific virtues; he passes from appreciation to narrative and back again. This method gains in literary freedom what it loses in logical system, but it is not Xenophon's way. The *Agesilaus* in respect to structure and technique exemplifies rhetorical doctrines, that, as has been remarked, are older than the *Evagoras* of Isocrates.

For information as to the milieu from which these doctrines emanated if not as to their inventor, one has but to turn to the *Symposium* of Plato. It will be remembered that the guests who had assembled at the house of Agathon, the young tragic poet who was celebrating a recent victory, are disinclined to the usual potations after the dinner is over. Hence they agree to a feast of wisdom in which each guest in turn shall pronounce an encomium on Eros or Love, the only God, it is alleged (177 A-C), who has not had such a tribute in poetry or prose. The ball once set rolling, each guest essays to do his part on that *nox ambrosiana*. When the turn of the host, Agathon, comes, he criticizes the previous efforts as faulty in method and proceeds with youthful dogmatism to lay down the law. The one correct rule for the composition of an encomium on *any* subject is to set forth characteristics, then activities.[16] In his speech this method is followed to the letter. The qualities of Eros are enumerated under successive rubrics, with scrupulous attention to lucid division; under each head, ordinarily phrased as a superlative adjective, the *tekmêria* or "proofs" are gathered. True to encomiastic convention, the four cardinal virtues form separate rubrics. The second of the two grand divisions of the speech deals with the benefits conferred by Love on man, Agathon's adaptation of the *topos* "activities" to suit the particular subject.

It is clear beyond all doubt that in Agathon's encomium appears an exact analogy to Xenophon's demarcation into deed and trait, as illustrated in the *Agesilaus*, and to his use of deeds to elucidate virtues, the plan followed in the second part of the *Agesilaus* and adopted previously by him in the encomium on Cyrus the Younger. Agathon, we know, had imbibed at the fountain of Gorgias. Hence, as the editors of the *Symposium* have shown, Plato's artful mimicry filled the young enthusiast's discourse with

[16] 195 A.

imitations of the sophist's manner. Finally, Socrates, whose discourse follows that of Agathon, rallies the poet with gentle mockery and asserts that his host's speech has the ring of the Gorgian eloquence (198 C).

The same evidence that emancipates Xenophon from the dominion of the *Evagoras*, does away also with Leo's view that, notwithstanding Xenophon's chronic dependence on Isocrates in other parts of the *Agesilaus*, the descriptive catalogue of virtues is a step taken by the volition of the author beyond his model. But here also Xenophon was applying a lesson that the young literati were learning from Gorgias at the end of the fifth century and the beginning of the fourth. The *Agesilaus*, as we have seen, has an individuality imparted to it by the author's penchants and temperament. However, this individuality has its play on the tracks laid by a rhetorical tradition that antedates the *Evagoras* and helped to form the methods of Isocrates as well as of Xenophon. If Leo and other critics[57] had not overlooked the importance of the *Symposium* as a document in evidence for the history of biographical encomium, the history of this form would not have had to be rewritten here. What has chiefly contributed to befog criticism is the obsession that the *Evagoras* really deserves to hold the authoritative primacy that Isocrates claims for it. This question and its bearings on our study will be considered in the next chapter.

[57] X. Hürth's assertion, "De Gregorii Nazianzeni orationibus funebribus, *Diss. philol. Argentoratenses* XII (1907), 11, 12, that Gorgias had not instituted a formal method of encomium cannot stand. It does not necessarily follow that the plan we know emanated from the school of Gorgias was the only scheme utilized by himself and his pupils; *see* Pohlenz, *op. cit.*, 268, n. 1."

CHAPTER IV

A QUESTION OF PRIORITY: THE PRETENSIONS OF ISOCRATES

"I first adventure: follow me who list
And be the second English Satyrist."
—Joseph Hall, *Virgidemiarum libri*, Prologue.

Isocrates, "that old man eloquent," whose house, in Cicero's words, "lay open to all Greece, as it were a school and work-shop of oratory,"[1] belongs to that clan of writers with whom it would seem to be a point of honor not to display undignified haste in coming to grips with a subject. The prefatory disquisition, in which the fortress of a theme is approached by sapping and mining, is characteristic of his manner. So the *Encomium of Evagoras* opens with a formal preface, quite in contrast to the crisp sentences with which Xenophon plunged into his eulogy of Agesilaus.

Isocrates first addresses to the son of Evagoras, Nicocles, some solemn platitudes extolling the literary tribute over other methods of paying honor to the dead. The serious attention of the student of Greek intellectual life is first engaged when the author begins to discourse for the benefit of the educated public, as Bruns[2] has well observed, on the

[1] *Brutus* 32. [2] *Op. cit.*, 116.

hindrances with which, as a eulogistic biographer, he finds himself confronted.

The thought of Isocrates unfolds as follows: Other writers ought to adopt the practice of eulogizing illustrious contemporaries. The gain would be twofold; first, because the dictates of veracity would necessarily be observed in biographical eulogies written for the attention of men whose lives synchronize with the life of the subject; secondly, a spirit of emulation would be stirred in the young if they could be sure that their virtues and deeds would find a chronicler. As it is, only the worthies of heroic antiquity meet with their just meed of praise in epic, dithyramb, and tragedy.[8] This condition of things is due to envy, which, nevertheless, is a curse chiefly to those who harbor it (5–7).

Eulogy in prose of the virtue of a man, Isocrates continues, is, to be sure, a difficult task. Proof positive is furnished by the procedure that has hitherto held good among men of letters and learning. A great variety of subjects has been treated in prose encomia, but no one has ever essayed a theme such as mine (8).

[8] I agree with E. Conrotte, "Pindare et Isocrate," *Musée Belge* II (1898), 178, and E. S. Forster, *Isocrates' Cyprian Orations*, note *ad loc.* and dissent from Fraustadt, *op. cit.*, 57, 58, in understanding the word ὑμνουμένους (6) as alluding to poetical compositions only. Coupled with a reference to a specific poetic form, tragedy, in which the great figures of antiquity were celebrated, allusion merely to other genres of commemorative poetry is to be expected. The combination ὑμνουμένους καὶ τραγῳδουμένους balances the previous phrase ποιούμενοι τοὺς λόγους (5), the connotation of which must be restricted to writers of prose since throughout the exordium λόγοι means "prose" only. Prose had been used as a vehicle for praising heroic personages of antiquity; there were the *Achilles* of Gorgias, for example (Arist. *Rhet.* iii. 17, 11) and Isocrates' own encomium of Busiris. Because, however, poetry had been the more obvious medium for such eulogy, Isocrates, intent on his main distinction between contemporaries and personages of the past, permitted the rule rather than the exception to control his phraseology.

In this context a source of mild surprise confronts the analytic reader. He has first been informed that the bar to eulogy of contemporaries in prose and verse alike is envy. For all that Isocrates says to the contrary, envy is the sole deterrent. We next learn that there has been another cause which has made against the eulogy of great men. The medium itself furnishes an obstacle. The poet can draw on the charms of situation and descant on the good old times when the gods had not yet withdrawn themselves from the walks of men. He can utilize embellishments of diction, trope, and meter. All these resources are denied to the encomiast in prose. Hence it is that *littérateurs* have refrained from extolling in this medium the good and great man, although they have so treated a motley variety of other themes.

How far is the value that Isocrates set upon his treatise as a pioneer achievement in literature authentic? During the three decades that have elapsed since the publication of Ivo Bruns's book on literary portraiture, the essential historicity of Isocrates' estimate of his services to the prose encomium has been well-nigh universally accepted by the critics with, it is true, certain unavoidable reservations. For even to be a literalist with respect to the pretensions of Isocrates, one has at the outset to enter this *caveat*. One must understand the orator as speaking of such prose encomia as were literary units complete in themselves and ignoring eulogies of men that formed merely an incidental fraction of some discourse. This is the reason why he does not take cognizance of his own eulogy of Alcibiades, which is formed on orthodox rhetorical lines and antedates by twenty years the composition of the *Evagoras*. The encomium of Alcibiades, it will be remembered, is included in the speech *On the Chariot-Span*. This procedure is in consonance with the conventional attitude of ancient literary criticism, which tended to recognize only literary priority manifesting itself in formal, sustained production, such as books or literary cycles, and took little or no cognizance of sporadic precedent. Horace's assertion of pioneership (*Carm*. iii. 30), based on the elaborated series of the first three books of the *Odes* and overlooking the experiments of Catullus in Aeolic lyricism, was justifiable from the ancient point of view.

With this reservation, Bruns[4] contended that there was no reason to look askance at Isocrates' assumption that he is creating in the *Evagoras* a new literary genre. Leo's great authority, acting on succeeding investigators, has assisted in perpetuating this as the all but canonical doctrine.[5] The *Evagoras* has not only been regarded as the first of its kind, but has been set up as a golden milestone from which the encomiasts of the next decades plotted their way.

Evidently the quietus could be put most efficaciously on the pretensions of Isocrates if one could point to the existence, prior to the *Evagoras*, of a specific prose eulogy analogous to it in choice of subject. This von Wilamowitz[6] essayed to do by

[4] *Op. cit.*, 118.

[5] Kaibel, *op. cit.*, 595; Drerup, *op. cit.*, p. cxliii (*see also* Münscher, Gött. gel. Anz. 1907, 775, 4); Hürth, *op. cit.*, 6; 10, n. 6; Fraustadt, *op. cit.*, 58–60; Gossmann, *op. cit.*, 52; J. B. Bury, *The Ancient Greek Historians* (New York, Macmillan, 1909), 153; Christ, *Gesch. der griech. Litt.* (ed. 6), I, 573, and n. 1.

[6] *Hermes* XXXV (1900), 533.

calling attention to the fact that in the first book of the *Rhetoric*[7] Aristotle mentions an encomium on one Hippolochus as the first composition of its kind. However, most subsequent critics for one reason or another have not accepted this evidence as administering the coup de grâce to the boast of Isocrates. The trouble is, we know too little about Hippolochus, too little about the nature of the encomium written in his honor. If this Hippolochus were, as von Wilamowitz arbitrarily assumed, the fair Thessalian youth for whose manly beauty, as the story is told by Plutarch,[8] the courtesan Lais forsook Corinth only to meet a tragic death early in the fourth century at the hands of her lover's jealous countrywomen, an encomium in his honor might antedate the *Evagoras*. To make this identification it is necessary to assume that Plutarch alone was right in giving the name of the lover of Lais as Hippolochus. He has other names in other writers.[9]

Because of these impediments the attempt of von Wilamowitz to localize Aristotle's Hippolochus must be deemed more romantic than convincing. The name is quite noncommittal as to epoch and nation notwithstanding the remark of von Wilamowitz: "Es klingt thessalisch." The name is as old as the Homeric poems and figures in both myth and history variously before the generation of Aristotle.[10]

Nevertheless, Hippolochus may be set down as an unknown quantity without affecting the possibility that Aristotle was actually by innuendo

[7] i. 9. 1368 A. 38. [8] *Erot.* 21. 767 F.

[9] Pausanias ii. 2. 4, calls him Hippostratus; Polemo *in* Athenaeus xiii. 589 A named him Pausanias; by the scholiast on Aristophanes *Plutus* 179 the name is given as Eurylochus or Aristonicus.

[10] *See P-W*, *s.v.*

disputing Isocrates' claim to be the inventor of the prose encomium of contemporaries. This interpretation of the cryptic bit of text[11] has indubitable allurements. Aristotle has but just quoted a passage from the *Evagoras*;[12] elsewhere[13] in the *Rhetoric* he draws illustration from it. The Stagirite was dealing with the encomium as a branch of epideictic prose, hence it is a plausible supposition that in referring to a matter of origins his thought would be focused on prose encomium only. It would be like his inquisitive scholarship to unearth an obscure fact of literary history in order quietly to puncture what he may have deemed a tumid and unwarranted generalization.

Of course it may be urged that after all Aristotle was chiefly concerned with illustrating a theme prescribed by him as apposite to encomium, namely, the distinction conferred upon the subject of a eulogy by the fact that some prize or honor was first established on the great one's account. As one instance of this sort Aristotle then cites the dedication of the first portrait statues to the tyrannicides, Harmodius and Aristogeiton. Having taken one illustration from the field of art, he passes to the field of literature and perhaps cites a tradition that had to do merely with the origin of the *poetic* encomium.[14] His language unhappily leaves the reader quite in the dark as to the literary character of the encomium of Hippolochus. Yet the more one reflects upon the comment of Aristotle and the more directly one faces this

[11] However, the conjectural emendation of Drerup, *loc. cit.* and the doubts expressed as to the general drift of Aristotle's meaning seem to me to be the results of an *ex parte* attitude.

[12] i. 9. 36.

[13] ii. 23. 12; 24. 2.

[14] The interpretation approved by Hürth and Fraustadt *loc. cit.*

particular word in this particular context, the more difficult it becomes for the impartial critic not to read into the passage a covert but deliberate revision of Isocrates' assertion.

Other prose encomia known to us as antedating the *Evagoras* cannot serve as cogent testimony making against the veracity of Isocrates. One who is minded to take the fundamentalist's attitude can in every instance plausibly rest his case on a literal interpretation of the language in which Isocrates phrases his self-assertion. Thus, encomia celebrating figures of mythology or famous courtesans, such as the *Nais* of the rhetorician Alcidamas,[15] can be rejected on the ground that they fail to meet one or more of the conditions expressed in Isocrates's description of his program, or properly to be regarded as implicit in this program. Restriction to personages of contemporary history, to manly virtue, to monographic form can in every case be invoked to save the good faith of Isocrates.

A year after the iconoclastic stand taken by von Wilamowitz, Leo[16] did not hesitate to reaffirm the traditional view and to rate Isocrates as the inventor and the organizer of the biographical genre to which the *Evagoras* belongs. This conservatism, exemplified, as has been said, by the majority of scholars since Leo's time, indicates that the minutiae of external evidence such as we have been discussing have not by themselves power finally to make or to mar one's conception of the place to be assigned to Isocrates in the development of the biographical encomium. Nevertheless, since Leo's book was

[15] Productions of this sort are listed in Fraustadt, *loc. cit.*

[16] *Op. cit.*, 91.

written, criticism in this field has progressed to a point that renders necessary a modification of former ideas. In our previous chapter we found it essential to recast the literary pedigree of Xenophon's encomia. The more one studies the background from which the figure of Isocrates has been made to stand out in such solitary prominence by those who have taken his words at their face value, the more poignant must become one's realization that the perspective has been unduly distorted, the relief made too high. This is to say without metaphor that the *Evagoras* does not deserve the unique authority as a model that has been attached to it. It is sheer folly to assume that other encomia on Agesilaus[17] of which we hear, and the multitude of similar tributes composed in honor of the heroic Gryllus, owed their origin and their nature to the example of Isocrates[18] alone. As to these treatises all we know is that they were written *after* the *Evagoras* was written; we do not know *how* they were written.

To gird at Isocrates as a mendacious braggart is as unsatisfactory a way in which to confute him as it is facile. That method promotes neither sound criticism nor fair play. It is desirable and feasible to take a step beyond von Wilamowitz and his converts, Frick[19] and Seyffert,[20] to all of whom the passage in Aristotle bulked sufficiently large to persuade them that Isocrates acted quite in character

[17] *See* notes 21 and 22, p. 74 above.

[18] As did Drerup and Leo.

[19] O. Frick, *Die Darstellung der Persönlichkeit in Xenophons Anabasis* (Höxter, Flotho, 1905), 1, 2.

[20] *Op. cit.*, 19. Pohlenz also is seemingly to be ranged with this group, since he expressed (*op. cit.*, 268, n. 1, 269, n.) his general agreement with Seyffert's findings and suggested that in the *Evagoras* Isocrates was following an older scheme.

in slipping lightly over the letter of the truth when there was a question of his enhancing his originality and literary achievement. Instead of merely dismissing his assertions as the unjustifiable boasting of a literary pretender, we should apply to him the standards of ancient criticism as well as study him in the light of the literary ethics of all classicism.

The accents in which Isocrates here speaks are typical of the to us naïf directness with which the ancient man of letters was prone to emblazon his own merits in his chosen field. Nowadays, taste and practice recommend at least a feigned self-effacement. In his heart an author may be convinced that he is doing something unprecedented in literature. He may secretly cherish the belief that he speaks as a voice yet unheard, tills virgin soil. For so the hackneyed metaphors have run almost since personal expression began in literature. But however seriously some of our contemporary craftsmen seem to take themselves and their artistic canons, it is not the mode for them to herald their uniqueness over their own signature. By our beautiful modern arrangements publishers' notices and the paeans of amiable and perhaps not wholly disinterested reviewers take care of the deserts of the author and commend him as an inspired innovator to the worshipful attention of the trusting reader. "Different from any book you ever read"; "Strikes a new note of strangeness and mystery"; "In 1915 Mr. Blank made a departure entirely new in literature . . . . ." The works in question may or may not have measured up to these assurances caught by an indolent eye on "book-jackets" and in weekly reviews during the past year. The point is that such assertions, whether made by and with the consent of the author or in spite of him, have an air of modest objectivity. There is the subtler tactic, too, of praising oneself by lauding the work of a friend who stands for the same artistic doctrine and can be depended upon to intone a eulogistic antiphony when his turn comes.

The ancients also had their societies for mutual admiration. None the less no false modesty stifled an author's expressing his own opinion of his originality and, it might be added, his high estimate of the appeal of his work, although this latter is a topic that we need touch but incidentally here. The assertion of Ennius that he was the first Latin poet of formal culture[21] was in the mode of both Greece and Rome. So were Cicero's repeated boasts that he was the first competent adapter of Greek philosophy to the Roman tongue[22] and Vergil's "Wend we our way to dells hitherto untrod."[23] Let us recall Horace's familiar claims to pioneership: "Dicar . . . princeps,"[24] with its neglect of the literary precedence of Catullus, and "Parios ego primus iambos ostendi,"[25] written in spite of Cato the Younger's adaptation of an invective from Archilochus.[26] The basis for Propertius'[27] declaration of priority in the field of Roman love elegy is quite subjective.[28] These

[21] *Annales frgs.* 214, 215 (Vahlen, ed. 2).

[22] *Tusc. disp.* i. 3. 5; *De nat. deor.* i. 4. 8.

[23] *Geo.* iii. 40.

[24] *Carm.* iii. 30. 10.

[25] *Epist.* i. 19. 23.

[26] Plutarch *Cato min.* 7.

[27] iii. 1. 3, 4.

[28] The professional classicist will recognize the fact that these are oft-cited instances; *see* W. Kroll, "Unsere Schätzung der römischen Dichtung," *Neue Jahrb. f. d. klass. Alt.* XI (1903), 3 ff.; G. Riedner, *Typische Äusserungen der römischen Dichter über ihre Begabung, ihren Beruf, und ihre Werke* (Nürnberg, Stich, 1903), 66–69.

utterances were not the outgivings of freakish genius or the eccentric mind. There is in them a store of literary convention doubtless surviving from the artless bidding of the old-time bard for the attention of his audience: "I have a new song to sing, my masters."[29]

Time was, in modern literature as well, when with their eyes on classical precedent authors were addicted to announcements of the same sort. The example that will first occur to the reader is Milton's "adventurous song" pursuing "Things unattempted yet in prose or rhyme,"[30] an echo of Ariosto's

> Cosa non detta in prosa mai, nè in rima.

Dante[31] and Spenser[32] both introduced the same motive which, as Joseph Hall's assertive challenge quoted above as a text of this chapter betokens, is not confined to poetry of the high style. Apart from conscious imitation of classical mode lies, I take it, Rousseau's self-affirmation: "Je forme une entreprise qui n'eut jamais d'exemple et dont l'exécution n'aura point d'imitateur." In the *Confessions*, as when Marie Bashkirtseff stressed the extraordinary standing of her work as a human document, we hear the assertive accents of the individual temperament, not free from morbid egotism.

Warned by the known truths of literary history we are aware that we must guard against attaching

[29] *See* Homer *Odyssey* i. 351.

[30] *Paradise Lost* i. 13–16. Similarly in *Comus*, 44–45, Milton declared that his theme "never yet was heard in tale or song"; see *The Poetical Works of John Milton*, H. J. Todd, ed. (ed. 4, London, Rivingtons et al., 1842), I, 403, notes; Ida Langdon, *Milton's Theory of Poetry and Fine Art* (New Haven, Yale University Press, 1924), 133, 134. The reference in Ariosto is *Orlando Furioso* i. 2. 1–2.

[31] *Paradiso* ii. 6.

[32] *Faerie Queene* vi. prol. ii.

too literal a value to these declarations of priority. They tend proverbially to be rhetorical generalizations; they are seldom founded on any such exhaustive knowledge of preceding literary effort as modern criticism insists on. Ideas, spirit, manner are elements of cardinal importance to us when we set out to determine what is original in an author's product. The ancient theory throughout sophisticated epochs was prone to place external attributes beside or even above inner essence. In the simple code of the Roman, owing to the derivative character of much of his artistic literature, that was original which for the first time was imported from Greek and domesticated in the native medium. To us essay, play, or novel will seem to merit the term 'satire' as rightly as do the *Dunciad* or Samuel Johnson's *London*. In our roster of world satirists we unhesitatingly assign a place to Aristophanes who satirized in drama and Martial who satirized in epigram. The ancient theory at its highest was not blind to analogies and differences in content. Aristotle, of course, in more than one passage of the *Poetics* grounds literary distinctions on subject-matter, as when he points out (i. 1447 B) the integral difference between Homer and Empedocles, distinguishes (ix. 1451B) poet and historian by his famous criterion of the possible and the actual in their respective narratives. Horace recognized the spiritual likeness between Greek Old Comedy and Lucilius (*Serm.* i. 4. 1–6); yet he spoke of satire as a *form* untouched by the Greeks (i. 10. 66).

Time after time it has been found that, where a question of literary innovation is involved, the accepted point of view in antiquity stressed form and medium above content. The wine skin was deemed more important than the wine. The utterances especially of the lyric poets of Greece furnish ample illustration of what was regarded as justifying claim to originality.[33] In the average instance the new departure involved not novelty in subject-matter but innovation in outward form, in rhythm and melody. This elevation of form over content had become firmly established in the literary practice of Greece by the fifth century. So at the end of the century Timotheos, following a custom traceable to Terpander, Alcman, and Pindar, declares that he does not sing the old songs and bids avaunt the ancient Muse;[34] yet the extant titles indicate that Timotheos set the traditional themes to new strains. This belief in the renovative effects obtainable by new departures in form and setting lived down to the days of eighteenth-century classicism. Indeed, the question of form *vs.* matter is eternally *sub judice.* "In poetry a new cadence means a new idea,"[35] averred not many years ago one of the advocates of 'The New Poetry.' What is this imagist's dictum but a virtual rejuvenescence of the old Greek view?

If the poets in actual usage paid homage to the dominance of form, the sophists, insisting on the

[33] These and other data on this point have been compiled by Stemplinger, *op. cit.*, 143–45, and, with due acknowledgment of his debt to Stemplinger, by G. C. Fiske, *Lucilius and Horace* (Madison, University of Wisconsin Studies, 1920), chap. 1. I have consulted both these works with profit.

[34] *Frg.* 21, U. von Wilamowitz-Moellendorff, *Timotheos, Die Perser* (Leipzig, Hinrichs, 1903); Bergk, *PLG frg.* 12.

[35] Quoted by A. Lowell, *Tendencies in Modern American Poetry* (New York, Macmillan, 1917), 239 *and* J. Erskine, *The Literary Discipline* (New York, Duffield, 1923), 47, from the preface of *Some Imagist Poets* (Boston, Houghton Mifflin, 1915).

infinite capacity for transformation resident in skilful and conscienceless use of discourse, elevated practice into rhetorical principle. In the pages of Isocrates the theory was transmitted as a literary program universally applicable to both prose and poetry. In the celebrated prooemium of his discourse entitled the *Panegyric*, Isocrates gives a veritable treatise on "Principles of Success in Literature"—to apply a modern title to an ancient disquisition. His principal thesis is that the possibilities of freshness attainable by improvements in form quite eclipse those obtainable by innovations in content. Isocrates had touched previously on this theme in his *Encomium of Helen* (1). He there vents his scorn on those rhetorical craftsmen who in their mania to achieve originality were given to treating bizarre and sensational topics. Developing this contention in the *Panegyric* (7–8), he maintains that no subject, however trite, is exhausted so long as the possibility of improving on the efforts of former speakers remains. He here preached what he practiced in the *Helen* and the *Busiris*. Each of these encomia was intended as corrective of what he deemed abortive attempts, made previously by other men of letters, to eulogize those two unpromising subjects for eulogy, the Greek beauty and the Egyptian tyrant.

The time is ripe, is his thought in the *Panegyric*, actually to choose old themes and to try to surpass one's predecessors (10). In making this constructive suggestion Isocrates must be credited with an insistence more rigid than the sophists of his time themselves exhibited in carrying to its logical conclusion the sophistic declaration of the metamorphic omnipotence of speech. By contact with its divers hues, content, chameleonlike, takes on the color of the individual author's mood and design. The old may be newly costumed, former valuations may be reversed, old emphasis shifted. Real artistic progress is furthered not by those who seek out virgin themes but by those who know how to speak beyond the chance of rivalry.

This Isocratean code is at once the product of stimuli originating in practice and theory before his time, and also an authoritative body of ordinances, affecting the growth of literature through centuries subsequent to his day. Since this is the case, the only justifiable method is to study Isocrates not in isolation and in terms of his procedure in any given instance, but to approach him as the result of previous tendencies and the prototype of subsequent practices in literature.

From this digression into regions that abut no more upon the realm of biography than on other territories of literature, one returns with a better right to an opinion as to the verities to be disengaged from the prooemium of the *Evagoras*. There can be no doubt that in the reckonings of Isocrates it was his proposed innovation in the form of the encomium that overshadowed all else. In his own eyes his great step would consist in making prose serve as a handmaid where poetry had served before. Hence his gaze was riveted on poetic encomia which he was proposing to transmute into a new medium. Under these circumstances it is highly improbable that he would deem it necessary to take precise cognizance of such specimens of prose encomium as antedated him and to scrutinize them in respect to subject-matter. There must have been such specimens, the fruit of forensic eloquence and political propaganda. However, unless these harmonized with his conception of how the prose encomium should continue the poetic tradition, he as judge and jury would rule them out of court.

In this connection the modern analogies to which attention has been called a few pages since are most instructive. We know that the grand scale of *Paradise Lost* and the superb sweep of its *epic* narrative are the features that differentiate it from such continental predecessors as the *Adamus Exul* of Grotius and the *Adamo* of Andreini, both *dramatic* in form.[36] Original in the rigorous sense of the word Milton was not. In Hall's case only his exalted opinion of his own greater fidelity to the spirit and the form of Juvenal's satires excuses his boast. If he were unfamiliar with the work of Donne, the chronological relations of whose satires to those of Hall is not free from uncertainty, there was Lodge's *A Fig for Momus*, published two years before the *Virgidemiarum Libri*, to dispute the claim to absolute priority.[37] Benvenuto Cellini's story of his own life and Cardan's autobiography brand Rousseau's proclamation of the unique character of his *Confessions* as "rhetorical self-assertion,"[38] the fruit of defective knowledge or subjective estimate.

[36] See *Paradise Lost, Books I and II*, A. W. Verity, ed. (Cambridge, University Press, 1910), liv.; Ida Langdon, *loc. cit.*

[37] R. M. Alden, *The Rise of Formal Satire in England under Classical Influence* (Philadelphia, published for the Univ. of Pennsylvania, 1899), 113–16; K. Schulze, "Die Satiren Halls," *Palaestra* CVI (1910), 122–24; *Cambridge History of English Literature*, IV, 329.

[38] A. R. Burr, *The Autobiography, a Critical and Comparative Study* (Boston, Houghton Mifflin, 1909), 25.

Returning to Isocrates, let us further observe that of all the divisions of a discourse the prooemium is the least promising place in which to look for statements on the literal historicity of which one can build. In antiquity at least the exordium was deliberately formulated to bid for the favor of the audience and to induce a frame of mind. No Puritanical sensitiveness to literal truth circumscribed the oratorical prologue. From Aristotle down to Quintilian and beyond, theory commended all possible instruments with which to play on the various humors of the listeners. They were to be conciliated, their interest was to be attracted, their understanding of the topic under discussion to be quickened or, if desirable, befogged.[39] Anything, in Quintilian's famous phrase, to render the hearer "benivolum, attentum, docilem."[40]

In the exordium of an epideictic piece such as the *Evagoras*, theory came especially to sanction an author's putting his best foot forward. According to Aristotle[41] the foreword should be comparable to the prelude in flute-playing. The musician strikes up first the melody that he can play best, thus to win the favorable attention of the audience. Then, by transitional modulations, he passes on to the movement of the piece proper. Thus the prooemium in epideictic oratory is a mere preliminary flourish, intended to display virtuosity and proverbially—"They all do it," wrote Aristotle—it consists of matter quite extraneous to the main body of the treatise.

[39] Aristotle *Rhet.* iii. 14. 7.

[40] *Inst. orat.* iv. 1. 5.

[41] *Op. cit.*, iii. 14. 1.

In advancing these reasons for tempering implicit faith in the literal credibility of the declaration of Isocrates, we are indicting him no more than we are the attitude of his forerunners and his successors. The famous maxim of Socrates, "The excellence of an orator consists in telling the truth,"[42] is pitifully at odds with Greek rhetorical theory, teeming with "ingenious hints on deception," as Theodor Gomperz[43] acridly described Aristotle's *Rhetoric*. The prooemium especially is the happy hunting ground for topical utterance and nonchalant generalization. By the end of the fifth century B.C. handbooks of model exordia had appeared, as for example Antiphon's work entitled *Prooemia* and *Epilogues*.[44] In later days even Cicero did not disdain resorting to such tinned eloquence.[45] Before the time of Isocrates repetition of the various commonplaces had made them so hackneyed that they furnished butts for the ridicule of comic poets. One of these *clichés* consists in the defendant's stressing the disadvantages under which he labors because of the wicked machinations and carefully elaborated speech of his accuser. In a play of Cratinus[46] produced in 423 this theme is parodied, but it did yeoman service in the exordia of orators for many years thereafter.[47] In the *Panegyric* (13) Isocrates in his didactic way pays his respects to the orator's habit of mollifying his

[42] *Apology* 1. 18 A.

[43] *Greek Thinkers* (London, John Murray, 1912), IV, 435.

[44] Cited by Suidas *sub* ἅμα and μοχθηρός. Thrasymachus and Critias composed similar books; *see* Blass, *Die att. Bered.* (ed. 2), I, 115.

[45] *Ad Att.* xvi. 6. 4; "Habeo volumen prooemiorum: ex eo eligere soleo" *et seq.* At any rate, these "movable prefaces" were his own handiwork.

[46] The Πυτίνη; *see* Kock, *Com. Att. Frag.* I, 69, no. 185.

[47] *See* O. Navarre, *op. cit.*, 170 ff.

audience with trite introductory formulas in which apology is offered for lack of time for preparation or for dearth of words suitable to the case at issue. Nevertheless, Isocrates could lapse like the crowd into the use of stereotyped material. A quarter of a century after he had written the *Panegyric* he himself introduced into the *Antidosis* (17–19) the overworked motive satirized seventy years before by Cratinus.

The rhetorical technician, as is true of the lyric poet and is said to be true of woman, belongs to the *genus semper mutabile.* His utterances, inspired by the mood of the moment, are often the results of ephemeral incentives. The prooemium of the *Evagoras* is redolent of the set flowers of language adapted to the specific circumstances attending its composition. It reveals the note of exaggeration characteristic of special pleading. For example, there are the words about the harm that envy can do and the sweeping assertion that great men of the present generation, no matter what their deserts, can never hope to have their praises sounded, since this honor is extended only to the heroes of yore. But the triumphs of the Spartan admiral, Lysander, had moved various poets in his lifetime to glorify his deeds in encomiastic poems.[48] These various panegyrics, produced at the beginning of the fourth century when Lysander's fame was at its height, antedated the *Evagoras* by two decades.

Likewise, the deprecatory words of Isocrates concerning the difficulty of the task he has set for himself in attempting a prose encomium are a version

[48] Plutarch *Lysander* 18; Pfister, *op. cit.* II, 556; 587.

of a traditional rubric.[49] In forensic pleading lack of oratorical address and experience, tender years—

"You'd scarce expect one of my age
To speak in public on the stage,"

as the old school declamation puts it—the unscrupulous cleverness of his adversary, and the like motivate the ancient orator's pretended discouragement and his bid for a considerate hearing. Thus, in making this appeal Isocrates was doing the conventional thing. Only the particular handicap under which he declares himself to labor, adapting to prose a form indigenous to poetry, is new.

One cannot but query how seriously he expected his readers to take this pronouncement. The assertion that the difficulty of prose eulogy of manly virtue is the reason why hitherto such a subject has not found a place among the wealth of themes treated in prose encomium has little or no grounding in logic. Encomia of worthies of the past, of divine and semidivine personages, had for a generation been couched in prose. From the time of Gorgias poetry had been influential in fixing both method and diction for the prose encomiast. The application of these precedents to a eulogy of a contemporary, which should form a literary unit, was one of expansion and development along lines that had previously been followed. Furthermore, the distinction between history and myth was so comfortably nebulous that the objects of personal encomia were not differentiated on the one hand, into figures of fable, on the other, into terrestrial figures of history. All were regarded in this age by most writers as persons

[49] *See* p. 83 above, n. 40.

equally historical, but belonging to different generations. Thus in the *Busiris* (8) Isocrates criticizes his literary rival, Polycrates, for garbling the genealogy of such denizens of the realm of myth as Aeolus and Orpheus.

Where rhetoric enters, truth flies out of the door. Since it is evident that in the prooemium of the *Evagoras* the rhetorical atmosphere is so pervasive, we cannot be sure that in any part of it we are transported to the clear ether of actuality. The motive of pioneership, the entrance into untrodden territory, was a commonplace cherished, as we have seen, throughout ancient classical literature. The orator's version of this theme was to proclaim the unprecedented significance of his case, the matchless rascality of his opponent. This, the sort of natural hyperbole that would fall in practice from the lips of the pleader, early in the history of rhetoric took its place among the typical themes of the prooemium.[50] As Aristotle puts the matter: "Men are attentive to important subjects, to those which concern themselves, to the marvellous . . . therefore the speaker must instil [in the prooemium] the notion that his subjects are of this kind."[51] The Stagirite, to his everlasting credit, well recognized the fact that only the intellectual crudity of the audience necessitated recourse to such shifts. Aristotle's term θαυμαστοῖς, "marvelous," comprehends, of course, 'new and strange.' The Roman theorists[52] introduce literally into their recipes, inherited from

[50] E.g., Lysias Κατὰ Διογείτονος 3; Isaeus Περὶ τοῦ Κίρωνος κλήρου 4; it is a favorite sentiment in Demosthenes; *see* Navarre, *op. cit.*, 215.

[51] iii. 14. 7, Jebb's translation.

[52] *Auctor ad Herenn.* i. 4; Cicero *de Invent.* i. 16. 23; Quintilian *Inst. orat.* iv. 1. 33.

the Greek handbooks, the terms *nova*, "new," and *inusitata*, "out of the ordinary."

Clearly, then, Isocrates's declaration of the unprecedented character of the *Evagoras* as a piece of commemorative literature is one of the conventional flourishes. It is to be judged by the standards of rhetoric, not hastily accepted as historical fact. Isocrates, with others, was influential in perpetuating these conventions, but he was not their originator. Many of them, as we have seen, had arisen and been codified before the *Evagoras* was written. There is thus every reason to suppose that Isocrates was comporting himself as the trained virtuoso in rhetoric, intent not on adhering to the objective facts of literary history but on magnifying his work in the eyes of his readers.

The precautions that have been taken to put the prooemium of the *Evagoras* in its proper setting do not exhaust the resources of demonstration, whatever effect they may have had upon the patient reader. There is still forthcoming a piece of more objective evidence bearing on this question of historicity. It is proposed to present this evidence because it is external in character and because it has never been projected upon the point at issue. Again we turn to the *Symposium* of Plato which, many other things though it contains—more, as Jowett has observed, than any commentator has dreamed of[52]—is also a dramatization of current rhetorical modes.

Because the dramatic date of the dialogue is the year 416 B.C., it does not, of course, follow that the piece is a historically accurate representation of the

[52] Translation of Plato, ed. 3, I. 515.

doctrines and practices that governed the composition of the prose encomium at that period. Like the literary fictions that Plato elsewhere plays with would be an imaginative transference back to an earlier time of facts of literary history holding good of a later period.[54] Hence conclusions as to the literary realism of the *Symposim* should not be pushed to extreme limits chronologically. At all events the date of composition approximated by the consensus of opinion[55] quite justifies our assuming that the work reflects a cultural era some years prior to the publication of the *Evagoras*.

A part of Plato's design was in his portrayal of Socrates to elevate truth-telling above rhetorical sophistries, spontaneity above elaboration. In his inimitable accents of ironical self-depreciation Socrates is made to enunciate a new program for the encomiastic art. He insists that he must be allowed to cleave to his benighted prejudice as to what the ideal encomium should be and, in contrast with the preceding eulogists, tell the truth about Love. This is a program which to the everlasting loss of ancient biographical art exerted no reformatory

[54] Cases in point are the astounding anachronism of the *Menexenus* and the fact that in the *Symposium* 193 A Aristophanes is made to refer in the year 416 to the dispersion of the Mantineans into separate communities, an event that most critics assume occurred in 385. Von Wilamowitz seems to be alone in his contention that the allusion is to the dissolution of the Arcadian Confederacy by the Spartans in 418, hence that no anachronism is committed. His latest utterance on the topic is to be found in *Platon* (ed. 2, Berlin, Weidmann, 1920), II, 176, 177). It is odd that the same person should be ready to explain the *Menexenus* as a deliberate attempt at mystification *à la* Bernard Shaw and balk at a similar hypothesis in the case of the *Symposium*.

[55] Placed by Hug (ed. 2; Leipzig, Teubner, 1884), in the interval 384–372 B.C., but at a date nearer 385; Pohlenz, *op. cit.* 390, n. 3, *circa* 380 B.C.; von Wilamowitz, *op. cit.* II, 178, in the period 381–378 B.C.; Christ, *Gesch. der griech. Litt.*, ed. 6, I, 686, says: "Im Jahre 385 oder bald nach her abgefasst."

influence on subsequent encomiasts. Furthermore, Socrates is made to disclaim all concern with rhetorical diction and the rules of formal arrangement. He will not and does not speak as the schoolmen who precede him speak.[56]

In order to motivate the protest of Socrates, Plato had to show by antithesis the prevalent fashions of the encomium. In composing the several exemplars he adapted them with consummate skill to the personalities of the speakers. It is also an exegetical commonplace that, especially in the discourses of Phaedrus, Pausanias, and Agathon, the different penchants of contemporary rhetoricians were mirrored.[57] The encomia of Eryximachus and of Aristophanes reproduce, not so much the *tempora et mores* of rhetoric, but rather the *ethos* of the speakers, the medico-pedant and the genial *farceur*. Yet Eryximachus develops his contribution with the same heed to heading and subheading that is visible in the speeches of Phaedrus, Agathon, and the other formalists. Even the mythical fantasy of Aristophanes preserves conventional elements of encomium.[58]

These *illuminati* are frank in their criticisms of one another's efforts. Each individual is wedded to his own idea of what an encomium should be. Plato has not painted a conflict of individual biases only; we hear the clash of rival theory and dissentient schools. There were in the golden age of intellectual Athens encomia and encomia. There was

[56] *See* von Wilamowitz, *op. cit.* 176.

[57] *See* Pohlenz, *op. cit.* 372; 397, 398.

[58] Note, for example, the superlatives at the beginning, esp. 189 D, and the rhapsodical epilogue 193 D.

an elasticity of plan comparable with that marking another realm of literature according to Kipling's jingle:

> There are nine and sixty ways of constructing
> tribal lays
> And every single one of them is right.

But with the *dramatis personae* of the *Symposium* only that is right as an encomium that squares with personal theory or school dogma.

Plato's picture thus shows the thorough ventilation that questions pertaining to the technique of encomium were receiving in the late fifth and the early fourth century at the hands of the protagonists of rhetorical art and their followers. It is incredible that the multifarious activity and the busy experimentation rife in the fifteen years following the death of Socrates had left unexemplified any possibility relating to the content of encomium, to the rules governing its composition, and (no matter what Isocrates asserts) to the range of subjects.

And so to our final point. When it comes the turn of Alcibiades to speak his encomium, he humorously insists that his subject must be Socrates. He cannot, he says, in the presence of Socrates praise anyone but Socrates—the Greek says "god or mortal"—and come off unscathed from the jealous ire of the master (214 D). This, to be sure, is badinage, and Alcibiades at his entry is portrayed as half-seas-over. But with consummate art Plato knew how to keep his characterization quite aloof from sottish horseplay and the broad realism of comedy. Alcibiades is drunk to a degree only. His speech, with its brilliant play of wit, its flashes of whimsical fancy, and its penetrating insight into the greatness of the character of Socrates well illustrates the Greek adage "Wine and truth." Plato took the precaution to warn even the dullest reader that the speech of Alcibiades is far removed from the illusory vaporings of a reveler deeply sunk in his cups, by hinting in the words of Socrates, "You are, in my opinion, sober," (222 C), that Alcibiades is captain of his own wits. At all events the encomium is one of the most inspired pieces of interpretative delineation in classical literature.

It was the device of an inspired biographer to show Socrates as he appeared to the eyes of the unregenerate Alcibiades. Pages of direct characterization could not have attained realism so completely. Moreover, in so doing Plato did not turn his back on the traditional topics of biographical encomium. Much of the disquisition of Alcibiades is an illustration, taken ostensibly from personal experience, of the 'self-control' of Socrates (216 D–219 D). 'Valor' and 'wisdom' also come in for eulogy (219 D). Like the rubric of 'self-control,' *karteria*, 'hardihood,' is developed by the citation of incidents of the conduct of the philosopher on the field of battle (219 D–221 B). Alcibiades makes play with the canonical device of *syncrisis* (221 C). Other touches preserve inimitably the atmosphere of set encomium, but we must pass them over here.

Nowhere in the repartee that precedes and follows the speech of Alcibiades does Plato introduce any suggestion to the effect that traditional practice is violated when an encomium is centered on a great contemporary figure. Nor at the end when Socrates proposes to eulogize Agathon does any one demur (222 E–223 A). Alcibiades' choice of theme is approved by the spokesman, Eryximachus (214 D), without any expression of surprise that praise of a contemporary should form the subject-matter of an encomium. Had this been at the period of composition an unprecedented departure from conventional principles, Plato must certainly have made the most of the point. The spectacle of an Alcibiades flouting the proprieties of rhetoric as he flouted most other conventions would certainly have moved Plato to put an apposite comment in the mouth of one of the interlocutors. Let us remember that Plato is partly bent on exposing the futilities of contemporary rhetoric and shattering its cherished axioms. In the company, as we have seen, were exponents of the cut-and-dried programs of the schools. These alumni were still at the stage of intellectuality at which rules and patterns are sacrosanct. Yet none of the auditors takes issue with Alcibiades over his choice of subject. Why? Because there was nothing revolutionary in devoting an especial encomium to a great contemporary figure.

This is the end of our demonstration. We have sought to prove that Isocrates, governed as he was by ancient criteria as to what constituted literary pioneership and obsessed by ideals of form and style, would not have hesitated to put a personal valuation upon his services to the biographical encomium in prose. His words, occurring in that haunt of exaggerated and *ex parte* expression, a prooemium, are not valid proof that to no sophist, logographer, or pamphleteer before his time had the thought of composing a prose eulogy of a figure of recent history presented itself. They indicate merely that he was ready to insist that no one hitherto had fashioned a prose, biographical encomium that accorded with his own theory as to the lines, schematic and stylistic, that such productions should follow. Judicious criticism must then rate his declaration of pioneership at the most as the expression of an arbitrary, subjective estimate, not as the irrefutable record of objective fact.

CHAPTER V

ARISTOXENUS AND THE EARLY PERIPATETICS

To watch the growth of a legend is a sad occupation.
—From the last writing of Joseph Conrad.

In a current book on the history of Greek philosophy we read: "Although biographies are the favourite reading of those who most despise philosophy, they could never have been written without its help."[1] This sounds like a retort elicited by some specific detractors of Mr. Benn's chosen field. Who the scoffers were, I know not. However, the assumption that there is a temperamental crevasse between confirmed readers of biography and the devotees of philosophy would, it may be imagined, take some proving. Nowadays, when reading biographies is a means of mental recreation only less popular than reading fiction, there is surely no lack of folk who are addicted to reading biographies, memoirs, and the various other sorts of personal chronicles, but who do not contemn philosophy.

On the other hand, it is credible that many minds should find greater profit and instruction from viewing the drama of terrestrial life, conduct, and fortunes as these have been lived, exemplified, or

[1] A. W. Benn, *The Greek Philosophers* (ed. 2; London, Smith, Elder and Co., 1914), 129.

encountered by human beings than in conning the problems of mortal existence by the comprehensive, impersonal methods of metaphysics and ethics. Among the Romans, for instance, the personal example of virtue, the concrete human precedents which it was the immediate business of the biographer and of the psychological historian to set forth, but which a Horace found as germane to his purpose as did a Nepos and a Tacitus to theirs, were more esteemed as guides to living than were the abstractions of philosophical speculation.

To assert that biographies *could* not have been written without the aid of philosophy is, nevertheless a *post hoc propter hoc* in which it is prudent not to indulge. For the purposes of literary history a recasting of the generalization will, at all events, suffice. Biographical writing among the Greeks came to owe much to philosophy; it was in part the result of incentives furnished by philosophy and philosophers. The intellectual movements centering around Socrates, Plato, and Aristotle stimulated and enriched biographical expression, precisely as the modern rationalistic spirit, with its elevation of the truth and its appreciation of the realistic, has wrought on English biography improvements amounting to metamorphosis. Yet there was English biography of a sort before the advent of critical intelligence. An account of the growth of Greek biography should be phrased in somewhat similar language. The channels of biographical impulse, by no means choked before, were widened and deepened in the age in which is localized the rise of formal biography among the Greeks.

As, in consonance with the point of view enunciated in previous chapters, the saving adjective 'formal' must be inserted, so the term 'philosophy' must be interpreted, not in any restricted sense but as the ancient world understood it. This seemingly obvious warning is inspired by the fact that a philosophical friend of mine, whose interests lie in the fields of psychology and metaphysics, confessed himself mystified at the notion that philosophy had contributed to the rise of biography. The learned gentleman was for the moment visualizing the content of philosophy in terms merely of those categories that represent the subject as it is subdivided in the modern university discipline. Of these branches ethics, of course, is the one that fostered especially the study of individual lives as exemplars of its precepts.

The affinity between ethics and biography is so natural and has been so frequently acknowledged that illustrations need not be multiplied. Throughout the centuries biographers have conceived it a proper part of their function to attach to the life of a good man the value of a lesson in human conduct. This moralistic and edificatory purpose is discernible in Nepos, Plutarch, and countless lives of the Christian saints. Sometimes it was uppermost or even exclusive. English biography in its inception was permeated by this spirit. Thus that pious optimist, Izaak Walton, genuflected reverently before the worthy subjects of his *Lives;* he saw himself as one who had "commended" their "merits to the imitation of posterity."[2] As Sir Sidney Lee has

[2] Quoted from the end of the *Life of Sir Henry Wotton.*

observed,[3] the morally unworthy, in Walton's judgment, lay outside the proper pale of biography. He resembled in respect to this prejudice the French impressionist, Eugène Carrière, who—I appropriate information given to me by one[4] learned in modern art—would only paint those whom he esteemed.

Had such ideals of biography been without exception dominant throughout the centuries, one shudders to think of the volumes that must have been added to the monotonous chronicling of impeccability—of a dearth of which the genre has never had reason to complain. Insistence on the didactic mission of biography was quite as characteristic of Samuel Johnson as were the clear-sighted views, which put the world of letters in his debt, concerning the duty of the biographer to avoid panegyric and respect truth and realism. Johnson was much given to stressing the paradigmatic usefulness of "judicial and faithful" record of almost any life.[5] The lexicographer followed out his principles logically in his own biographical work and consciously set a utilitarian value on the portrayal of the career of an evil liver, such as Savage. His own *Lives of the English Poets* he was fain to hope were "written . . . in such a way as may tend to the promotion of piety."[6]

Ethically intentioned biography starts from a moral life as a concrete example and proceeds to the more or less formal application of the lesson in human conduct taught by that life. The swing of the indicator on the dial did not always tend in this

[3] *Principles of Biography*, 19.
[4] F. J. Mather, *Estimates in Art* (New York, Scribner's, 1916), 189.
[5] *Rambler*, no. 60.
[6] *Boswell's Life of Johnson*, G. B. Hill, ed. (Oxford, 1887), IV, 34.

direction. In the course of the development of the study of human life among the Greeks general ideals of behavior, abstract definitions of character, or descriptive treatments of modes of human existence formed the points of departure. Human types and individual exponents had at first the subsidiary value of illustrations. In popular thought we still have a way of assuming that a kind of graphic classification is applicable to the several modes of living, '*bioi*' as the Greeks styled them. Everyday speech at least recognizes in its terminology the 'Intellectual Life,' the 'Religious Life,' the 'Strenuous Life.' Books have been written to commend and illustrate these kinds of life, as, for example, that classic for brain-workers, Philip Gilbert Hamerton's *Intellectual Life*. The author constantly cites specific examples in order to buttress his general precepts, a method for which there are Greek prototypes in plenty.

The Hellenic precedents for this demarcation of the possible areas of existence, however, mapped them out with an ethnographic precision rivaling the fashion in which the old geographies divided the descendants of Noah into white, black, yellow, brown, and red races. Aristotle's philosophy, recognizing as it did the 'Life of Pleasure,' the 'Life of Action,' and the 'Life of Contemplation,' applied the principle with harder analysis than should we and posited more rigidly a mutual exclusiveness among the *bioi*. The concept was seemingly older than Aristotle, since the Pythagoreans had made tentatives in diagraming the sectors of human life. The famous comparison of mankind to the three classes of people that assembled at the Olympic Games, namely, chaffering tradesmen, contestants, and spectators, emanated, if not from Pythagoras himself, at least from Pythagorean circles.[7] This is an early instance of drawing paradigms from the world of men in order to elucidate human living. The method of assessing the different values of life by illustrative recourse to types of humanity and ultimately to individual figures is a device which Greek ethics naturally made its own.

The *Dialogues* of Plato reveal a complete comprehension of this illuminative power of exemplars gleaned from observation of types of people and individuals. The figure of Socrates as limned by Plato is in truth an all-compelling example of a way of life, an ethical pattern as masterful in its effect as are the doctrines this unique personality is made to enunciate. In Plato's work the human element is pervasive. The *Dialogues*, as every one knows, owe the pictorial charm that sets them off from the less colorful pages of Aristotle to the panorama of human society manipulated by Plato. It was this recognition of the didactic efficacy of concrete illustration that led Plato to put on the stage of his ethical dramas those homely folk, "cobblers and fullers and cooks and doctors," at whom Callicles jeers;[8] to typify the unjust man who yet is happy by sketching the crimes by which a personage of recent history, Archelaus, ruler of Macedon, rose from lowly origin to the throne;[9] to justify the contention that Athens had never owned a good statesman by analyzing the

[7] John Burnet, *Early Greek Philosophy* (ed. 3; London, A. C. Black, 1920), 98, n. 3.

[8] *Gorgias* 491 A. [9] *Ibid.* 471 A-D.

careers of supposedly eminent uplifters of the state, Pericles and others.[10]

Thus in the ethical perceptions and the methods of literary presentation formulated by Socratic philosophy the conviction that character can be most graphically outlined when it is shown incarnated in characters is firmly imbedded. Later descriptive ethics carried the method farther. When the pursuit of learning and the study of morals took up a joint abode in the Peripatetic community, Aristotle and his pupils kept adding to the store of applicable examples. The several objects of life, reprehensible and commendable, were studied and presented in terms of their mortal exponents, individual or corporate. Take, for example, the work of Heraclides Ponticus, dubbed Pompicus ('The Parader') by wags poking fun at the fleecy raiment he affected and his plethoric habit. The gods, however, had made Heraclides' body thick but not his wits. He was a pupil of Plato, an associate of Aristotle in some formal or informal position of discipleship,[11] and was thus a "link between the two intellectual realms." Among the products of his industrious brain were treatises on *Pleasure*, *Temperance*, *Piety*, *Valor*, *Virtue*, *Happiness*, and *Justice*.[12] These tractates, in which he resorted freely to the chatty and anecdotal dialogue form, teemed, as extant fragments suffice to show, with lessons drawn from the lives of historical personages. An example or two out of many:

[10] *Ibid.* 515 C–516 D.

[11] O. Voss, *De Heraclidis Pontici vita et scriptis* (Rostock, Adler, 1896), 13, 14, explains the report that Heraclides was a pupil of Aristotle as inspired by the intellectual leadership of the latter when both were disciples of Plato.

[12] Diog. Laert. v. 86–88; Athen. xii. 512 A.

In *Concerning Pleasure* the ruinous effects, financial and mental, of a life spent in dalliance are rendered concrete by the citation of Pericles' bankruptcy, induced, we are to believe, by the bright eyes of Aspasia;[13] the remorseful self-mutilation of Dinias, the perfume-vender, was another horrific warning.[14]

The ferver with which the busy minds of this period devoted themselves to separating the various threads in the tangled skein of existence gave rise also to many books treating the various modes of living. Περὶ βίων was the stock title and such works came from many hands.[15] Heraclides wrote under this caption, but since the work in question is listed by Diogenes Laertius (v. 87) among works dealing with psychology and the world of nature, its contents may have differed from those of other books on this theme.[16] Theophrastus and Clearchus[17] of Soli in Cyprus, another pupil of Aristotle, addressed their works on the subject to the life of mankind. Another Peripatetic savant, Dicaearchus of Messene, made an interesting application of the theme in his Περὶ τοῦ τῆς Ἑλλάδος βίου,[18] in which he sketched in chronological order the several upward steps of Greek civilization. Books of this sort were ethical preachments as well as tentatives in the history of culture. Their content was rich in human examples; the paradigm, hortatory or monitory as the case might be, was also gleaned from the lives of peoples whose

[13] Athen. xii. 533 C = Voss, *frg.* 4.

[14] Athen. xii. 552 F = Voss, *frg.* 8.

[15] *See* Leo, *op. cit.* 97, 98; E. Bickel, *Diatribe in Senecae philosophi fragmenta* (Leipzig, Teubner, 1915), I, 216.

[16] Voss, *op. cit.* 31 follows H. Schrader, *Philol.* XLIV (1885), 241, in regarding the work as a treatise on natural history.

[17] Müller, *FHG* II, 303–10.

[18] Müller, *op. cit.* II, 232–40.

culture exemplified one ideal or another. The advantages of sobriety over excess, simplicity over luxury, justice over injustice were preached by acquainting the Greek world with the pernicious results of the Sybaritic existence elected by the Medes,[19] Lydians, Tarentines, and other supposedly self-pampering races.

There was another direction taken by descriptive ethics, fruitful in its results both for ancient and modern literature, namely, the sketching of social types. A first furrow in this field was turned in the fourth book of the *Nicomachean Ethics* where various types of human character, the liberal man, the magnanimous man, the arrogant man, the buffoon, and others, are partitioned off, their emotional reactions under certain circumstances, their conduct, and sometimes even their external attributes portrayed.[20] After Aristotle came Theophrastus to mirror in the *Characters* the *comédie humaine* with mellow realism. The book catalogues and delineates some thirty embodiments of stock human traits that darkened the sunshine of Athenian social life. Some of the figures, 'The Late-Learner,' and 'The Newsmaker,' for example, are the more or less offensive nuisances that mar daily serenity in all ages; others, however, such as 'The Coward' and 'The Avaricious Man,' fall into the range of ethical ideas.

Thus in the fourth century life in the mass and life in the individual came to be an engrossing concern. The realization that a great part of "the proper study of mankind is man" fostered naturally

[19] *See* e.g., Athen. xii. 512 A.

[20] Thus slow step, deep voice, and stately language are declared to be attributes of the magnanimous man, iv. 3. 1125 A. 34.

the study of mankind in men. The Greek citizen was finding himself more of a personal entity than he had been in earlier times. In the fifth century the careers of the normal citizenry, bound to the life of the state, had been marked by a uniformity inherent in the common civic responsibilities of assembly and law court, of official and military service. The man belonged less to the state in the fourth century, more to himself, his family, and his friends.[21] The average life was no longer a bubble borne onward in the flow of the main current but one that might circle in eddies apart.

It is axiomatic that the differences in the plastic art of the two centuries exhibit the contrasting values set by the one age and the other on individuality. The portrait sculpture of the fifth century deals in types in which the variety of specific likeness is mostly lost in idealization. In the fourth century verisimilitude prevails in delineation of the human subject; a god as well becomes under the hand of a Praxiteles a creature susceptible to mood and with an aspect of human charm. Scopas depicted with an anatomical clearness the tense play of emotion on the warrior's visage. Lysippus, chosen sculptor of Alexander the Great, wielded a master's touch in characterization. No wonder then, with the spirit of realism that pervaded the age, the greater distinctness of the individual in the scheme of things, and the competence given by ethics to estimate personal worth and conduct, that literature responded by extending and refining that sculpturing of personality in the round which the prose encomium had

[21] M. Wundt, *Geschichte der griechischen Ethik* (Leipzig, Engelmann, 1911), II, 47 ff.

already begun. Formal biography was the finished product.

There is always peril in the endeavor to be strictly logical and entirely comprehensive when one is engaged in tracking the antecedents of a literary phenomenon to their lairs. Yet we must, I think, take account of another impulse that was bound to lead to the study of men's lives, namely, the polymathy of the day. Quite apart from its obvious utility as a means of ethical indoctrination that commended biography, an epoch so catholic in its scholarly inquiry would have been driven by the mere thirst for knowledge and its mania for docketing men in relation to their times and their pursuits to carry on the investigations in which the fifth century savants had made a beginning. Biography became an ancillary device in those provinces of human cognition that we should now term the history of science, the history of arts and letters, and the history of civilization and government. Inquiry into these fields naturally carried with it study of inventors and contributors together with the facts of their lives. A title such as that of Heraclides' *On Poetry and Poets* tells its own story. This, so far as our knowledge goes, is the first instance of a combination in one work of the history of a genre and its representatives.[22]

Present-day criticism has agreed to assign a dominant force as a formative and inventive influence on Peripatetic biography to a single brain, that of Aristoxenus of Tarentum. As his initiative is estimated, we find him occupying a position analogous

[22] Leo, *op. cit.* 101.

to that usually assigned to Isocrates as an agent in the development of the prose encomium of historical personages. The extent of the originative service of Aristoxenus and of his sphere of influence is stated now more, now less comprehensively. Leo called him the "Founder of Literary Biography."[23] Christ enlarged the range of this definition and characterized Aristoxenus as the "Founder of Peripatetic biography with all its weaknesses."[24] However, both these scholars unite in picturing his influence, whether on succeeding biographers of men of letters or on Hellenistic biographers in general, as a sort of visitation of paternal iniquities upon the children. In other words, whatever traits reprehensible to modern canons of truth are found to mark the biographies of the Alexandrian era, are alleged to be inherited from the prejudices and the intransigent temper of this so-called prototype.[25] The question is whether these views have not darkened counsel. One is left with an uneasy feeling that this picture of Aristoxenus as the evil genius of biography has been drawn with strokes too decided and that fine shades of distinction have been thereby blurred. It all sounds too simple.

Among all the delvers in the field of learning in the Alexandrian period whose names belong in a history of biography, the figure of Aristoxenus is the most arresting to the modern mind. This appeal is

[23] *Ibid.* 102.

[24] *Gesch. der griech. Litt.*, ed. 6, II, 1, 71.

[25] A typical expression of the traditional view is the following assertion of A. Gercke, *Einleitung in die Altertumswissenschaft* (Leipzig, Teubner, 1910), II, 330: "Damit [i.e., as a result of the slanderous attacks by Aristoxenus on Socrates and Plato] kam der Klatsch in den Peripatos hinein."

not due to his prodigious industry (453 books[26] are attributed to his authorship), nor to the versatility of his scholarly interests. These qualities were proverbial of his age and school. But he was the great rhythmical and musical theorist of antiquity; this connection with one of the universal arts has insured him contacts independent of time. Furthermore, ancient tradition has attached to his career the always picturesque circumstance of disappointed ambition, to his personality a realistic human trait, asserted with the easy logic of ancient literary history to be the result of a kind of inferiority complex. A brief sketch of his life that has come down to us in the *Lexicon* of Suidas avers, at least, that, embittered because Aristotle decided in favor of Theophrastus as his successor in the headship of the Peripatetics, Aristoxenus vented his chagrin by defaming the memory of his master. He is pictured as a second Heraclitus, a veritable "foe to laughter."[27] Conspiring with this piquant characterization of Aristoxenus as a backbiter and kill-joy to cause him to stand out as a flesh-and-blood personage, the victim of intelligibly human weaknesses, is the notoriety that has accrued to him through the ages because of his depreciation of two of the great ones of all time, Socrates and Plato. The old Adam that is in most of us turns instinctively a readier ear to the disparager who seeks to bring to light in biography the dross in the character of a man or woman than to the orthodox panegyrist. According to our conviction as to where the sane balance lies between a

[26] Not, of course, comparable in length to our books; they were tantamount to chapters or pamphlets.

[27] Aelian *Var. hist.* viii. 13.

biographer's telling the truth as he sees it and paying loyalty to a friend, we approve or deplore, say, Froude's Carlyle or Henley's Stevenson. But—we read the exposures of the heretical critic and do not forget him. The shafts launched by Aristoxenus at his shining marks were gathered up centuries after by the Christian Fathers, notably Cyril of Alexandria and Theodoretus of Cyrrhus, and served these apologists in their assaults on Paganism. Thus Aristoxenus long continued to enjoy the sensational prominence tending to attach itself to the subverter of cherished idols.

In the previous chapter we have had to quarrel with that mode of criticism that connects innovations in biographical writing too credulously with a single name instead of rating his work as a product, conspicuous but not solitary, of literary evolution. Further volubility on this theme may overtax the reader's patience. Nevertheless for science's sake there must be expressed the conviction that the vividness with which as compared to less colorful co-workers Aristoxenus presents himself to our eyes has contributed to overemphasize his originality and the range of his influence. This at least is certain: loose exaggeration only can ascribe to him priority covering the whole field of Peripatetic biography. His Βίοι ἀνδρῶν—this is the title assigned by Plutarch[38] to the work on which the fame of Aristoxenus as a biographer chiefly rests—did not stand as the sole specimen emanating from the first generation of Aristotle's disciples. There was at least one fellow-pupil, Phaenias of Eresus in Lesbos, the extant fragments and titles of whose works indicate so full a

[38] *Non posse suaviter vivi* 10. 1093 C.

response to the intellectual stimuli of the day as easily to bracket his services to nascent biography with those of his more celebrated compeer. Phaenias, Theophrastus (famous compatriot of Phaenias), Dicaearchus of Messene, and Aristoxenus were members of the same literary coterie[29] and flourished in the same period. No literary pioneership can be assigned rightfully to Aristoxenus over these others.

Phaenias shared the versatility of scholarship sought by the Peripatetics but his especial predilection was for history and chronology. Hence he naturally was moved in the course of his biographical work to treat the lives of men of action, a territory that Aristoxenus did not enter at all. His work *On the Tyrants of Sicily*[30] exemplifies the chronic fascination that the personalities and the acts of potentates have exerted on mankind throughout political history. This plan of a homogeneous biographical series illustrated in the work had had, as we have seen, precedent in the studies of Damastes and Glaucus. Phaenias applied it to the lives of rulers. The *Tyrants of Sicily* was thus in one respect a forerunner of the biographical cycle of Suetonius on the Caesars.

In another work of Phaenias, *On the Socratics*, we have the first instance known to us of the application of the method of encyclopedic biography to a philosophical school. By attaching as he does a biographical character to this treatise Leo[31] by implication placed Phaenias on a level with Aristoxenus in

[29] Aristoxenus, Phaenias, and Dicaearchus are mentioned in the *Vita Marciana* of Aristotle (*see* V. Rose, *Aristotelis qui ferebantur librorum fragmenta* (Leipzig, Teubner, 1886), 435) as pupils of the Stagirite; in Suidas' life of Aristoxenus we read that he and Dicaearchus were contemporaries.

[30] Müller, *FHG* II, 297.

[31] *Op. cit.* 110.

the field of literary biography, notwithstanding the previous assertion of the latter's initiative. However, Leo's attitude toward another work of Phaenias, namely, *On Poets*, the title of which certainly relates it to biography, was in stricter consistency with his belief in the pioneership of Aristoxenus. This book, together with others of similar title and coming from various hands, Leo compared to Aristotle's dialogue *On Poets* and described them as studies in the history of literature rather than as biographies.[32] Former scholarship in this field had been, to be sure, hasty in attributing to books cited as Περὶ τοῦ δεῖνος or Περὶ βίων a biographical character merely on the strength of their titles.[33] In his proper revulsion against such an uncritical procedure Leo was inclined to go too far to the other extreme, especially when the traditional prestige of Aristoxenus' *Lives of Men* was at stake. The discovery some fifteen years ago of the *Life of Euripides* by Satyrus (of which more in the following chapter) gave us the first real insight into the elements entering into Peripatetic literary biography and the methods by which its exponents combined biography and literary criticism. As a result of this extension of our knowledge Leo afterwards revised his original opinion of the content of Aristotle's work *On Poets* so far as to admit that "It can no longer be doubted that the dialogue of Aristotle was concerned essentially with the poets as persons.[34] The inference is quite as applicable to the treatise of Phaenias *On Poets*.

[32] *Ibid.* 105.

[33] J. Luzak, *Lectiones Atticae* (Leyden, Luchtmans, 1809), 142, erroneously termed Theophrastus the inventor of biography on the basis of such titles.

[34] *Nachrichten der Gesellschaft der Wissenschaften zu Göttingen*, philol.-hist. Klasse, 1912, 275.

To the monopoly of the fame of literary inventor that Aristoxenus has enjoyed a well-known passage, preserved by Jerome[35] but undoubtedly deriving in substance from the *De viris illustribus* of Suetonius, has been made to contribute.[36] In this context Aristoxenus is placed fourth in a list of Greek biographers—Hermippus, Antigonus of Carystus, and Satyrus precede in the order given—and is dubbed *longe omnium doctissimus*. However, this estimate, to say nothing of the fact that it is one that falls easily from a Roman's pen, involves general reputation for scholarship; the writings of Aristoxenus on music and other topics, his tireless literary activity would help to justify the compliment.[37] Even if it be assumed that in this passage Suetonius was putting this superlative valuation on the merits of Aristoxenus as a literary biographer, it does not follow that the latter is properly to be viewed as the founder of the genre. The list is illustrative, not exhaustive. That it should rise to a climactic stress on Aristoxenus would naturally follow from his eminence—earned we have seen how—as *one* of the Greek prototypes of literary biography. Aside from the interpretation put upon this passage there is not a scintilla of evidence to warrant the assumption that he is in any exclusive sense the founder of literary biography.

The obsession that has led to exaggeration of the formative agency of Aristoxenus also affected, it must be believed, Leo's estimate of the work of Dicae-

[35] *De script. eccles.* prol. Migne, *Patr. Lat.* XXIII, 631.

[36] Leo, *Die griech.-röm. Biographie*, 102; 136.

[37] Gellius *Noct. Att.* iv. 11. 4, calls him for the same reason *vir litterarum veterum diligentissimus;* see also E. Zeller, *Die Philosophie der Griechen* (Leipzig, Reisland, 1879), II, 2, 883, n. 5.

archus of Messene. This other Peripatetic held in the commonwealth of learning a position no less commanding than did Aristoxenus if we may accept the judgment of Cicero, who hails Dicaearchus "My particular pet" and is given to coupling him and Aristoxenus together as bright luminaries of erudition.[38] Logically associated with the interest in mankind in the large that moved Dicaearchus to write his great work on the Greek modes of life would be such group biographies as other members of his circle were producing. As a matter of fact Diogenes Laertius[39] does cite in his life of Plato from the first book of a work by Dicaearchus, Περὶ βίων, such a biographical detail as Plato's competing in the wrestling match at the Isthmian Games. Similar data are found in the ancient lives of Sophocles and Euripides. There can be no reasonable ground for doubt that the references to Plato's poetical compositions and to his interest in painting, points that directly follow upon the allusion to his athletic prowess, also revert to Dicaearchus.[40] Farther along in Diogenes' chapter are two additional citations from Dicaearchus, but without reference to bibliographical source. One of these items is a slur on the *Phaedrus* of Plato, disparaged as a banal composition.[41] The other records the interesting information that Plato admitted women to his lecture-hall and that one of these cultured ladies was wont to wear men's clothes[42]—an assurance as to the antiquity

[38] *Tusc. disp.* i. 77; i. 41; *Ad Att.* viii. 4. [39] iii. 4.

[40] In the context in Diogenes the sources, Neanthes and Timotheus, from whom was obtained the subject-matter immediately preceding and following the reference to Dicaearchus, are expressly named. The intervening matter, it naturally follows, derives from Dicaearchus.

[41] iii. 38. [42] iii. 46.

of sex equality in education and apparel that ought to arouse in us a responsive thrill. Such material betrays the fondness for censorious fling and gossipy detail typical of much of ancient biography. The statements concerning the philosopher's athletic and artistic abilities are of a kind with subject-matter constantly forming a *locus* of ancient biography, namely, pursuits of boyhood and youth prior to embarkation on life-work.

It is not then adventurous to conclude that Dicaearchus composed a life of Plato which formed a division of a biographical group dealing with philosophers. Aristoxenus and Phaenias addressed themselves to biographical studies in this field. Diogenes, having on his first recourse to it in his life of Plato, cited the work by name, dispensed thereafter with surface reference, needless since the provenience of other material for which Dicaearchus is named as authority would be self-evident. The lone citation Περὶ βίων without further descriptive limitation will not, of course, persuade one who, as was Leo,[43] is an uncompromising adherent to the traditional doctrine of Aristoxenan supremacy. That attitude tends to make critics purblind to any possibility save the one.

[43] In doubting the existence of a purely biographical work by Dicaearchus which was comparable to that by Aristoxenus, Leo (*op. cit.* 105) was perpetuating the view of E. Köpke, *De Chamaeleonte Peripatetico* (Berlin, G. Lange, 1856), 11, who assumed that the fragments of Dicaearchus having a biographical content are to be attributed to Περὶ τοῦ τῆς Ἑλλάδος βίου. After I had arrived at my own opinion as the result of independent study of the ancient evidence, a process that I have sought always to follow in the preparation of this book, it was reassuring to find in the course of verification that in *P-W* V 1, 552–53, Martini had unhesitatingly assigned to Dicaearchus the authorship of an extended biographical treatment of philosophers and thus made at least two "founders" of literary biography. (But what of Phaenias?)

The true picture of the rise of Peripatetic biography should thus present the composite efforts of men who had been baptized from the same intellectual font. The flow of biography was along conduits laid by several hands. The qualities of literary technique, the facts of contents, the attitude toward truth characteristic of Hellenistic biography in general, are not unique in Aristoxenus. There is no reason to believe that because he had been dogmatic in his partisanships and had spiced his narrative with censorious anecdote, subsequent literary biography owed to him alone its perpetuation of these "weaknesses."

If we except Porphyry and the Christian Fathers, Aristoxenus' picture of Socrates has met with scant credence through the centuries of world thought. These are the chief counts in the old indictment: Socrates was in his youth the corrupted favorite of his teacher Archelaus (25);[44] as a man he was abnormally sensual (25 *b*, 27 *a*, 28); he was unlettered (27 *a*); he had a canny acquisitiveness (26) and a temper which in its outbursts betrayed him into transgressing all bounds of decent speech and action[45] (27 *b*, *c*); lastly and the most famous exhibit from the

[44] The numbers in the text designate the fragments according to Müller, *FHG* II.

[45] One Christian writer, Synesius, in kindlier portraiture represents the ungovernable temper as a failing confined to the younger years of Socrates; *Calvitii encom.* 81 *in* Migne, *Patr. graec.* LXVI, 1196, 1197. In the narrative of Aristoxenus, however, the paroxysms of rage formed an item of the information derived, as we shall see, from his father Spintharus, who, a younger contemporary of Socrates, could have known him only as he was in the last decade or two of his life; *see* Cyril, *Contra Iul.* vi. 185, after Porphyry, = Müller, *FHG* 28. Furthermore, the bigamy story was used by Aristoxenus, if we may judge from Porphyry as quoted by Cyril, *op. cit.* vi. 186 = *FHG* 28 b, and Theodoretus, *Graec. affect. cur.* xii. 174, as a proof of the incontinence of Socrates. Obviously, the bigamous Socrates was the adult Socrates; cf. E. Zeller, *Die Phil. der Griech.* (ed. 4; Leipzig, Reisland, 1889), II 1, 63, n. 5; 65, n. 3.

secret museum of the private life of Socrates, he was a bigamist (29, 30). These impeachments sound like ludicrous aberrations when set over against the figure of ethical grandeur that emerges from the pages of Zeller's minute analysis[46] and that is comprehended in such appreciations as: "A great moral teacher;" "A man who led a blameless personal life and in his teachings held up the highest ideals of conduct to others;" "A man of the noblest character and of the simplest life . . . accepting no fees, he acquired no wealth." It is portraiture of this kind, abstracted for illustration from two recent English handbooks,[47] that the world at large has been given to contemplating as the true likeness.

A book written over a century ago by the Dutch scholar, John Luzak,[48] remarkable though it is for occasional fantastic hypotheses,[49] for quaint verbosity and the emotional style which it shares with so many of the old-time diatribes, has remained the classic refutation of the story of Socrates' bigamy. Luzak gave Aristoxenus a wholehearted castigation as the source of libels on Socrates repeated by such later biographers as Hieronymus of Rhodes and Satyrus. The original attack on the philosopher was according to Luzak merely the reflex of the literary and the intellectual rivalries that throughout Peri-

[46] *Op. cit.* and *Grundriss der Geschichte der griechischen Philosophie* (ed. 12; bearb. W. Nestle, Leipzig, Reisland, 1920).

[47] R. B. Appleton, *Greek Philosophy from Thales to Aristotle* (London, Methuen, 1922), 55; W. T. Stace, *A Critical History of Greek Philosophy* (London, Macmillan, 1920), 131.

[48] *Op. cit.*

[49] E.g., the assumption that Aristoxenus, through the personality of Polyarchus, the voluptuary (*Life of Archytas, frg.* 15) is really lauding subjectively a life of sensual pleasures. In Luzak's eyes the Peripatetic also put himself beyond the pale of all respectable morality by his doctrine that the soul was a "harmony" (*Lect. Att.* 215–18).

patetic biography continued to wreak havoc on veracious portraiture. Luzak's conception of the perverting effects of these "apostolic blows and knocks" on the substance of ancient biography was undoubtedly exaggerated. Quite characteristic of former criticism, which inherited the tradition from Alexandrian scholarship, was the proclivity to imagine adherents of different isms as standing always with daggers drawn. Modern opinion is not so ready to twist intellectual differences between—let us say—Plato and Aristotle, between Aristotle and his pupils Aristoxenus[50] and Dicaearchus into acrimonious personal feuds. By and large, however, the evil reputation of Aristoxenus as a scandal-monger in his delineation of Socrates and Plato remains about where Zeller left it.[51] The seeming absurdity of the charges has been generally regarded as constituting their own refutation. A critic such as Professor Burnet, who has not been content merely to cling to flat rejection of the testimony of Aristoxenus, at the most goes to some pains to motivate the hostility of the assumed fabricator.[52]

Nevertheless, in classical research as well as in other fields of scholarship few doctrines are so sanctified as to preserve immunity unassailed by some tough-minded skeptic. Thus it is that one scholar,

[50] Aristoxenus' reputed assaults on Aristotle are not borne out by the facts; *see* R. Westphal, *Aristoxenus von Tarent* (Leipzig, Abel, 1883–93), II, proleg. ix.

[51] *Die Phil. der Griech.* II, 2, 883, "seine fabelhaften und theilweise offenbar aus Verkleinerungssucht entsprungenen Angaben über Sokrates und Plato;" A. Busse, *Sokrates* (Berlin, Reuther und Reichard, 1914), 119; J. Burnet, *Greek Philosophy* (London, Macmillan, 1914), Part I, 124; 129 n. 2; Gercke, *op. cit.* in various terminology brand Aristoxenus as a scandal-monger. Westphal's classic treatment of the life and character of the biographer is distinctly rehabilitative in mood.

[52] *Op. cit.* 153.

von Mess,[53] a stimulating contributor to the study of the origins of ancient biography and psychological historiography, some ten years ago dared to essay a rehabilitation of Aristoxenus and his biographical merits. According to our critic Aristoxenus was no libelous iconoclast,[54] but a genuine precursor of modern realistic methods. In his work we are to see nothing less than the first unfolding of psychological biography. Naturally correlative with this position is the view that the Socrates, not only of the inspired Plato but of the matter-of-fact Xenophon, is a figure impossibly idealized, a glorified phantasm very different from the real conversational loiterer of the Athenian market-place. There is by now ample precedent, of course, for a more realistic estimate of Socrates as man and teacher.[55] The efforts of twentieth-century scholarship to penetrate behind the veil of idealization to the personality of the historical Socrates have ranged from a clearer humanization to nihilistic rejection,[56] as a creation of

[53] In the article already referred to, p. 9, n. 15.

[54] This view is not entirely revolutionary, but is to a certain extent a resuscitation of the ancient estimate sponsored by W. L. Mahne, *De Aristoxeno Peripatetico* (Amsterdam, 1793) to the effect that the biographer was a judicial narrator who followed a path midway between the eulogists and the vilifiers of Socrates.

[55] The essay of R. von Pöhlmann, *Aus Altertum und Gegenwart* (neue Folge, Munich, Beck, 1911), is a vigorous protest against the contradictions into which modern scholarship has been betrayed by its frequent failure to recognize the Platonic and the Xenophontic Socrates as in great measure a product of "hieratic" idealization.

[56] E.g., Gercke's view (*op. cit.* 380) that almost nothing connected with the career of Socrates save the fact of his execution is guaranteed history; to E. Dupréel, *La légende socratique et les sources de Plato* (Brussels, Robert Sand, 1922), even the condemnation is romantic fiction, a position befitting a scholar who finds in Protagoras, Hippias, and Prodicus the sole creators of what we call Platonism and makes Plato merely a consummate literary artist; *see esp.* 419 ff. In spite of the Baconians it seems that we are still to have a Shakespeare.

idolaters' fiction, of the Socrates whom the centuries have revered.

The method invoked by von Mess is, briefly stated, to project upon the several items of the biographer's account such corroborative evidence as can be gleaned by reading not so much the lines as between the lines of the other ancient sources of information, notably, of course, Plato and Xenophon. Thus the cataclysmic outbreaks of rage, it is maintained, are intelligible in a temperament capable of the cold martial wrath exhibited by Socrates to the awe of the enemy in the retreat from Delium.[67] The berserker ire of the battlefield thus betokens capability of "seeing red" on other occasions, our critic contends, especially (it is hard here to repress the lift of a democratic eyebrow) in the case of a man who had risen from the lower social strata.

Similarly, in respect to the frailties of the flesh which are attributed by Aristoxenus to Socrates, it is asserted that the veneering touch of the Socratic disciples did not hide entirely the genuine man. The real Socrates was congenitally of a strongly sexed temperament; he triumphed over his baser impulses by rigorous self-discipline.[68] No prude in his attitude toward the vivid half-world of Athenian society, he adopted the tolerant language of his time when speaking of homosexual relationship. In short he was a sound human animal who saw no reproach in his robust naturalness.

[67] *Op. cit.* 91.

[68] This picture of Socrates as a man endowed with a fiery temperament, naturally subject to intensities of emotion but self-schooled to continence, is essentially that given by Th. Gomperz, *Greek Thinkers* (Eng. trans. Scribner's, 1905), II, 48, and Ed. Meyer, *Geschichte des Altertums* (ed. 2; Stuttgart and Berlin, Cotta, 1915), IV, Book III, 435.

Evidently it cannot be our primary concern to fulminate against a conception of Socrates that savors of the Walt Whitman philosophy. Every one has a right to his own Socrates, and it is particularly the case that modern reconstructions of the man and his teachings are bound to be affected by one's estimate of the relative value of sources and by one's own cast of mind. The several items of unfavorable characterization that derive from Aristoxenus have been sifted by Zeller's painstaking scholarship[59] and their plausibility dismissed, I think, correctly. Attempted refutation of von Mess which would be based merely on Zeller would be gainless repetition. It is only for the purpose of establishing to our own satisfaction the ideals and methods of Aristoxenus and his kind that we shall dwell longer on his delineation of Socrates. In so doing we shall follow a line of reasoning which is apart from Zeller's discussions.

The circumstances attending this particular problem are in a way typical of the perplexity in which one who is striving to distinguish truth from fiction through most of ancient literary biography is often involved. The extant lives of philosophers, poets, orators, and ancient men of letters in general teem with data that more frequently titillate our appetite for the picturesque than command credence as history. Exact demonstration of truth by recourse to additional source or variant version is seldom feasible. To try to determine by means of weighing divergent testimony whether Empedocles' death was due to a broken thigh, whether he hung himself,

[59] *See* the more recent evaluation by H. Dittmar, *Aischines von Sphettos*, *Philol. Untersuch.* (hgbn. Kiessling und von Wilamowitz-Moellendorff), XXI (1912), 170–72 and n. 32.

precipitated himself into the sea or into Aetna[60] is to put moonshine on the scales. In the case of Sophocles there is a choice among three modes[61] in which he is reputed to have met his end; the number of the narrated fashions in which Plato expired[62] almost rivals the number of cities that claimed Homer dead. Is one to believe that the ailing Aristotle bathed in warm oil or merely comforted himself by applying a bag of the heated fluid to a distressed portion of his anatomy?[63]

Luckily that vital representation of human character and its accomplishments which is the business of biography and autobiography does not depend on whether details affecting the purely external incidents of a life are thus or so. The merits of Thucydides' history remain what they are irrespective of whether he composed the work in the shade of a plane tree or not.[64] Rousseau's famous confusion of the dates of his birth and baptism does not necessarily vitiate the self-revelatory candor of the *Confessions*.[65] But it is different when the point at issue has power to make or mar our reconstruction of the man as artist or thinker, our plotting of the psychic sources from which flow the streams of his influence on thought and literature. A Socrates who was tempted by the seductions of petty doles, who was morally not above

[60] Diog. Laert. viii. 69; 73; 74.

[61] In the *Vita Sophoclis*, A. Westermann, *op. cit.* 129, 60–65; the *Vita* has been most recently edited by A. C. Pearson, *Sophoclis fabulae* (Oxford, Clarendon Press, 1923), in which *see* sec. 14; Westermann, 130, 65–68 = Pearson 14; Westermann, 130, 69 = Pearson, 14.

[62] Müller, *FHG* III, 44.

[63] Diog. Laert. v. 16.

[64] *Vita Marcellini*, Westermann, *op. cit.* 191, 25.

[65] A. R. Burr, *The Autobiography*, 45–47; H. Beaudouin, *La vie et les oeuvres de Jean-Jacques Rousseau* (Paris, Lamulle et Poisson, 1891), I, 1.

his milieu would be well-nigh an ethical disaster. The stories of Euripides' connubial infelicity and of Lucretius' fits of madness carry profound implications to one who is considering the inevitable reactions of emotional life upon a poet's work.

In attacking questions of this sort, to pit source against source and to base inferences on likelihood, as Zeller did in his treatment of Socrates, are procedures that by no means exhaust the resources of method. We can and should probe deeper. When it is possible, study must be comparative; we must use as touchstones our available knowledge of ancient modes of ratiocination, the proclivities that tended to hold sway over the narrative and to render receptive the imagination of the biographer.[66] The corpus of ancient biography betokens frequently what analytic minds have delighted to point out is true in other fields: The machinery of human inventiveness is set in motion by common impetuses and tends to run in fixed grooves. One cannot, of course, emulate for biography the beautiful precision that has kept dramatic critics talking since Gozzi's day about the thirty-six possible situations in drama.[67] Nevertheless, one can point to stock features of narrative, conventional items of characterization, and kindred impulses reflecting themselves in the biographies of different men.

The reader will unprompted recall the inevitability as a topical rubric of the portents that come

[66] Karl Lehrs showed the way here; *see* "Ueber Wahrheit und Dichtung in der griechischen Litteraturgeschichte," *Populäre Aufsätze aus dem Alterthum* (ed. 2; Leipzig, Teubner, 1875), 385 ff.

[67] Georges Polti, *Les trente-six situations dramatiques* (Paris, édition du "Mercure de France," 1895).

to cluster about the birth of a great man and foretell a brilliant future for him. An inveterate human instinct lies behind the introduction of such motives. In the reference Mark Twain's authorized biographer makes to the great comet that appeared in the sky at the time of the humorist's birth, to "return no more until the day when he should be borne back to the far spaces of silence,"[68] survives something of the spirit that made Apollo the father of Plato, endowed also Alexander, Scipio Africanus, and Augustus with supernatural progenitors,[69] pictured bees as swarming about so many infant bards.[70] Such material became a part of biographical paraphernalia and the commonplaces were repeated and transferred with uncritical freedom where their appositeness commended them. We can understand how ill-natured gossip made the father of Horace a monger of salted provisions because the father of that ancient Swift, Bion of Borysthenes, was said to have plied the same trade. Two satirists, between whom there was a literary kinship, must needs have fathers who spent their days in the same pungent atmosphere and exhibited the same plebeian personal habit.[71] The picturesque story of the death of Euripides, reputed to have been torn to pieces by the hounds of Arche-

[68] A. B. Paine, *Mark Twain. A Biography* (New York, Harper and Bros., 1912), I, 12.

[69] Diog. Laert. iii. 2; Plutarch *Alex.* 2, 3; Gellius *N. A.* vi. 1. 2–5; Suetonius *Vita Divi Augusti* 94. 4 Ihm; Cassius Dio xlv. 1. 2.

[70] D. R. Stuart, "On Vergil Eclogue IV 60–63," *Class. Philol.* XVI (1921), 226, 227.

[71] Diog. Laert. iv. 7. 46; Suetonius *Vita Horatii* 297 Roth. To say that one's father "wiped his nose on his forearm," was a thrust treasured in ancient billingsgate; R. Heinze, *De Horatio Bionis imitatore* (Bonn, Georg, 1889), 1 ff.; W. Süss, *Ethos* (Leipzig, Teubner, 1910), 257 and note.

laus in pursuance of canine vengeance,[72] appealed to romantic imaginations as the meet end for the atheistic. So it was related that Heraclitus, like Euripides a pitiless castigator of popular beliefs, had been devoured by dogs:[73] a late and pious legend consigned the scoffer Lucian to a like ignominious end.[74] There are other illustrations that could be added. Suffice it to say that one is justified in viewing with suspicion any statement the nature of which suggests that it may be a page taken from the universal concordance of stock incident or feature, may be the result of fusion or transference of legend.[75] Both the eulogistic and the censorious delineations of personality had their phrase-books of topical themes.

The picture painted by Aristoxenus of Socrates' moral character shows but too clearly the stereotyped strokes freely utilized for aspersion in various sorts of literature. Licentiousness and sexual perversion were pet themes in the invective of orators and the raillery of comedy. 'Ἀσέλγεια became a stock word in partisan appreciation of ἦθος or 'character.' There can be no doubt that frequently these gibes were mere *façons de parler*, not to be taken seriously,

[72] *Vita Euripidis*, Westermann, *op. cit.* 135, 46–136, 58; Satyrus, *Life of Euripides*, *in* H. von Arnim, *Supplementum Euripideum*, 9. A modern version of "The Dogs' Revenge" is accredited by Boswell (*Life of Johnson*, ed. G. B. Hill [Oxford, Clarendon Press, 1887], II, 232) to Goldsmith who ventured in the presence of Johnson to remark that, eating dogs being a custom in China, "a dog-butcher is as common there as any other butcher, and when he walks abroad, all the dogs fall on him." Whereat Johnson "fell on" this and another tall story related by poor Oliver with a rationalization drawn from personal experience.

[73] Neanthes *frg.* 11, *in* Müller, *FHG* III, 4.

[74] Suidas *in* Westermann, *op. cit.* 345, 8.

[75] Further examples of biographical *clichés* are to be found in H. Diels, *R. M.* XXXI (1876), 13 ff. and in K. Jex-Blake and E. Sellers, *The Elder Pliny's Chapters on the History of Art*, xlvii, xlviii.

so hackneyed were they. The aspersions cast by orators such as Demosthenes and Aeschines upon each other's moral character do not represent splenetic narrative of truth; these imputations, appealing to the Rabelaisian sense of humor and feeding the vulgar appetite for scandal, were primarily bids for jurymen's votes.[76]

The list of alleged sinners against modern standards of continence that can be compiled from biographical literature is as impressive in respect to the persons involved as it is imposing in its length. The accusation was brought against Pericles by the biased Stesimbrotus;[77] against the poets Alcman,[78] Anacreon,[79] Ibycus,[80] Cratinus,[81] and Menander.[82] The philosophers Socrates, Bion,[83] and Arcesilaus,[84] the orators Isaeus,[85] Hyperides,[86] Demosthenes,[87] Aeschines,[88] and Isocrates[89] also figure in this rakes' gallery. Evidently in this sort of thing there was a deal of catering to a prurient curiosity. The biographical narratives appropriated the "hits" of comic caricature and generalized therefrom.[90] In the ancient

[76] Süss, *op. cit.* 249 ff.; 254–58.

[77] Plutarch *Pericles*, 13–14; Athenaeus xiii. 589 D, E.

[78] Athenaeus xiii. 600 F.

[79] Westermann, *op. cit.* 103, 16–17.

[80] *Idem*, 106, 63.

[81] *Idem*, 164, 9.

[82] *Idem*, 179, 61.

[83] Diog. Laert. iv. 53.

[84] *Idem*, iv. 40.

[85] Westermann, *op. cit.* 261, 6–11; according to the Γένος Ἰσαίου the excesses of this orator were the wild oats of youth.

[86] *Idem*, 314, 56.

[87] *Idem*, 289, 1–4; 309, 2–5; Idomeneus *frg.* 13, *FHG* II, 492; Hermippus *frg.* 59, *FHG* III, 49.

[88] Westermann, *op. cit.* 267, 2.

[89] *Idem*, 252, 35 ff.

[90] Thus the comedians, always prone to jests at the expense of the amorous dotard, made merry over the liaison formed by Isocrates in his old age with the courtesan Lagisce; Westermann, *op. cit.* 255, 44 ff.; 256, 77 ff.

lives of the orators and statesmen the accusation was often only the repercussion of charges with which partisan speakers had made the welkin ring. In the case of the poets deduction could be made from their own utterances.[91]

The discreditable construction put on the relationship of the youthful Socrates and his reputed teacher Archelaus also falls into one of the stock categories of vilification. This is the *erastes-paidika* motive into which any association, literary or political, of an older man and a younger protégé could be so easily turned by a biographer or historiographer. We need not call the roll in political history where the report is affixed to the pairs Harmodius and Aristogeiton, Hamilcar and Hanno, Caesar and Nicomedes. In literary biography it was the mode thus to interpret intellectual or artistic association; as the names of Socrates and Archelaus are linked together, so are connected Empedocles and the physician Pausanias, addressed in the Περὶ φύσεως;[92] Marsyas (*sic!*) and Olympus;[93] Aristotle and Palaiphatus;[94] Scipio, Laelius, and Terence.[95] Every student of Vergil knows how the sentimental pose of

[91] In the case of Alcman we can point to an especially instructive illustration of the manner in which such a characterization as καταφερὴς περὶ γυναῖκας, sounding harsh enough when standing by itself in a biographical sketch, took its rise in a generalization from lyric utterance. In Athenaeus xiii. 600 F. (a passage in which Alcman is made the inventor of erotic poetry) mention of the trait, repeated by Chamaeleon from an earlier source, Archytas, is followed by the quotation of Alcman *frg.* 36 (Bergk, ed. 4) on which the generalization was based; *see* E. Köpke, *op. cit.* 38. The text of the citation from Chamaeleon is not entirely clear, although the sense is.

[92] Satyrus *frg.* 12, *FHG* III, 163.

[93] Westermann, *op. cit.* 110, 43.

[94] *Idem*, 221, 90. Add Archebulus and Euphorion, Suidas, *sub* Euphorion.

[95] Suetonius, *Vita Terenti*, 292, 9 ff. Roth.

the *Second Eclogue* was made into a historical page of the poet's reputed eroticism.

Wholesale rehabilitation is not the aim of the preceding paragraphs. That which is called a spade at any time in the history of human morals may be indubitably a spade; if it deserve the name, it should be so designated. Only an incorrigible idealist would try to sever all recorded instances from crass reality. Our object has been to show that in his description of the morals of Socrates Aristoxenus was writing *à la mode* and thus to indicate the background against which this part of his delineation should be contemplated before it is rated as realistic portraiture. Von Mess suggests that in the famous likening of Socrates to the satyr Silenus, which forms the contribution of Alcibiades to the encomia in the *Symposium*, Plato meant subtly to hint at the corporeal side of the real man. Quite as plausible is the inversion of the reasoning: The satyrlike visage, masking, we believe, a soul so different, may well have formed the pretext of, as certainly it would add point to, stories of a temperamental proclivity proverbially attaching to the satyrs. Spintharus, the father of Aristoxenus and a musician of sorts, who in the course of a stay in Athens had some personal association with Socratic circles (how close the acquaintance was and how long continued we cannot tell) and who, if we are to believe the son,[86] passed on to him autoptic information about Socrates, was chronologically in no position to give a contemporary's testimony as to Socrates' deportment in youth or early maturity. The association of Socrates

[86] Zeller, *op. cit.* II 1, 65, n. discredits Aristoxenus' veracity in regard to this detail, a skepticism that is shared by Dupréel, *op. cit.* 415, but Dupréel is always skeptical.

and Archelaus, as learner and teacher, if this relationship be historical, would have antedated the birth of Spintharus by many years.[97]

In one context of Aristoxenus (28) censorious characterization is joined with what might at first sight seem a complimentary estimate. It is told that Spintharus reported that he had met few men who had greater powers of persuasion than had Socrates; voice, gestures, personality alike were elements in this effectiveness; this was true, however, only when Socrates had not been provoked to wrath. Once inflamed by rage, he displayed an utter lack of decorum. So far the gist of the passage. This concession to the magnetic powers of Socrates is not phrased in the language of unbounded enthusiasm. In our imperfect knowledge of the original diction and context the complimentary intention is by no means free from doubt. The tribute is paid to Socrates' art in exposition, not to the intrinsic merits of his subject-matter. To attribute an expounder's hold on his audience to the charms of elocution and the nicely calculated appeal of personality is to damn with faint praise. Here it may well have served as a positive weapon of detraction precisely as we are informed in the Suetonian life of Vergil that an unfriendly critic asserted that the poet's verses, paltry and inarticulate, owed their appeal to the Mantuan's voice and dramatic ability.[98]

[97] Zeller, *op. cit.* II 1, 49, rejects the tradition that Socrates and Archelaus stood in the relation of pupil and teacher. Ed. Meyer, *op. cit.* Book III, 440, regards the story as derived from a reputed visit of Socrates and Archelaus to Chios when the former was a young man; *see* Ion of Chios *frg.* 9, *FHG* II, 49. It seems, however, overskeptical to doubt the historicity of the tradition; *see* Burnet, *op. cit.* Part I, 124 and note; Busse, *op. cit.* 79, also accepts it.

[98] *Vita* 29, Diehl.

The count against the psychological insight of Aristoxenus and against his credibility becomes perhaps most decisive when we face candidly his assertion that Socrates was unlettered and ignorant.[99] This point is of capital importance if we are to have a different Aristoxenus, a pioneer in the biographical art who viewed his subjects judicially and imparted realism to his portraiture. The silence preserved by von Mess concerning this cardinal feature of the biographer's character-sketching goes far to vitiate elsewhere elaborate efforts at amendatory criticism. Here if anywhere in the fragments of Aristoxenus the signs of animus are clear. Certainly this was the impression made on Plutarch, who may have known the Βίοι ἀνδρῶν in its entirety and who saw in the life of Socrates, instead of an equitable balancing of the subject's virtues and defects, a wily attempt by means of slight tempering of condemnatory utterance to lend an air of sincerity to a censorious estimate. Various points appertaining to the education of Socrates and his intellectual contacts in his formative years are controversial, to be sure. It might be urged that Aristoxenus was applying to Socrates the formal criteria of rhetorical and philosophical schooling. Even so a biographer capable of weighing a Socrates in such a balance and finding him wanting cannot be esteemed an acute appraiser of real values. It is on the whole more complimentary to Aristoxenus to assume that he was wilfully shutting his eyes to the real significance of Socrates' confessions[100] of deficient training in order to make capital of them than to suppose that he was purblind in comprehension.

[99] Plutarch, *De Herod. malign.* 856 C = Müller, *FHG* II, 27 a.

[100] Plato, *Apol.* 17 B; *Sympos.* 199 A; Xenophon, *Sympos.* 1, 5.

In his repetition of the puerile fabrication of the bigamy of Socrates, Aristoxenus, von Mess would have it, was merely led astray by a tradition that took its rise in later misunderstanding of the social regulations and domestic conditions existing in Athens at the time of the Peloponnesian War. However, our rehabilitating critic is forced to admit that the bias of the Peripatetic, inured to the acceptance of fees and desirous of defending the practice, led Aristoxenus to endeavor to fix the practice of receiving doles on Socrates. As I read them, neither the remnants of the life of Socrates nor the very meager remains of the life of Plato justify essential modification of the prevalent view of the shortcomings of Aristoxenus as a biographer. His leanings toward Pythagoreanism moved him to eulogistic treatment of the founder of the brotherhood. Here he did not work as a critical biographer. His life of Socrates was to some extent the obverse expression of his philosophical convictions.

It is certainly more prudent to join Professor Burnet[101] in seeking the key to the biographer's animus in a feeling of hostility engendered by a belief that Socrates and Plato had misrepresented Pythagorean doctrines than to read into his delineation of Socrates merely the emotional reactions of a jaundiced temperament. Doubtless there developed in antiquity an "Aristoxenus Legend" that tended to romantic distortion of his personality and of the motives to which his literary life responded. However, the tone of his biographical work should not be entirely severed from his disposition. A tempera-

[101] *Op. cit.* 153.

mental attribute on which we can build with confidence, for the reason that its presence in the man's make-up is unmistakably reflected in extant work other than the fragments of his biographies, was an intellectual arrogance that prized highly divergence from received knowledge and strove to earn a reputation for originality.[102] In various passages of the *Elements of Harmony* we find him censuring his predecessors for their faults of omission and commission, while with "his pompous reiterations of 'Alone I did it' "[103] he heralds the novelty and value of his contributions to musical science. This was precisely the mind that would strain to paint not necessarily the true Socrates, but a different Socrates.

[102] Adrastus characterized him in the second century A.D. as a man who strove for novelty in utterance and point of view; *see* Proclus *In Timaeum* iii. 192 A.

[103] The comment of H. S. Macan, *The Harmonies of Aristoxenus* (Oxford, Clarendon Press, 1902), 87, apropos of such passages as i. 3; 4; 35–38 Meiboom.

CHAPTER VI

THE ALEXANDRIAN CONTINUATORS

Critics I saw, that other names deface,
And fix their own, with labour, in their place:
Their own, like others, soon their place resign'd
Or disappear'd, and left the first behind.
—Pope, *The Temple of Fame.*

Sundry incentives that lay behind the making of biographies by the Greeks have been noted here and there in previous chapters. Nevertheless, in order further to clarify understanding of the phases through which Hellenic biography evolved it will not be amiss to reflect for a moment on one or two tendencies that marked the course of its crystallization. Our distinctions will be to some extent matters of degree, our contrasts somewhat broad. There is an overlapping among the several types of biographical literature in respect to literary purpose and character that renders precise demarcation not easy to achieve.

Between the *Memorabilia*, the *Evagoras*, and its like on the one hand, and on the other the biographical output of the Peripatetic researchers, there is, to say the least, one intrinsic difference. The former were, as we might say, works of occasion. They were written because Xenophon, Isocrates, or somebody else desired to keep green the memory of persons whose deaths had been recent events and who had lived their lives in times of which the author himself had personal knowledge. Xenophon especially had been intimately associated with the men whose lives he recorded and he wrote of scenes in their careers of which he had been in some degree an eye-witness. Encomiast and defamer had, it is true, harked back to remote ages in their choice of subjects. But they had been moved by the promptings of rhetorical bravura rather than actuated by a serious informative or commemorative purpose. The figures treated were drawn from the well-thumbed directory of legendary history. That Busiris, Helen, Theseus, and Achilles were personages known "*lippis et tonsoribus*," that popular tradition had formulated them in respect to character and deeds were postive recommendations. In the program of the Peripatetic biographers differences in time were obliterated. Personages belonging to the distant past and to recent generations appealed equally for biographical presentation, just as is the case nowadays when a life of one of the Medicis seems quite as normal a product of the biographer's pen as does a life of a recent president of these United States. Thus it came to pass that a life of Pythagoras and a life of Plato fell into the same biographer's scheme.

Gradations in what the world calls fame have by now become of secondary importance in biographers' calculations. Their projects are no longer controlled by the view which W. D. Howells makes one of his characters apply to the work of the novelist: "You can paint a man dying for his country, but you can't express on canvas a man fulfilling the duties of a good citizen."[1] Our modern taste for realism, our appreciation of the literary value of pictures of humdrum existence—"cross-sections of life" as we say—long since domesticated in fiction, have wrought their effects on biography. Classical biography did not pay its respects to the John Does of antiquity so far as to become habituated to devoting long books to the records of their lives. So far as comparative obscurity had a place accorded to it in ancient biography, its entry was due to encyclopedic presentation of the history of art and of the various branches of knowledge. Naturally it was as true of antiquity as of modern times that a person's connection with some kind of human accomplishment would secure him the attention of the encyclopedic or group-biographer aiming at a complete survey of that field. Already in the fifth century, as we have seen, technical biography began in the study of poetry and music. As the various branches of art and science attained a formal parity in the kingdom of knowledge, biography extended along with the widening flow of scholarly inquiry. Lives of flute-players[2] and lives of the painters,[3] for example, are gathered into special works as well as the lives of philosophers and men of letters.

Thus ancient biography anticipated the two main directions that the genre has continued to follow, namely: (1) Studies of commanding figures who played a great part in some major domain of human life; in the composition of these the biographer has

[1] *The Rise of Silas Lapham* (Boston, Houghton Mifflin, Riverside Press edition), 284.

[2] Aristoxenus *in* Müller, *FHG* II, 285, *frg.* 59 b.

[3] Duris of Samos *in FHG* II, 487, *frg.* 77.

before him the interests of the general reading public and may well seek to impart to his work some of the charms of belles-lettres. (2) Biographies designed primarily to purvey information to readers who are in quest of specialized knowledge; in biographies of this sort style tends to subordinate itself to subject-matter.

Another fact worth while to observe in the development of Greek biography, with Aristoxenus and his compeers as points of departure, is the growth in promiscuity of interests. Aristoxenus found in biography a vent for his personal detestations and enthusiasms. With less certainty the same remark is applicable to Dicaearchus. At least, so far as we can reconstruct his work in biography, it is evident that he shared with his correspondent and intellectual associate, Aristoxenus, partiality for the Pythagoreans and hostility toward the Socratics. These predilections were, in the case of Aristoxenus, closely linked with the accidents of birthplace and parentage, in the case of Dicaearchus with birthplace alone. Tarentum, where Aristoxenus was born, was in the later days of Pythagoreanism the chief center of the brotherhood. Sicilian Messene, whence Dicaearchus came, was also in the sphere of what amounted to the "Western Church" of Pythagoreanism. The interest in music inherited by Aristoxenus from his father formed another bond between him and the school of Pythagoras. In the earlier part of his career Aristoxenus imbibed from personal relations with such survivors of the sect as Xenophilus a sincere admiration for the Pythagorean tenets and mode of life that he did not relinquish in his later association with Aristotle. Hence his lives of Pythagoras and the Pythagoreans were preachments in which he sought to glorify the master and the ideals for which the master stood, and to correct the vulgar errors according to which popular belief had deformed the Pythagorean way of life. Thus his treatment of Pythagoras had much of the color of a saint's life. It was a natural step for his partisanship, using the same literary vehicle, to proceed to an antipodal study of the lives and doctrines of Socrates and Plato. Dicaearchus, it seems safe to conclude, followed in these respects the same lines as Aristoxenus. Closely articulated also with the author's own interests were the cycles composed by Aristoxenus on flute-players and tragic poets[4]—works that inevitably incorporated much material of a biographical sort—and his life of the dithyrambic poet Telestes.[5]

Two of the early exponents of formal biography thus found in it to a considerable extent a medium of self-expression. Choice of subjects followed the bent of philosophical conviction and literary specialty. The biographical activities of Phaenias, likewise, as we have seen, in the first wave of the literary movement, owe much of their impetus to his intellectual propensities. A disciple of Aristotle, like his two fellow-pupils he turned naturally to exposition of philosophers' lives. Because he was interested in history he wrote about the tyrants of Sicily. It is more than likely, too, that the ethical and admonitory element entered into this work, since it was the way of his times to utilize tyrants as exemplars of the life of luxury and in their persons to hold up

[4] *FHG* II, 283, *frg.* 40. [5] *FHG* II, 282, *frg.* 36.

before the eyes of men the excesses of absolutism. Nevertheless, when we add to these two products of biographical composition the treatise *On Poets* to which it is folly to deny a large admixture of biographical material, conjectural though the character of the work be, it would seem that in the versatility of Phaenias begins the appeal of biography *qua* biography. At all events, as the growth of the form advances through the next generations, biography comes more and more to attain an existence as an end in itself. Ultimately an individual biographer ranges freely among the various categories of persons whose life-histories qualify them to be the natural objects of universal interest.

An early indication of the objective appeal of biography is found in the work of Duris of Samos who belonged to the generation following Aristoxenus and Phaenias. In his early years an adept boxer victorious at Olympia, Duris attached himself as a pupil to Theophrastus, and developed into a prolific writer of history and of various special studies on divers topics. It is interesting to observe that in his case a youth marked both by intellectual ardor and athletic prowess was the harbinger of a manhood combining the literary ubiquitousness fostered by his Peripatetic training with a participation in the affairs of active life. In the late fourth or early third century B.C. he became the ruler of his native island.

The biographical writings of Duris included a work on that conventional theme, the tragic poets, in his case restricted to treatments of Sophocles and Euripides.[6] More symptomatic of the increasing

[6] Athenaeus iv. 184 D.

catholicity of biographical inquiry were his books *On Painters* and *On the Plastic Art.*[7] This latter work, despite its title, was not a technical treatise on engraving and sculpture but dealt with the history of these arts in connection with their exponents.[8] In this ancient Vasari, appreciation and record of artistic production was everywhere jostled by anecdote. The superabundant interest of Duris in the personal traits of his craftsmen and the scenic occurrences of their careers have been convincingly established by those scholars[9] who have addressed themselves to reconstructing the spirit of his work. He took in the characteristic fashion of the Peripatetic moralists a keen delight in the ethical aspects of human fortunes as these were illustrated in his subjects' lives. None the less his approach to biography was for its own sake. No artist himself, he was the first to write about artists from the lay point of view. Thus the impulse that inspired his biographical studies of painters and sculptors was obviously different from that which moved the Peripatetics of the preceding generation to discourse on the lives of philosophers, or Aristoxenus, the musical theorist, to treat flute-players.

In the first half of the third century B.C. the emergence of the blanket-title Περὶ ἐνδόξων ἀνδρῶν or *Concerning Famous Men* marks another step in the progress of biography toward the status of an independent, objective art. Neanthes of Cyzicus, bred

[7] *FHG* II, 487, *frg.* 79.

[8] L. Urlichs, *Ueber griechische Kunstschriftsteller* (Würzburg, Thein'schen Druckerei, 1887), 22.

[9] Urlichs, *op. cit.* 21 ff.; F. Münzer, *Hermes* XXX (1895), 531 ff.; K. Jex-Blake and E. Sellers, *The Elder Pliny's Chapters on the History of Art* (London, Macmillan, 1896), xlvi ff.

by his teacher Philiscus in the Isocratean tradition, wrote under this caption which sounds sufficiently comprehensive. Yet the fragments[10] plausibly attributable to the work deal, with the exception of one evidently deriving from a life of that romantic figure Timon the Misanthrope, with men great in literature and thought. Neanthes was a historian, an annalist, a rhetorician, and an antiquarian;[11] doubtless, as was the way of the Hellenistic chronicler, he had in historiography his say about the personalities and the careers of public men. We can but speculate as to whether in his biographical series he included the lives of men of action. Certain it is that such a combination had not been the practice of the Peripatetics, who thus observed in biography the distinction between the closet and practical existences enunciated in ethical theory. Thus Phaenias in his *Tyrants of Sicily* and Idomeneus of Lampsacus, friend of Epicurus, in his *Civic Leaders* (Περὶ δημαγωγῶν—[12] had treated rulers and statesmen as classes apart from representatives of learning and the creative arts. Presumably whatever lives fell into the scope of Neanthes' work were grouped under the usual categories, philosophers, poets, and the like. At all events the epoch was at hand at which the noteworthy career in any walk of life was to furnish the biographer sufficient excuse. The stimulus was to act from without, whereas at the start it had acted

[10] *FHG* III, 4, *frgs.* 8–16.

[11] I follow Leo, *Griech.-röm. Biog.*, 112, and Christ, *Gesch. der griech. Litt.* (ed. 6), II, 1, 211, in attributing this literary versatility to *one* Neanthes, the pupil of Philiscus.

[12] *FHG* II, 491–94. The title rests on a generally accepted restoration of Sauppe.

from within. Biographers were to pursue their work as a literary vocation instead of as a parergon.

How far biographical composition had become a literary profession is best exemplified in the work of Hermippus and Satyrus, the last important representatives of the Peripatetic manner. With these men we have come to the close of the third century B.C. It is true of both of them that biography formed the major portion of their literary labors and that their reputations rested in antiquity on the voluminous lives that they composed. The surviving fragments of their work surpass in richness those of any other representative of their school. In Satyrus there is completely realized the attitude that no life the memory of which is worth transmission is foreign to the biographer. So in one elaborate work, quoted as *Οἱ βίοι*,[18] were included divisions on monarchs, statesmen, orators, sages and philosophers, and poets. If this list is completely representative of the biographical work of Satyrus—a not improbable conjecture—we must acknowledge that he confined his studies to the types of human activity for whom niches are reserved throughout all time in the hall of fame. Celebrity itself, in other words, constituted the thread of unity on which the biographer could string the beads of his narrative.

The output of Hermippus, too, took cognizance chiefly of such orthodox classes as lawgivers, sages, rhetoricians, orators, and, as there seems no cogent reason for doubting in view of the sweep of his

[18] The actual wording of the title is controversial. A. Gudeman, *P-W* III[ter] Hbd. 2[te] Reihe, 233, 234, argues cogently against Hunt's assumption, *Oxyrhynchus Papyri* IX, 126, that Ἀναγραφὴ τῶν βίων was the formal title. Ἀναγραφὴ in the papyrus seemingly meant as usual an 'index' or 'table of contents.'

biographical interests, poets.[14] However, there is not lacking evidence that he went afield from the traveled road of biography in a work which bore the mystifying title *On Magi*,[15] "knowledgeable men" as they might be called in the idiom of the Irish folk-story. Hermippus and his age being what they were, the consensus of scholarship has not hesitated to assign to this work a biographical character.[16] Hermippus was the author of an exhaustive work on the magic art and of a commentary on the writings of Zoroaster.[17] Interest in such lore is thoroughly in keeping with the easy credulity and the appetite for the marvelous reflected in the indisputably biographical writings of the man. Hermippus was termed not only 'Peripateticus,'[18] an epithet applied also to Satyrus[19] and modified from its original philosophical connotation to describe any savant who was a continuator of the Peripatetics' biographical and literary methods; he was likewise dubbed

[14] Athenaeus vii. 327 C, *FHG* III, 52, *frg.* 74, cites from a work Περὶ Ἱππώνακτος. In the *Anonymous Vita* of Euripides (Westermann, *op. cit.* 138) Hermippus is cited as authority for the story that, after the death of Euripides, Dionysius the Elder paid a talent for the poet's lyre and writing implements. This may well derive from a *Life of Euripides*, though it is ascribed to a *Life of Dionysius* by H. Frey, *Der* ΒΙΟΣ ΕΥΡΙΠΙΔΟΥ *des Satyros und seine literaturgeschichtliche Bedeutung* (Gotha, F. A. Perthes, no date but *circa* 1920), 26, 27. In view of the wide range of the biographical work of Hermippus, it seems over-skeptical to doubt that he treated poets; see Heibges, *P-W* VIII 1, 847.

[15] Diog. Laert. i. 8.

[16] H. Diels, *Doxographi Graeci* (Berlin, Reimer, 1879), 151; F. Susemihl, *Gesch. der griech. Litt. in der Alexandrinerzeit* (Leipzig, Teubner, 1891) II, 492, 493 n. 9; 494 and n. 13; Heibges, *P-W* VIII 1, 846. Corollary with this view is the attribution of the work to Hermippus the Alexandrian instead of to a later Hermippus who flourished in the time of Hadrian and produced biographical cycles on physicians and on slaves who had made a name for themselves in letters and learning; *see FHG* III, 36, 51.

[17] Pliny *Nat. hist.* xxx. (2), 4. [18] Hieronymus *De script. eccles.* prol.

[19] Athen. vi. 248 D; xii. 541 C.

'Callimachius.'[20] Callimachus, like Dr. Johnson, poet and polymath, had set on foot the construction of immense bibliographical rosters of the Alexandrian libraries. In these 'Pinakes' were catalogued, according to the kinds of literature to which they had contributed, the writers of the past and their works. Whenever the information was forthcoming, brief biographical details accompanied the various names. No follower of Callimachus, we may be sure, would have failed to organize a work bearing the title *On Magi* after the chronological and biographical mode. As for the rest, the biographical works of Hermippus formed an impressive collection in respect to quantity. Our knowledge of the whole rests upon fragments, but an idea as to the fecundity of this writer of lives may be gained from the provenience as well as from the number of the remains. The series on lawgivers is cited into the sixth book;[21] one fragment[22] from a treatment of the seven sages comes from the fourth book; a cycle on philosophers was so exhaustive as to extend from Pythagoras down to the Aristotelians; finally, under the branch devoted to the lives of orators the pupils of Isocrates were treated as a separate division.

In this account of what was, roughly reckoned, a century of biographical work, our aim has been to sketch the broad phases of development. It has so happened that the names of most of the practitioners of the art during this period have emerged into notice. One is painfully aware that even the mention of some of these persons must strike the unpro-

[20] Athen. ii. 58 F; v. 213 F.

[21] *FHG* III, 37, *frg*. 7.

[22] *FHG* III, 40, *frg*. 20.

fessional reader as an evocation of osseous nonentities from the pit of oblivion to which, so far as popular fame is concerned, they have perhaps been deservedly consigned. I have wished to contrive that they should serve primarily the illustrative purpose. A record of the external points of their careers and their personalities, unless these facts directly affected their literary attitudes and methods, must here be dispensed with. Intellects jaded from following the minutiae of biographical reconstructions essayed for creative genius of any age in the remote or not too distant past, and dismayed, as the mind often is, after many pages to find how fluid the lines of portraiture really are, how lacking in solid substance knowledge of the real man or woman is, will take refuge in Professor Santayana's sentiments concerning "Prying Biographers": "Ignorance of the life of a great writer is not . . . much to be regretted. His work preserves that part of him which he himself would have wished to preserve."[23] What then shall be said of these men, not "Greeks but Greeklings," when measured by the golden standards of Hellenic creative art? They were exegetes, compilers, and critics, the genus which nature has a way of fashioning, as some one has said, "from the chips that were left when authors were manufactured and patented." Their significance for us lies in what they did as early experimenters in an art that by now has a long and an increasingly honorable history. For what we need to know about them their writings are the men themselves.

Most ideals of manner and method that are exemplified by the representatives of Peripatetic

[23] *Little Essays* (New York, Scribner's Sons, 1920), 159.

biography may be described as attributes of the school. As these qualities are ordinarily set forth by modern appreciators, a positive note or an undertone of disparagement is always apparent.[24] Modern rationalism, wedded to the doctrines of higher criticism and adhering uncompromisingly to historical method or its own conception thereof, tends naturally to judge first and last these biographers by its own standards. Nevertheless, the disapprobation that they merit in respect to acumen and veracity should not extend to utter condemnation or merely patronizing estimate of their contribution to the biographical art. Indeed, when certain traits of the school are characterized, the language is not far removed from the phrases in which the aims of modern biography are now being couched by idealistic critics. More and more the new biography is pushing a claim to consideration as a branch of high literature. A few English biographies, more memoirs and autobiographies *are* endowed with the merit of universality. Their appeal to the reader is quite apart from their nature as chronicles of a life. Read Professor Dunn's[25] retrospective account of biographies that enjoy an independent place in the domain of letters and his prophecies, already in the way of fulfillment, of a closer approach of the genre to literary graces in the future.

This at least must be set down to the credit of the Peripatetic biographers from Aristoxenus to

[24] Gilbert Murray's judgment of Satyrus in *Euripides and His Age* (New York, Henry Holt, 1913), 24, may serve as a typical example: "Satyrus wrote a series of *Lives of Famous Men*, which was very popular, and we are now—since 1911— in a position to judge how undeserved its popularity was."

[25] *English Biography*, 264–86.

Satyrus and Hermippus: All alike had a conception of biography that differed from the dry recording of the events of a man's life and the facts of his personality that literary biography came to be in succeeding generations under the scholarly hands of Alexandrian philologists. Yet it is the fashion of our serious-minded criticism to decry the effort of the Peripatetics to present information about a man in a readable form; to deplore their discursiveness, and their predilection for interspersing their narrative with anecdotes and quotations. There is distinctly another side to this matter. It is at least due to the Peripatetics to say that, in trying to impart to biography the charms of belles-lettres, they anticipated present tendencies by two milleniums and over.

English biography in its eagerness to give revelation of all sides of a personality (the "Three Johns," according to Dr. Holmes's mellow analysis: John's ideal John, Thomas's ideal John, and the real John, "known only to his Maker,"[26]) has long prided itself on its recourse to anecdote, conversations, and kindred devices of presentation which found favor with the Peripatetics and their followers. Even before the generation of Aristotle the memoirists had learned to prize the racy incidents of human intercourse, the apt retort, and the like, not only for their intrinsic interest, but, as Plutarch says, as "signs of the soul in men."[27] "It is my opinion," says Xenophon at the beginning of the *Symposium*, "that not only such acts of gentlemen as belong to the serious side of life are worthy of record, but likewise their lightsome moments." It was like Xenophon to

[26] *The Autocrat of the Breakfast-Table*, iii. [27] *Alex.* 1. 3.

insert in the *Hellenica* (ii. 3. 56), though apologizing for its inclusion in the pages of formal history, the famous story of how Theramenes met death with a sarcastic fling at Critias, his political rival and accuser. Xenophon's plea that he judges it admirable that in the face of death neither Theramenes' self-possession nor his sense of humor deserted him, shows more than an inchoate consciousness that such data furnish openings by which to penetrate beneath the external crust of personality. Montaigne, that shrewdest knower of men and life, rose no higher when he affirmed that in judging of other men's lives he was wont to observe how they carried themselves at the end.[28]

True, the average ancient delineator of personality was not given to philosophizing about these matters so extensively as modern practitioners are fond of doing. Yet he grasped pragmatically the self-revelatory value of a man's *obiter dicta* and *obiter facta*. What recognition of the principle could be more satisfactorily complete than that contained in Plutarch's words?

> In the most illustrious deeds there is not always a manifestation of virtue or vice, nay, a slight thing like a phrase or a jest often makes a greater revelation of character than battles where thousands fall, or the greatest armaments or sieges of cities.—*Alexander* 1, 2.

Let it be recalled that in this famous passage Boswell sought the inspiration of the method by which he planned to enable his readers "to see Johnson and to live over each scene with the great man." It is no small distinction for ancient biographical technique

[28] *Essays* i. 18.

thus to have kindled a torch that the first great English realistic biographer caught directly from the hand of an ancient bearer, one, moreover, upon whom the mantle of the Peripatetics had fallen. For there is much in Plutarch's conception of the biographical manner that undoubtedly reverts to Peripatetic models. The ethical note, the spacious and discursive treatment of material, stylistic attractiveness, in short all the various elements by which the Peripatetics sought to impart to biography aesthetic charm and popular appeal are hall-marks of Plutarch's *Lives* as well. Hence, with all the hard words that must be said about the laxity of the Peripatetics' critical methods, their adherence to conventions of legend, their naïve acceptance of material drawn from such biased sources as comedy and oratory, as technicians in the biographical art they were by no means devoid of merit.

Reconstruction of the nature of Peripatetic biography until about a decade and a half ago had to rest on evidence piecemeal to a degree. This evidence consists of a motley array of quotations and testimonia gleaned from later writers. Furthermore, stores of material, more frequently unacknowledged than accredited to a specific source,[29] sifted from the Peripatetics down into those epitomized lives of the various representatives of literature, poets, orators, and historians, to which the stock title applied in the manuscripts is Γένος καὶ βίος, "Lineage

[29] The *Anonymous Vita* of Sophocles is unusually rich in such surface references; it cites Neanthes, Aristoxenus (twice), and Satyrus (three times). The *Vita* of Euripides, on the other hand, we now know drew, more probably indirectly than directly, from Satyrus; nevertheless it contains no mention of Satyrus but frequently introduces material deriving from him by the general formula φασί.

and Life." These little biographies, not infrequently to be found prefixed to modern texts of ancient authors, revert to originals composed by scholars of the Alexandrian period to accompany editions and works of exegesis. These savants, whose object was to convey information for its own sake, abridged the expansive narratives of their predecessors into the brief compass appropriate for an article in a biographical dictionary and adapted their style to their purpose. Under their hands literary biography was shorn of aesthetic pretension and became soberly didactic.

The gaps in our knowledge of the spirit and methods characterizing the work of the Peripatetic biographers have not been so hopelessly large as might be expected from our sporadic and indirect sources of knowledge. Scholarship has found it possible to discover and list the various topics touching outer and inner life that these narrators felt should enter into their delineations of their subjects. They of course included the themes essential to the biographer's exposition in any age, namely, nationality, parentage, parents' walk in life, pursuits engaged in prior to entrance on career proper, education and teachers, death and place of burial. Such data were naturally the common stuff of biography, whether the man treated was a personage in literature or a personage in government and politics. To the list of rubrics, applicable in common to all subjects irrespective of any difference in career, belong also animadversions on scale of living, morals, and the imbroglios of gallantry involved in such narration; this last, as we have seen, was a canonical topic.

Inventions and innovations affecting human culture and literary mode formed also stock material pertinent alike to the lives of men of action, of philosophers, and men of letters. Thus Aristoxenus (*frg.* 10) related that Pythagoras introduced weights and measures into Greece. Satyrus (*frg.* 6) asserted that Sophocles was the first to make a curved staff a feature of the actor's costume. Certain innovations in music and harmony are attributed by Phaenias (*frg.* 17) to the musician Stratonicus. Idomeneus (*frg.* 4) credits the sons of Pisistratus with the introduction of banquets and revels into Athens. Hermippus (*frg.* 1) declares that a citizen of Mantinea invented the usage of single combats. Neanthes (*frg.* 15) is authority for the doubtful[80] information that Antisthenes, the founder of Cynicism, first wore his mantle doubled.

In the lives of literary men and philosophers this topic of priority, on which Peripatetic scholarship laid so much stress, naturally initiated discussion of sources of information and inspiration—'literary influences' as we say. Almost never is the intention latent in the presentation of this theme neutral, much less complimentary, as is the case in the report of Aristoxenus (*frg.* 2) that Pythagoras derived the great body of his ethical doctrines from Themistoclia, priestess of Delphian Apollo. To equip Pythagoras with an Egeria was obviously to magnify his teachings, since he was thus made the vessel of divine inspiration. Ordinarily the rubric of literary influence was so handled as to discredit the originality of poet or thinker. Thus Hermippus, whose treatment

[80] *P-W* I, 2, 2540.

of Pythagoras shows plain traces of the scoffer,[31] asserted that this philosopher merely domesticated Jewish thought in Greece (*frg.* 2; *frg.* 21), a point of view that in after times naturally won for Hermippus the enthusiastic praises of the Jewish historian, Josephus.[32] According to this not impartial judge Hermippus was the most celebrated authority on Pythagoras and a painstaking investigator. The latter estimate is, at all events, an expansion of the facts.

The door lay always open for the prejudiced narrator to translate the interplay of two minds into stories of collaboration injurious to the fame of a genius, to launch accusations of plagiarism and of palming off as one's own literary material questionably acquired by some sordid means or other. Aristoxenus (*frg.* 33) averred that Plato had taken almost the entire *Republic* from the *Contradictiones* of Protagoras. To such fantastic extremes of statement could the indubitable Pythagorean elements in the teachings of Socrates give rise that Hermippus is found asserting that Plato bought from the relatives of Philolaus, one of the last leaders of the school of Pythagoras, a work of Pythagorean content and transcribed the *Timaeus* from it (*frg.* 25). How little they really knew about the matter is clear from the circumstance that Satyrus (*frg.* 16) represented the opulent Plato as commissioning his friend Dion to purchase *three* books from Philolaus. This is the ordinary version of the story, which probably reverts

[31] The comment of E. Rohde, *R. M.* XXVI (1871), 562, "Eine giftige Satire auf Pythagoras," is almost as true as it is tart.

[32] *Contra Apion.* i. 22.

to Aristoxenus.[33] From a like soil sprang the tradition handed down by Idomeneus (*frg.* 2) that Plato, out of hostility to Aeschines the Socratic, assigned to Crito in the dialogue of that name the part really played by Aeschines, as well as gossip to the effect that Aeschines had sold as his own dialogues of Socrates acquired from the widowed Xanthippe. In the *Vita Euripidis* we find the story, founded on a jest of the comic poet Teleclides, that Socrates was a collaborator of the tragedian.[34] To the slave Cephisophon is also ascribed literary (as well as connubial) partnership with Euripides, just as in Roman literary legend—so tenacious of life was the motive—Terence's relations with Scipio and Laelius were interpreted to the discredit both of his moral character and his literary originality.[35]

These biographers did not confine themselves to narrating the events and performances of a life, and to dealing with the man on his intellectual side. They were ambitious to display as completely as possible the manifold facets of personality. They told of the man as the world saw him, of his manners and disposition, his outward traits as a physical being, his dress and deportment. It is true that, until we come to the later generation of biographers, the fragments are not very rich in touches belonging to photographic description. It may well be that, as biography matured, the tendency to iconistic portrayal gained impetus. This kind of material

[33] On this famous scandal see J. Burnet, *Greek Philosophy* I, 339; *Early Greek Philosophy*, ed. 3, 279 ff.

[34] Westermann, *op. cit.* 134.

[35] Suetonius *Vita Terentii*, 292, 293 Roth.; Leo, *Plautinische Forschungen* (ed. 2; Berlin, Weidmann, 1912), 64, 65.

became increasingly available as the scope of biography was extended and cycles were carried down to periods contemporary with the biographer's own times or not far anterior to them.[36] Hence it is that of our extant fragments those of Hermippus and of Antigonus of Carystus, who flourished in the generation of Hermippus and Satyrus and wrote lives of philosophers with whom he was contemporary, show an especially nice eye for iconographic details.[37]

Tradition, of course, had preserved some general information concerning the outstanding traits of personality and physique of persons who had made in past generations a deep imprint upon the world. The personal attractiveness of Pythagoras, for example, was a part of the biographical tradition. According to his eulogists he was richly endowed by nature; he was lordly and tall, had a gracious disposition and a charming voice.[38] As the fragments of Ion show, personal description found a place in the works of the memoirists of the fifth century. The surviving allusions in Aristoxenus' delineation of Socrates to deportment and elocution point to an extensive treatment, not only for Socrates but for other worthies included in the Βίοι ἀνδρῶν, of those features of individuality and character that the Greeks included in the terms τρόπος, ἦθος, and εἶδος. Therefore, since these elements were at home in the

[36] The rise of iconistic description and its development among the Peripatetic and later biographers has been recently treated by Geneva Misener, *Class. Phil.* XIX (1924), 97–123; *see* esp. 107 ff.

[37] *E.g.*, in Diog. Laert. v. 67, Antigonus' description of Lyco's sturdy, athletic frame and battered ears; *see also* G. Körtge, *In Suetonii de viris illustribus libros inquisitionum capita tria*, *Diss. philol. Halenses* XIV (1901), 270.

[38] Dicaearchus, *FHG* II, 244, *frg.* 29.

earliest period of Peripatetic biography, it is plausible to assume that they were invariable and that it is due merely to the accidents of survival that their presence is not completely attested for all members of the school. These biographers thus anticipated the niceness of personal description with which Suetonius and Plutarch paint their subjects.

In the following fragment of Hermippus there is a veritably photographic effectiveness: "At the set hour Theophrastus, sleek and groomed to perfection, would arrive at the lecture-portico. He would then take his chair and set forth his discourse, which he delivered with an animation of movement and a vividness of gesticulation that stopped short of nothing. Thus on one occasion, when he was imitating a gourmand, he protruded his tongue and licked his lips."[39] The same biographer's account of the foppery of Lyco, famed for his spotless attire and for the soft and gleaming fabrics that he affected,[40] suggests a prototype of an eminent and well-dressed Hellenist, belonging to the past century, of whom a waggish person remarked: "All the time he could spare from the study of Greek he spent on the adornment of his person." In a fragment of Satyrus,[41] too long to be quoted here, there is an iconistic description of Alcibiades with his surpassing beauty and his luxuriant tresses of which he was inordinately vain. We are told that he affected a particular style of foot-gear, named after him precisely as the Iron Duke gave Britain the Wellington boot.

[39] *FHG* III, 46, *frg.* 43. [40] *Ibid. frg.* 47.

[41] Athenaeus xii. 534 B. Frey, *op. cit.* 37, n. 4 holds that the part of the context containing the description of Alcibiades may derive, not from Satyrus, but from a *Vita Alcibiadis* in which Satyrus was cited.

In my attempt to characterize briefly the generic traits of the Peripatetic biographers I have touched on aims, manner, and materials. These are the features of their work in connection with which it is possible to talk of trends observable in all alike. Individual variations, such as of course there were, can at least be estimated by class standards. These men were human entities and there are penchants discernible in individual instances that do mark one man's predilections apart from the general characteristics of the school. Thus Hermippus parades his erudition by citing an array of sources upon the existence of which, apart from the imagination of the biographer, skeptical scholarship has cast grave doubts. The fragments both of Hermippus and Neanthes so abound in stories of strange, not to say prodigious deaths as to indicate on the part of these two an especial weakness for that kind of sensational tradition. The interest of Duris in matters of costume and his mode of indulging in minute descriptions of the spectacular and the dramatic befit a historian of art and a student of tragedy.[42] Yet, even if the flight of centuries had dealt less destructively with the works of these gentry, it is unlikely that distinguishing bents would be so marked as to remove any individual from the community of attributes now discernible in respect to the main features of their biographical productions. The *disiecta membra* that we possess seem to have belonged to very similar bodies.

Now, until comparatively recent years it was a hopeless task to discover from extant material the

[42] R. Schubert, *Geschichte des Pyrrhus* (Königsberg, Wilh. Koch, 1894), 15–21.

fashion in which any Peripatetic biographer articulated the complete structure of his life-chronicles. Clear as it has been that they favored certain kinds of subject-matter, were addicted to certain methods in amassing their material, and followed certain literary ideals, scholarship had no means of determining in any individual case how material was organized, what was the relation of narrative and characterization, what were the proportions of these two elements. Herein are involved criteria important for all biography but fundamental for ancient biography, prone as it was to schematic arrangement of its material. To us the chronological method of presentation is the natural mode. We as a matter of course prefer to follow the life of a man as it unfolds from year to year, to view his personality through the processes of its growth, to see it developed by circumstances, affected by chance and environment. So obvious are these points of view that it is hard to realize that they have not always seemed so inevitable. The ancient biographer was, on the contrary, chiefly interested in the man as he was when he had emerged a finished product. The chronicler tended to see in character and personality static things that it was his task to analyze and describe, but with the evolution of which he was only incidentally concerned.

A welcome glimpse at the way in which one of the most famous of the Peripatetics put his life-stories together was furnished by the oddments of papyrus unearthed not many years ago from an Egyptian rubbish heap and containing parts of

Satyrus' *Life of Euripides*.[43] These remains gave us some new information, though tantalizingly little, about the tragedian's life and furnished some additions to the fragments of his poetry. However, the student of biographical technique finds in these fragments interests aside from the historical and the aesthetic. Their discovery did not fulfil Mahne's fervent wish that some of the lost works of Arixtoxenus might be brought to light;[44] nevertheless it furnished us our only first-hand survival of a Peripatetic biography. The work is cast in the form of a dialogue. This fact caused more surprise[45] when the papyrus first became known than on sober second thought is justified. The dialogue form had become, in the course of its development under the hands of the Peripatetics, a popular means for vivifying the exposition not only of philosophy but of a wide variety of other subjects. Aristotle had chosen so to organize his work *On Poets*, in which he must have dealt not only with matters of literary criticism but also with biographical details. There are other analogous examples.[46] Hence Satyrus was not an innovator but a follower of literary precedent. The thought of imparting the dramatic atmosphere to biography was a natural outcome of the desire actuating the Peripatetics to make a life-story readable literature. The romantic biographical studies of the

[43] The *editio princeps* is contained in *Oxyrhyncus Papyri* IX (London, Egypt. Explor. Fund, 1912), 124–82. The important fragments have been made conveniently accessible by H. von Arnim, *Supplementum Euripideum* (Bonn, Marcus und Weber, 1913).

[44] *Diatribe de Aristoxeno*, cap. iii, sect. 27, 94.

[45] "The method is a singular one to apply to biography."—Hunt, *Oxy. Pap.* IX, 126.

[46] Leo, *Nachr. d. königl. Ges. d. Wiss. zu Göttingen*, 1912, 275, cites Praxiphanes *On Poets* and Clearchus *On Modes of Life*.

present day are responsive to a like impulse. There have come down to us in the lives of the saints some later outcroppings of the idea of making dialogue the vehicle of biography, most notably in the *Life of St. Chrysostom* written by Palladius of Helenopolis about the year 408 A.D.[47] Apparently there was no direct literary contact between these later biographies and the method adopted by Satyrus for his *Life of Euripides* and doubtless utilized by him elsewhere. As has often happened in the history of world literature, there was a renascence in other surroundings of an old idea.

Of the two or, as most critics assume, three interlocutors that appear in Satyrus' dramatized biography, one at least is a woman, Euclia.[48] This device of having a woman participate in a dialogue expository of the life and works of Euripides has an especial piquancy in view of the poet's traditional though unmerited reputation for misogynism. In the setting of the dialogue are reflected the conditions of Alexandrian society in which women had attained to a higher degree of social and intellectual emancipation than was ordinarily their lot in classical days. Euclia, I infer, was not a later Aspasia, but a virtuous

[47] Other examples to which my attention has been directed by my colleague, Dr. Paul Coleman-Norton, are: *A Life of St. Benedict*, comprising the second book of the *Dialogues* of Gregorius Magnus and the *Life of St. Martin* implicit in the *Dialogues* of Sulpicius Severus; P. R. Coleman-Norton, *The Journal of Theological Studies*, XXVII (1926), 388–95.

[48] Leo, *op. cit.* 276, following Hunt, assumed the presence of three interlocutors, namely, Diodorus, Euclia, and a chief interlocutor, unnamed but, perhaps, in accord with the Aristotelian practice afterwards followed by Cicero in the *Brutus*, Satyrus himself. Christ, *op. cit.* II 1, 83 and Gudeman, *op. cit.* 230 agree. H. Gerstinger, *Wiener Studien* XXXVIII (1916), 61, n. 1, following von Arnim, accepts only two speakers, the chief interlocutor, A, and a woman, Diodora, surnamed Euclia. Frey, *op. cit.* 17, n. 1, rejects von Arnim's substitution of a Diodora for a Diodorus.

dame who can wax warm against one whom she esteems a libeler of her sex because of her own sense of rectitude.[49] She is neither devoid of learning nor opinions. She drives a point home by a reference to Plato's *Republic* (*frg.* 39, xiii, 31), for example.

By good fortune it happens that, scraps of the original though these fragments are, the relative position of enough of them can be determined to reveal the sequence in which material was arranged through a considerable portion of the whole work. It is possible to mark successive divisions of the *Life*, to reconstruct the manner in which Satyrus developed the topics treated by him, and to note how one section was linked to another. Fragment Eight preserves the transition from the discussion of the dramatist's art to the treatment of his nature as a man—his temperament, personality, and intellectual convictions. The former topic closes with a resumptive formula quite after the manner of Xenophon, and a spirited touch is added at the end by a pertinent quotation from Aristophanes: "Such was the man as regards literary technique, whence it is that Aristophanes desires to measure his tongue 'By which such subtle utterances were expunged.'" Then follows the initial sentence of the succeeding rubric: "He was also great of soul." (8. ii. 20.) Evidently there was an orderly grouping of material, at least under broad captions, as to the limits and the content of which the reader was carefully orientated.

[49] *Frg.* 39, xiii, 23-xiv, 27, rightly attributed to the feminine interlocutor by Leo, *op. cit.* 284. Hunt erred in putting the defense of woman in the mouth of Diodorus. That Euclia comes to the defense of her sex is clear from the fact that she is congratulated by name on her plea, xiv, 31.

This principle of careful, topical development was also extended to the subdivision of a main theme. Thus, the delineation of the poet's *ethos*, a subject that occupies nearly half of the main fragments of the papyrus, was unfolded point by point. There are discussed Euripides' religious and philosophical views (37–38. i.), involving the influence of Anaxagoras upon him; the poet's estimates of such matters as wealth and virtue (38. ii–39. i.), from which there is a transition to the homage paid by Euripides to Socratic teachings (39. i. 20–39. ii. 23). Consideration of the contacts between the political views of Euripides and those of Socrates naturally leads to discussion of the tragedian's ideals of government and citizenship (39. ii. 23). Quotation of a comic poet's rehabilitation of the *demos* against the strictures of Euripides (39. iii–39. iv. 21), finally passes by natural association to the indebtedness of New Comedy to the dramatic and stylistic devices of the poet (39. v–39, vii.).[50] The *Life* then seemingly presented further exposition of the literary influence of Euripides as illustrated in the case of Demosthenes. As to the substantial accuracy of our outline there can be no misgivings, since many of these themes are in actual juxtaposition on the largest fragment (39), which also contains the end of the biography. Other pieces are plainly the relics of a text once continuous and immediately preceding the large fragment.

[50] I follow in the main Gerstinger's reconstruction of the thought sequence. The provenience of the quotations in 39, v-vi is not free from controversy. Leo, regarding this context as primarily incorporating the poet's warning, addressed to the youth, against vices, agrees with Hunt and von Arnim in attributing 39, vi, 1–15 to Euripides himself; by Gerstinger the citations are attributed to some comic poet.

Toward the close of the analysis of Euripides' character and characteristics was introduced his preference for the *vita solitaria* as betokened by the days passed in writing and meditation in a grotto on the island of Salamis (39. ix.). From this picture of lonely, brooding genius the biographer passed by an easy step to the popular disfavor likely to be visited on a man who holds himself aloof from his fellows and wields an iconoclastic and radical pen. The general dislike of Euripides is set forth under two heads, namely, the hostility of the Athenian men toward him and that of the women. In each case the cause of the animosity is adduced. The women's quarrel with him was naturally treated in greater detail because the alleged feud between the poet and the sex as well as the spicy stories concerning his experiences as an injured husband, which were assumed to have soured him against womankind, were motives precious to the Euripidean legend. Next comes the rehabilitation of feminine virtue against the carpings of Euripides. After this interlude a return to the main thread of the biography is lucidly indicated thus: "So much for our defence of women: let us now return to Euripides."—(39, xv. 14–20).

The chagrin of the poet caused by his unpopularity with his Athenian audience, as well as the injuries done to his self-esteem by his necessary competitions with poetasters and heightened by the jokes cracked at his expense by the comedians, motivate his departure to the court of Archelaus of Macedon[51]

[51] I cannot accept Frey's interpretation (*op. cit.* 39) of 39, xvii, 7–13 as the ribald jest of a "gallery-god." The words following the citation *οὗτοι μὲν οὖν, ὅπερ εἶπα, πρὸς τὴν τῶν πολλῶν ἐπολιτεύοντο χάριν*, must hark back to the concerted attacks of his literary critics, the comedians.

(39. xvi. 21–39, xviii. 23). A chronological phrase, the only one of definite fixation in the papyrus and to be translated "During the following winter" (39. xvi. 30–31),[52] indicates that some attention was paid to temporal sequence in narrating the events culminating in the dramatist's emigration to a land where he was welcomed as befitted his genius. The honors accorded to him by Archelaus and his vogue elsewhere than in Athens (39. xviii. 27–39, xx. 21) form the next theme; this is succeeded by the famous story of the ignominious death of the poet, mangled by the royal hounds (39. xx. 25 ff.). The transition to the narrative of his end is indicated by another deictic sentence (39. xx. 22–25): "Such was the course of Euripides' life; he met a death" *et seq.*

The papyrus ends with an account of the friendship between Euripides and Timotheos, and the assistance extended by the older master to the younger craftsman. But this is no haphazard appendage, the addition of which at this point constituted a departure from the principle of orderly arrangement governing elsewhere the composition of the life. We know from the anonymous *Vita* of Euripides that the authorship of the pretty epigram beginning "All Greece is Euripides' monument though Macedon holds his bones," was ascribed variously to Thucydides and Timotheos.[53] Herewith we have the clue to the context in the papyrus. The account of Euripides' relations with Timotheos,

[52] According to the probable restoration of von Arnim. Apropos of the critical difficulties involved in making the temporal phrase apply to the date of the *Ino*, from which the parodied passage is taken, and the last winter spent by Euripides in Athens, *see* Frey, 39–40. Satyrus may well have dated the piquant parody to suit himself.

[53] Westermann, 135, 35 ff.; Schwartz, 3, 4–10.

a topic which might conceivably have been introduced under the caption of literary influences, was logically linked with the quotation of the epigram. Satyrus declared for Timotheos as its author and hence explained why the poet discharged this pious function.[64]

As the death of Euripides and the circumstances preceding and attending it mark the end of the biography, the composition opened, of course, with the data concerning parentage, birth, and early life preserved for us in abbreviated form in the *Vita*. Here the nature of the case would demand that some attention be paid to chronology and historical sequence. However, in the delineation of the matured figure of the man to which the bulk of the treatise was devoted, categories instead of chronology governed presentation. To all intents and purposes this is the topical scheme of arrangement that the student of the classical literatures finds most strikingly exemplified in the biographies written by the Roman Suetonius. This gossipy but methodical chronicler framed in this fashion his lives of literary men and his lives of the Caesars. Normally the body of each biography consists in a record of deeds and a description of all manner of characteristics, thematically organized, and forming a huge parenthesis, as it were, inclosed between chronological narratives treating the preliminary stage of a career and its closing phases. Suetonius used the scheme by deliberate preference, in full consciousness that it involved a large neglect of chronological grouping. Thus he openly says: "Having given, as it were, a

[64] Leo, *op. cit.* 286.

summary of the life of Augustus, I shall now take up the various phases one by one, not in chronological order but by categories (*per species*), to make the account clearer and more intelligible."[55]

One of the main contentions of Leo's book is that this biographical form is identical with that after which were composed the Alexandrian grammarians' *Vitae* of literary men; imported into Roman scholarship by the learned Varro, it was adopted by Suetonius for his lives of savants and authors, and then consciously utilized in an unprecedented way by him when he transferred the same scheme to the lives of the Caesars. The merits of this atavistic explanation will be passed on in a future chapter. For the present let us be content with emphasizing what the discovery of the papyrus fragments of Satyrus have contributed to our knowledge of the currency of the thematically written biography: We now realize that it was struck out before the rise of the Alexandrian learned biographies and that the philologists who wrote these lives not only gleaned material from but also followed the structural form of their Peripatetic forerunners. It is unlikely that Satyrus was the sole exponent of this method of marshaling data or that his *Life of Euripides* was the only one of his biographies fashioned along these lines. The form was quite as applicable to his other lives of literary men and (why not?) may well have been found equally adapted to his biographies of men of action.[56] And it

[55] *Div. Aug.* 9. The translation is in substance J. C. Rolfe's, *Loeb Series* (London, Heinemann, 1914).

[56] Athen. xii. 557 B = *FHG* frg. 5 indicates that in the life of Philip of Macedon Satyrus grouped the several wives of this much-married monarch in one context. This is precisely the Suetonian method; *see* e.g., *Aug.* 62; *Claud.* 26; *Nero* 35; *Vesp.* 3.

is too logical an outgrowth of the processes of ethical analysis and delineative classification of personality with which philosophy had ushered in Peripatetic biography to justify limiting it to one representative of the school, and a late *diadochus* at that. The encomiasts, in their own way, from Gorgias on had organized their tributes also in an orderly, topical way. In principle their method does not differ from that of Satyrus.

"If it is true, it is in Plato," saith the ardent classicist. It is wholesome for our pride of intellect now and then to have exposed as only resurgents from the classic world points of view and procedures fondly cherished as the new progeny of modern enlightenment. So it is that these ancient practitioners of the biographical art pitched upon a method that bears more than a passing likeness to the style of human portraiture cultivated by Mr. Gamaliel Bradford and others. Mr. Bradford is too versed in biographical literature to claim for his "psychography" entire novelty as a technical device. It is described as a refinement and extension of methods that, in substance, have been previously employed. In contrast with biography which "is bound to present an elaborate sequence of dates, events and circumstances," and to strive for completeness, there is, writes Mr. Bradford, "a gain in swinging clear from this chronological sequence altogether and in attaching oneself solely to the presentation of a man's *qualities of character, arranged and treated in such logical sequence* as shall give a total impression that will be most effective and most enduring."[67] If the

[67] *A Naturalist of Souls* (New York, Dodd, Mead, 1917), 5; 18, 19. The present writer is responsible for the italics.

Peripatetic biographers ever became articulate expounders of the theory governing their actual practice in delineating personalities, they would have said words very like these. If they did not "swing clear" entirely from the chronological method, they and Suetonius after them made it subsidiary to their chief concern, the topical diagraming of characters and careers.

CHAPTER VII

THE ANTECEDENTS AND PRIMITIVES OF ROMAN BIOGRAPHY

The Romans thought that good men should be praised for all the virtues displayed in life and not alone for a glorious death.—Dionysius of Halicarnassus, *Antiquitates Romanae*, v. 17. 6.

The historian of biographical composition as practiced by the classic peoples must sometime in the course of his narrative cross, as did Aeneas, to the land west of the Adriatic. Once there he may, if he so elect, limit his responsibilities to those productions that according to formal literary criteria fall under the genre. If a complete catalogue[1] of all the exponents of biography among the Romans be his ambition, his book at the start is doomed to become caviar to the general on many a page. To be sure, biographies such as the *Lives of Illustrious Men* by Cornelius Nepos, and the *Agricola* of Tacitus, owing to their centuries' old place in the classical regimen, will be something more than names to many cultured readers. The *De viris illustribus* of Suetonius Tranquillus and, still more, his *Lives of the Twelve Caesars*, books which set a mode that endured among pagan and Christian biographers through Einhard to Petrarch and the Renaissance, have made good their own claim to literary renown. The *Twelve Caesars*,

[1] Such as the work of L. Wiese, *Commentatio de vitarum scriptoribus Romanis* (Berlin, Druckerei der König. Akad. der Wissenschaften, 1840).

we are told, was a treasured work on Mark Twain's "five-foot shelf"—recommendation enough for its intrinsic appeal. But aside from these exponents that bulk largest in a comprehensive account of Roman biography, there is a long list of representatives in which even to the specialist the learned Varro and his analogue in literary biography, Santra, Tiro, freedman and biographer of Marcus Cicero, Cicero's friend, Atticus, Julius Hyginus, imperial librarian of Augustus, Marius Maximus, and the *Scriptores Historiae Augustae*, successors of Suetonius in the gossipy pages of imperial biography, are celebrities in comparison with most of those writers who are known to us as having recorded the lives of men during the late Republic and under the Empire. The *Scriptores*, of course, like Suetonius, exist for us *in extenso*. In the study of the rest we are condemned to that grim necessity of dealing with fragments and testimonia, *undique decerpta*—fascinating and tantalizing diversion of technical scholarship.

Leo by no means regarded the fashioning of a repertorium of Roman biographers as his task.[2] He was engrossed in demonstrating as sweepingly as possible the descent of Roman formal biography from Greek ancestral origins. In Leo's view Isocrates stood to the *Agricola* of Tacitus, the Alexandrian grammarians to Varro and Suetonius as for Vergil Ilium stood to the *Urbs Aeterna*. *Veterum volvit monimenta librorum*, if we may venture a paraphrase. Naturally, therefore, he drew a line between biography employed consciously by the Romans as a literary device and such native revelations as there were among them of the biographical impulse.

[2] *Die griech.-röm. Biographie*, Vorwort.

The study of Roman forms in their relation to the Greek is, of course, a large part of the function of the critic of Latin literature. Yet the annals of the spread of Hellenic suzerainty over Roman letters cannot afford to omit inquiry into the original trends and accomplishments of the Roman people in literature. Hence those frequently plaintive speculations, conventional in our histories of Latin literature, as to what Roman beginnings in epic, drama, and the lyric might have brought forth had the native plodders not been overtaken in their pedestrian progress, caught up, and whirled away by the soaring Greek chariot. There is also the question of the survival, in various literary forms, of Roman ingredients. So in the case of biography our study would be incomplete if we should fail to take cognizance of the primordial phases of Roman attitude and practice.

There are only two Roman biographers of whom on the basis of extant utterance it can be said that they contemplated their specific projects as standing in any relation to the history of biographical writing. The orbits of these two, Tacitus and Suetonius, by a coincidence worth passing mention, intersected with circles of culture in which another arch-biographer of antiquity, Plutarch, moved for a time at Rome. In the opening sentences of the *Agricola* Tacitus writes that in his age the custom of recording for posterity the deeds and ways of eminent men was still observed. Even decadent modernity—to paraphrase his thought—is not wholly averse to celebrating the memory of men whose worth and achievements have been outstanding. But in the eyes of a Tacitus, the times were out of joint for that form of literary production. The palmy days had been *apud priores*—"amongst the forefathers." Then no chronicler of departed virtue felt called upon to apologize for taking pen in hand. Even autobiographers, such as Rutilius Rufus and Aemilius Scaurus, did not have to fear censure or incredulity on the part of the reading public.

To these examples of writers of autobiography Tacitus might have added another instance, the versatile Q. Lutatius Catulus who had a pretty touch in epigram as well as in less frivolous forms of literature. These three men were contemporaries. They lived and wrote in the period of mad party strife succeeding the days of the Gracchi. Thus we can localize exactly in time the epoch with which Tacitus was contrasting the end of the first century A.D. His glance went back to a period approximately two hundred years before his own time, but no farther. In essaying in this instance his favorite roll of *laudator temporis acti*, he had in mind, furthermore, biographies of the good and great only, to which in publishing a life of his father-in-law he was to add another specimen. In short, so far as his language goes, in these prefatory sentences Tacitus did not pass beyond the eulogistic type of biography; he likewise confined himself to a retrospection entirely national.

In contrast with Tacitus the attitude of Suetonius toward precedents in the field of biography paralleled the thought of the Horatian adage, which, threadbare though it has been worn by quotation in books like this, I venture to repeat: "*Graecia capta ferum victorem cepit.*" In a previous chapter[3] allusion has

[3] *Supra*, p. 135.

been made to the list of four representative Greek biographers of literary men, Hermippus, Antigonus, Satyrus, and Aristoxenus, which critics[4] unite in considering not the fruit of independent research on the part of the holy Jerome but erudite plumage appropriated from Suetonius' preface to the *De viris illustribus*. This roster also included, we believe, four Roman biographers, namely, Varro, Santra, Nepos, and Hyginus, the whole being a kind of brief "Who's Who" in literary biography anterior to Suetonius' own work in the field. The formation of a symmetrical canon of eminent predecessors—four on the Greek side and four on the Roman—is partly due, doubtless, to the passion for organization of data that was characteristic of the orderly mind and formal methods of Suetonius. However, national pride had long since found gratification in balancing in various kinds of literature groups of Roman celebrities against Greek and other alien counterparts. In this spirit Varro in his *Imagines* or "Portraits" and Nepos in his biographies had organized their work. A like homage to the principle we should expect to find exemplified in a writer like Suetonius, who strove to be the Varro of the age of Trajan and Hadrian.

Leo was doubtless correct in assuming that Suetonius credited Varro with the introduction to Roman soil of biography after the Greek models. Here is revealed the attitude typical of the Hellenized Roman man of letters, eager to link national progress in formal literature with the *exemplaria Graeca* and

[4] A. Reifferscheid, *C. Suetonii Tranquilli praeter Caesarum libros reliquiae* (Leipzig, Teubner, 1875), 367; U. von Wilamowitz-Moellendorff, "Antigonos von Karystos," *Philol. Untersuch.* IV (1881), 27; G. Körtge, "In Suetonii de viris illustribus libros inquisitionum capita tria," *Diss. philol. Hal.* XIV (1901), 191; Leo, *op. cit.* 136.

to emblazon by such appeals his own accomplishments. Students of classical antiquity all have their desiderata among the lost parts of Greek and Latin literature. A rescue of the *opera omnia* of Suetonius from the ravages of time would not be the preference of many—nor is it mine. Still one would wish to be informed less scantily than is the case concerning the prefaces with which the biographical treatises opened. As it is, one can but speculate as to what themes, if any, the industrious and erudite chronicler of lives may have touched upon over and above his terse account of the precedents for formal literary biography among the Greeks and the Romans.

The sophisticated standards adopted after the Hellenization of Roman literature did not per se blind the Roman critic to the indigenous forms and national capabilities antedating the transforming touch of Greek artistry. Cicero[5] tried to carry his history of Roman oratory back to the expulsion of the kings. Reasoning inferentially from the traditional accounts of the influence wielded by such men as L. Brutus and M. Valerius, he concludes that they must have been endowed with the gift of eloquence. Livy and Horace found the germs of drama in the rude verse dialogue, replete with rustic jest and billingsgate, which formed on days of festive merriment the outlet of the inborn Italian genius for raillery. The latter writer[6] also put on record, as native traits making for aptitude in the field of tragedy, the Roman's bent for the sublime and his capacity for emotional intensity. Suetonius opened his biographical conspectus of grammarians with

[5] *Brutus* 52 ff. [6] *Epist.* ii. 1, 164–67.

observations touching the lack of early interest in the subject, the reasons, and the informal beginnings of the study in Italy.[7] In the preface to his work *On Poets* forming one of the categories of his biographies of literary men, he philosophized concerning the folk-origin of poetry and linked, in a derivative vein, its growth with the rise of the religious consciousness.[8] Thus it would not have been unlike him to touch briefly in the preface of either of his two biographical works on traits of national genius and folkways that affected the biographical impulse.

At all events, from the earliest moments at which the Roman genius can be clearly visualized, there are attributes, if not congenital certainly inveterate, adhering firmly to it. Only a superficial view would deny that the Roman of the early Republic possessed imagination. However, this power of fancy found by preference its scope in such fields as law, statecraft, and religion, provinces where a sense for the niceties of formula and for ritualistic subtleties is challenged and where generalization has to be framed dexterously to cover multifarious instances. The imaginative faculty of the Roman was not of the sort to urge him at first to high literary creation. His instincts were to take his world as he found it and to arrange his life accordingly. The intellect of the Roman was not spurred as the Greek mind was to try to spell out the cosmic enigma, to contemplate the course of man as part of a mundane spectacle, and to see, as the Greek poet intuitively envisioned,

> Beyond his passions' widest range
> Far regions of eternal change.

[7] Roth, 257. [8] *Idem*, 290–91.

Still, there are emotions and desires so common to humanity that they are bound to manifest themselves spontaneously in the intellectual development of any race that rises above the levels of brute existence. The Roman, like the Greek and many other races, needed no suggestion other than native impulse to set it to chanting lays in praise of ancestral heroes and intoning dirges or *neniae* over the dead. These forms of commemorative literature, their roots imbedded in the soil of universal racial experience, are biography in embryo. They may or they may not survive beside later, documented outgivings of the impulse that sponsors alike prose and poetic tributes to personality. The rendition at banquets of songs extolling the deeds and the virtues of famous men was, we know, a usage obsolete among the Romans by the time of the Elder Cato, but in earlier days an established custom. It is only in respect to questions relating to the extent of this ballad literature, its survival in the stories of Roman history, and the persons who actually rendered the songs[9] that scholarly opinion has varied since the days when Niebuhr was fain to reconstruct a Roman counterpart of the Greek epic. The most detailed description of the content of these sagas is given by Cicero,[10] who learned all that he knew about them from the Elder Cato's *Origines*. *Clarorum virorum laudes et virtutes*, writes Cicero, after Cato—"eulogies of famous men and their virtues." Cato himself was reporting a practice of bygone generations. Under the circumstances, therefore, this characterization of

[9] *Pueri modesti* were the singers according to Varro, *De vita populi Romani*, in *Nonius* 77 M. I, 107 Lindsay; Cicero, *Brutus* 75 and *Tusc. Disp.* iv. 3 reports that guests rendered these songs.

[10] *Loc. cit.*

the ballads has only the value of a generalization such as might be applied to the tenor of almost any heroic narrative poetry.

The words *laudare* and *collaudare* were used to describe the function both of the dirge[11] and of the prose funeral eulogy.[12] The genetic kinship between the two is apparent; they respond to the same commemorative and laudatory desire.[13] The prose eulogy, we shall see, deserves to be placed on a substantial parity with encomiastic biography. Yet since the word *laudare* has a connotation that can embrace a rhapsodical tribute, quite general in content, as well as a detailed recital of deeds and virtues, it is evident that it would be folly to infer that the content of the primitive Roman dirge rivaled in wealth of truly biographical material the funeral speech. The *nenia*, arising as an impromptu, crudely but sincerely voicing the praise of the dead and the sense of loss felt by surviving intimates, degenerated by the time of Naevius[14] into an old wives' "keening." The banalities of hired mourners, *praeficae*, made it the butt of Plautine humor[15] even though, in spite of the disrepute into which it had fallen, the tradition of the dirge as an honorific tribute lasted to later and more sophisticated epochs.[16]

[11] Naevius 129 *in* Ribbeck, *Comic. Rom. frag.* (ed. 3), 34; Plautus, *Truculentus* 495; Festus 163, p. 155 Lindsay.

[12] Cicero *De legibus* ii. 62; Tacitus *Annales* iii. 5, 2; Suetonius *Aug.* 100; *Claud.* 1.

[13] This very identity in purpose may have worked to discredit the dirge. It could scarcely hope to compete with the greater range of the *laudatio; see* H. de la Ville de Mirmont, "La nenia," *Études sur l'ancienne poésie latine* (Paris, Fontemoing, 1903), 395–97.

[14] *Loc. cit.* [15] *Loc. cit.*

[16] Certain senators proposed to dignify the funeral of Augustus by a *nenia* rendered by the children of leading citizens; Suetonius, *loc. cit.;* Tacitus, *loc. cit.*; recall the wicked parody of the usage in the *Apocolocyntosis.*

Granting as we must the noncommittal character of the Romans' own references to the content of both the primitive narrative ballad and the dirge, we may still assume plausibly that these vanished specimens of commemorative poetry must have reflected the typical tendencies of the national temperament. No Roman Simonides or Pindar arose to lay the Midas touch of idealistic artistry on the dirge and to translate the particular into the universal and representative. It is impossible to imagine the ancestors of the men who composed the epitaphs of the Scipios as straying far in any metrical narrative from dry recital of the specific and the personal.[17] The racial mentality tended in historical times too conspicuously to careful, unimaginative chronicling of *res gestae* and virtues.

This very deficiency of the Roman in artistic fancy was in a way to the advantage of biography. The memoranda touching the life of a man, the compilation and preservation of which as well as of those touching the life of the state, were positive fetishes, would remain matter-of-fact appraisals of what he did and what he was. Partisanship or family pride might take liberties with veracity, but such distortion of facts would leave the essential literary character of a record unchanged. When the Romans were still in literary nonage, they had attained intellectual maturity in other respects. Desire for an orderly tabulation of officials and events led to the codification and filing of records. These

[17] E. Galletier, *Étude sur la poésie funéraire romaine d'après les inscriptions* (Paris, Hachette, 1922), 195–98, seeks traces of the content and language of the dirge in certain metrical epitaphs, especially those of children and those emanating from the unlettered bourgeoisie. The suggestion is interesting, though demonstration is scarcely possible.

various *libri*, *commentarii*, *acta*, and *annales*, the output of sundry priestly colleges and civil magistracies, were not due merely to the antiquarian spirit. The chroniclers that produced them were animated by the prudential regard for the value of precedent, the solid conviction that the past must prescribe for the future and point its way. To this day the visitor to the Roman Forum cannot fail to mark a huge edifice towering above him on the brow of the Capitoline. This impressive structure is the *Tabularium*, the state repository of records. The massive stonework of substructure and walls serves as a convincing reminder that the Roman of the Republic built for the ages when he housed his records. Many a casual tourist has looked

> And felt the hillside haunted even then
> By not dead memory of the Roman men.

The Roman pragmatism reponded also in private life from early times to the impulses that shaped the practices of civic life. As the state had its *Tabularium*, the substantial Roman householder had, adjacent to the atrium, a repository of family archives. Here were preserved records of various sorts, such as chronicles of deeds done in office by members of the family who had functioned as magistrates, funeral orations delivered over the illustrious dead, and the like. This ingrained zeal for the perpetuation of documents that centered about the family fostered the production of memorials of its great personages' careers. In all this there was something analogous to the workings of the principle of self-esteem that, carried to greater lengths in Arabian civilization, estimates, we are informed by students of Islam, every man as a great personality and has stimulated a veritable exuberance of biographical composition among the Moslems.[18] In the Roman family the will to edify and to guide by the torch of example the footsteps of posterity was associated with the impulse to commemorate the deeds of its great members. Influential also in the composition and preservation of biographical monuments were the dictates of religion, the pious regard for his ancestors that moved the Roman to try to keep unsevered the ties binding the living and the dead.

Furthermore, long before the literators of Rome had become acquainted with specimens of formal Greek biography, many a citizen of the governing class did not have to unroll a manuscript in order to read biography *in parvo*. As every student of Roman life is aware, the very walls in the houses of noble families exhibited a kind of monumental biography. Arranged in closet-niches in the atrium were portrait masks of ancestors. Each effigy was accompanied by a painted inscription, *titulus imaginis*, identifying the subject, recording his father's name, and presenting an *aperçu* of the offices, civil and priestly, which he had held. In case he had been a victorious commander and had celebrated a triumph, this honor and the war in which it had been earned would also be specified.[19] Lines drawn from likeness to likeness indicated relationship and descent. The origin of these partly pictorial, partly literary biographical compends lay far back in Roman his-

[18] A. Sprenger, *Das Leben und die Lehre des Mohammad* (ed. 2; Berlin, Nicolai, 1869), III, Vorrede cxxv.

[19] Livy x. 7, 11.

tory. The time came when the bronze and marble handiwork of Greek sculptors intruded into the sacrosanct portrait gallery; this artistic improvement stirred the Elder Pliny[20] to adopt his not infrequent vein of retrospective moralizing. To him art's gain was virtue's loss—he was not the first or the last Puritan to indulge in this plaint. At any rate, certain of the externalities of human portraiture which are common both to rudimentary and matured biography, namely, ancestry, descendants, honors, and personal appearance were perennial elements.

So natural a place does appraisal of character have in the commemorative utterances of all ages that one is led to ponder whether brief estimate of a man's worth, terse tributes to his standing in the community were ever included in these titular life-summaries. What knowledge we can gain of the primitive Roman practice in mortuary record comes, of course, not from any surviving *titulus imaginis*, but from the testimony of the analogous tomb inscription. The earliest form of Roman epitaphs as it is known to us[21] reveals that the original Roman disposition was to deem a bare enumeration of the offices a man had held sufficient testimony as to his merit. The matter-of-fact laconicism that in the fourth and the third centuries B.C. tended to restrict inscriptions set up in honor of victorious generals to a clipped account of *res gestae*[22] and left amplification and eulogistic estimate to literary history and documentary record, must also have exerted its effect on

[20] *Nat. hist.* xxxv. 2. 6–7.

[21] The allusion is to the prose *tituli* on the oldest sarcophagi of the Scipios, *C.I.L.* I, 1 (ed. 2, 1918), nos. 6 and 8.

[22] See *ibid.* p. 386, col. 2.

the content and diction of private memorial. At some time not far removed in either direction from the ending, in 241 B.C., of the First Punic War, the bleak dignity of the prose tomb *titulus* was felt to be inadequate. This more effusive mood expressed itself in the poetic epitaph, couched in the rude native Saturnians. The increased expansiveness naturally attending this innovation made general appraisal or ethical appreciation of the dead as conventional a part of the subject-matter as parentage and honors had been.

Of this fact there is ocular demonstration in the famous *elogia* of the Scipios.[23] These epitaphs have perhaps been most largely utilized by philologists as indices of the phenomena of early Latinity and metrics. However, quite apart from these aspects of the study that has been expended on them, they reflect, when they are examined in their chronological sequence, in an unmistakable manner the gradual unfolding of the Roman literary habit and the changing phases of commemorative attitude. There has been some erudite altercation concerning the dates of the epitaphs and a consequent divergence of views as to what the two oldest in particular may or may not have owed in respect to diction and theme to Greek precedent. That most acute of Latinists of the last generation, Eduard Wölfflin,[24] believed that even the earliest of the *elogia* was not cut until

[23] *C.I.L.* I, 1[2] nos. 7, 9, 10, 11, 15.

[24] *Revue de philologie* XIV (1890), 113–22; *Sitzungsber. der bay. Akad. der Wissensch.*, phil.-hist. Kl. 1892, 188–219. The late E. W. Fay endeavored unsuccessfully to prove that the two oldest Scipionic epitaphs were archaizing *elogia* for which Scipio Metellus, contemporary of Cicero, was responsible; *see* "Scipionic Forgeries," *Class. Quart.* XIV (1920), 164–71 and the refutation by T. Frank, *Class. Quart.* XV (1921), 169–71.

after the battle of Zama (202 B.C.) when the Scipios, at the height of their fame, desired to dignify the memory of comparatively obscure ancestors in a manner befitting the newly won family prestige. Hence a poet, perhaps none other than Ennius, was commissioned to supply for the tombs of the old Barbatus, consul in 298 B.C. and his son, Lucius Cornelius, consul in 259 B.C., grave epigrams of a character more elevated than the brief prose *tituli* which had been formerly deemed sufficient in a simpler age unmoved by the artistry expended by the Greeks on their sepulchral epigrams.

The oldest of the epitaphs is a metrical memorandum betokening the bent of the early Roman temperament for unvarnished, straightforward chronicling. Modern English does scant justice to its quaintly archaic Latin. A version should be spelled and pronounced in the fashion of Shakespeare's time in order to approximate the effect that Latin of the third century B.C. would have wrought on the ear of Tacitus or Suetonius:

> Here lies a man amongst good men the very best, most Romans do agree, Lucius Scipio, Barbatus' son. Consul, censor, aedile was he amongst you. Corsica and Aleria town did he take in; to weather gods gave he in thank-offering temple he had vowed.

The methodical arrangement, three verses devoted to appraisal and parentage and three to honors and deeds, testifies to the deliberately contrived symmetry of composition. In the second verse of the epigram the juxtaposition of *duonoru*[*m*] *optimo*[*m*] betrays a studied effort for rhetorical effect. This was due to the unassisted light of nature and not, *pace* Wölfflin, to the impact on the writer's mind of Greek stylistic precedents.[25] Like the antithetical phrasing in the first line, *oino[m] ploirime*, the collocation is one of those simple rhetorical devices that inevitably developed in the growth of a language that through centuries of practice was worked into the form requisite for the cogent and arresting discourse demanded in senate, court, and comitia.[26]

Even if the composition of the *elogium* be assigned to a period subsequent to 240 B.C.[27] and thus localized in the epoch in which Livius Andronicus in his translation of the *Odyssey* was putting Greek content into Roman meter and in his plays adapting Greek metrical forms to the Latin tongue, the character of the epitaph is genuinely old Roman. A conventional native mode had been struck out of which the *elogium* of Lucius Scipio is a specimen. This is proved by the striking similarity of its first two lines with the opening couplet of the *elogium* engraved on the tomb of A. Atilius Calatinus, consul in the years 258 and 254 B.C. By a happy chance Cicero[28] twice quoted in his extant works the beginning of the epitaph of Calatinus:

> Here lyeth one whom all mankind agree
> Rome's first and greatest citizen to be.
> —Rackham's translation.

There can be no reasonable ground for doubting that the *elogium* conformed to the type illustrated by the epitaph of Lucius Scipio and appended to the honorific estimate of Calatinus his *cursus honorum*

[25] Wölfflin, *op. cit.* 211.
[26] Fr. Leo, *Gesch. der röm. Lit.* 34 ff., 45, 46.
[27] *Ibid.*; Lommatzsch, *C.I.L.* I, 1², p. 379.
[28] *De fin.* ii. 116; *De senec.* 61.

and *res gestae*. Wölfflin's[29] theory that the earliest of the Scipionic epitaphs was an imitation of the *elogium* of Atilius, carved on his tomb soon after 240 B.C., has nothing to commend it. Incidentally—a fact which does not seem to have concerned Wölfflin—the theory does not exactly add to the poetic luster of Ennius. Verses devoid of literary quality—"*sermo merus*" except for the jolting meter—are fathered upon him, and furthermore it is work shaped in a mold formed by an uninspired Roman predecessor. Rather is it the case that the two *elogia*, and others the existence of which may be assumed, were all extracted from the one crucible of native Roman predilection and literary capability. The *elogia* provided from the death of Regulus down to the siege of Saguntum for the tombs of such great families as the Metelli and the Servilii, whose sepulchers as well as those of Calatinus and the Scipios met the wayfarer's eye outside the Porta Capena,[30] would not have varied in substance from one traditional type.

Architectonically the *elogium* of Scipio Barbatus, father of Lucius, which a less archaic syntax and spelling show was cut some years after the son's epitaph, is still true to the old national custom. Three verses devoted to name, father's name, and to appreciation are followed by three recording offices and achievements. Within the conventional framework, however, when we read:

> Lucius Cornelius Scipio Barbatus, from a sire Gnaeus sprung, brave man and sage, whose goodly aspect his virtue quite did match,

[29] *Rev. de Philol.* XIV (1890), 117. [30] Cicero *De fin.* i. 13.

we are conscious of an increased fluency in idea and phrase over the older epitaph. Hence a Greek aroma has been scented in the adjectival pair *fortis sapiensque*,[31] and in the assertion that Barbatus was "as good as he was fair to look upon."[32] *Sapiens*, however, did not connote to a Roman eulogist in the years just prior to the Second Punic War merely a man versed in Greek letters and learning.[33] The dictum of Cato in the *Origines* that such epithets as *fortis atque strenuus*, *bonus atque strenuus* were among the Romans of the old days the customary recognition of the possession by a citizen of the ideal civic virtues,[34] is the kind of generalization that should not be endowed with exclusiveness, especially when the informant is so consistent a praiser of former times. Surely it is conceivable that a Roman, unprompted by the Greek partiality for physical beauty, would be quite capable of voicing his appreciation of another's bodily perfections by the general word *forma*. A race that had been through centuries habituated to the sight of manly vigor as this was displayed in feats of arms and in the hardier exercises favored along the Tiber would certainly have developed of itself an eye for the male "form divine." Therefore, even though the attribute 'preliterary'

[31] Compared by Wölfflin, *ibid.* 121, to the Greek καλοκάγαθός, *sapiens* being construed as referring to Greek culture, of which from the elder Africanus on, the Scipios were champions. If one be determined to find Greek influence in the epitaph, the line *quoius forma virtutei parisuma fuit* is much closer to καλοκάγαθία.

[32] Galletier, *op. cit.* 151.

[33] Thus in the extract from the *laudatio* of Metellus preserved in Pliny *Nat. hist.* vii. 43. 139 and delivered in 221 B.C., *sapientes* means little more than 'sensible.' A *vir sapiens* here is one who spends his life not in the acquisition of Greek culture and philosophy, but of fame, honors, and riches, as well as wisdom.

[34] Aulus Gellius *N. A.* xvii. 13, 3; Festus, p. 201.

must be denied to the *elogium* of Barbatus, its content as well as its form may fairly be regarded as completely redolent of the original Roman spirit.[35]

Two of the four Scipionic *elogia* written in Saturnians[36] fall in a period well along in the victorious advance of Hellenism. Ennius died in 169 B.C. After the battle of Pydna (168 B.C.) the library of King Perseus of Macedon was brought to Rome by his conqueror, Aemilius Paulus, and became a rallying place for the Grecophile circle of Scipio Aemilianus and his bosom friend, Laelius. The senatorial edict of 161 B.C., denying residence in Rome to philosophers and rhetoricians, and the fulminations of Cato, sworn foe to the Greeks and all their works, were futile efforts to stem the resistless tide of the new culture. Such were the surroundings in which the later elogium has by scholarly consensus been placed; the composition of the other stands, if not within the period, at least on its threshold.[37]

The literary character of the epitaphs registers plainly the impact of the new ideals on such a proverbial stronghold of conservatism in literary tendency as mortuary poetry. They have more the nature of the eulogistic tribute, less that of the biographical memorandum. Generalities of appreciation and stylistic flowers replace the plain facts and the simple directness of their predecessors, as witness:

> Death brought to pass that all things thine were short, honors, fame, virtue, glory, talents, too. Had it been vouchsafed to thee in a long life to make the most of these, featly thy ancestors' feats hadst thou surpassed. Wherefore with good will into her bosom, Scipio, doth Earth receive thee, Publius Cornelius called, Publius thy sire.

[35] Leo, *Gesch. der röm. Lit.* 46. [36] *C.I.L.* I, 1², nos. 10, 11.
[37] *Circa* 170 B.C. Wölfflin; 164 B.C. Mommsen.

The tropical flight in the last sentence is clearly an echo of Greek figurative language: γαῖα κόλποις ἐδέξατο.[38] Nevertheless, the dictates of oldtime usage are still effective; this *elogium* and its fellow are a blending of the archaic and the *nouveau*. Adherence to the Saturnian meter in despite of the fact that Ennius had flouted the "sylvan crudeness" of the earlier Latin bards, was one point carried by tradition. Furthermore, each epitaph in its original form was six verses in length; the first verse of the *elogium* of Publius Cornelius, in which is recorded the fact that he was *flamen Dialis*, or chief priest of Jupiter, was prefixed as an afterthought, and was hence omitted in the English rendition just attempted. Comparison with the two third-century specimens indicates that a dimensional convention had been established and that this had to be observed, if possible. When, as is true of the two later Scipios, a member of the family had died too young to attain to the fulness of years and honors, some padding would be inevitable. Eulogistic generalities had perforce to be substituted for specific achievements. Thus the different flavor of the two later *elogia* is due partly to intrinsic causes and not alone to artistic choice. Moreover, each epitaph, so far as conditions permitted, lived up to the stress placed by Roman civic ideals on a man's services to the government. Hence the prefixed line referred to above. Also in the case of L. Cornelius Scipio, who died at the age of twenty years, the passer-by is informed that no record of offices held is possible since none was given to the dead youth's charge.

[38] Cicero *De leg.* ii. 63; F. Bücheler, *Carmina Latina epigraphica*, I, p. 7.

Memorial *titulus* and *elogium* as well were epigraphical condensations of biographical matter that was elaborated in the funeral speech with its wider scope. Of all the biographical primitives that Roman folkway produced, the *laudatio funebris* came nearest to the norm of formal biography as the ancients, with less rigorous standards than ours, understood it. For centuries during the Republic and the Empire delivery by some chosen speaker of a sustained prose tribute, commemorating the career and the virtues of a person whose life had ended, was a national institution of Roman life. The first instance known to literary tradition[39] is the eulogy of Brutus, the first consul, which was spoken by his fellow-consul, Valerius Publicola, in the forum before the assembled people. This story may be only the result of the tendency of ancient historiography definitely to localize the origin of a usage. At all events the record purports to give only the first known occasion of the delivery of a funeral oration at a public funeral. Dionysius of Halicarnassus had the critical judiciousness to confess his ignorance as to whether this was an innovation introduced by Publicola or a custom carried over from the age of the kings. The one thing, says the historian, of which his researches have made him certain is that the custom was of Roman origin and was not imported from the Greeks.[40] Modern scholarship is entirely in accord with him as to the truth of this assertion.

[39] Dionysius of Halicarnassus *Ant. Rom.* v. 17; for other references *see* Fr. Vollmer, "Laudationum funebrium Romanorum historia et reliquiarum editio," *Jahrbb. f. class. Phil.* Supplbd. XVIII (1891), 478.

[40] Dionysius, *loc. cit.*

The movement of the *laudatio funebris* was one of extension. Arising in response to the same natural impulse that produced the dirge, having, as there is every reason to believe, originally a place in the usages of private life as one of the tokens of respect paid to a dead man by patrician families, the *laudatio* became a public ceremony when the deceased had held official position and deserved well of the State. Hence members of plebeian families came in due course to a share in this honor. By the last century of the Republic the double standard, as it may be called, was broken down and women of illustrious families gained rights in this sphere. At the tender age of eleven the young Octavius eulogized his grandmother, Julia, in the crowded assembly.[41] One would like to know how that mordant critic of adolescent orators, Juvenal, would have reacted to the maiden effort of this precocious eulogist. The emperor Hadrian attained to such a peak of gallantry as to deliver a *laudatio* in honor of his mother-in-law![42]

Of greater moment than the narration of those incidents in the history of the *laudatio* that induce to frivolous reflections, are its literary significance in the annals of Roman biographical productivity and its formative influence. Consideration of these questions is linked with the study of certain specimens of Roman biographical writing that fall into the purview of the next chapter, and hence will be postponed. As an essential preliminary it will be in order here to discover the extent to which the *laudatio* in respect to content partook of the nature of biography.[43]

[41] Suetonius *Aug.* 8. [42] *C.I.L.* XIV, 3579.

[43] The material collected by Vollmer, *op. cit.* forms the basis for this, as it must for any other discussion of the *laudatio*.

Undoubtedly it is the result of accident merely that among our surviving fragments of Roman funeral discourses the earliest in which the theme of ancestry receives specific treatment comes from Julius Caesar's eulogy of his aunt, Julia. The speech was delivered by the future dictator in his quaestorship in the year 68 B.C. The lineage of Julia was accredited by the orator to kings on the mother's side and to the gods on the father's. The speaker then continued:

> Our stock therefore has at once the sanctity of kings, whose power is supreme among mortal men, and the claim to reverence which attaches to the Gods, who hold sway over kings themselves.[44]

This fable, which came from the same pen that later was to be moved by the fantastic tales of the zoological marvels of the Hercynian Forest to an immortal bestiary, has the florid content of the Greek encomium. Nevertheless, it is incredible that the topic of ancestry could ever have been passed over by a Roman eulogist, even in the early days before the extravagances of aetiology and the myths of noble Romans' descent from Trojan families had established themselves in literature.

The theory of the *laudatio* prescribed that praise of ancestors be coupled with praise of the recently deceased. This at least held good in the days of that acute and sympathetic observer of Roman institutions, the Greek Polybius, who came to Rome in the year 167 B.C. In what is our earliest and fullest account of the Roman funeral rites Polybius says (vi. 52, 11–54) that, when the officiating eulogist

[44] Suetonius *Iul.* 6 (Rolfe's translation).

had paid his tribute to his subject proper, he recounted the exploits of the dead man's ancestors beginning with the most remote. At first thought it might appear that so long as this eulogistic afterpiece held a place in the funeral ritual, any account of the dead man's ancestors and their prowess would be superfluous in the *laudatio* itself. We have no information as to whether the usage endured down to later times. Indefinite continuance would have its inconveniences as generation after generation added to the ancestral roster. Perhaps it was the primitive practice that was witnessed by Polybius. In any case some preliminary account of the dead man's lineage would be essential to the *laudatio*, if only for orientation, when the speech was delivered. Certain it is that when these speeches were consigned to writing and thus took permanent form as literary units, each separate specimen must have contained as an integral feature a rehearsal of ancestral descent and glory sufficient to locate the man in the family series and to lead up to discussion of his own life and personality. One of the incentives that led Roman households to preserve funeral speeches in documentary form was the utilitarian aim of resorting to older specimens as models and sources of information whenever a death in the family necessitated a similar panegyric.[45] This very fact is evidence, if any be needed, that pedigree and ancestral achievement were inevitable topics.[46] As to the position of the theme in the *laudatio* our only specific testimony comes from the days of the Empire in the

[45] Cicero *Brutus* 62.

[46] Vollmer, *op. cit.* 476, 477.

statement of Tacitus[47] that the funeral eulogy composed by Seneca for Nero to deliver in honor of Claudius enumerated at the beginning the ancestors of the dead princeps, their consulships and triumphs. Logical procedure would always tend to introduce this matter at the beginning of the *laudatio* proper, just as in the Greek biographical encomium and in the average modern biography.

Record of the official career was, of course, an element as essential in the *laudatio* as we have seen that it was in the skeleton biography presented by *titulus* and *elogium*. The presence of these data is attested, indeed, by our earliest surviving fragment of a funeral speech. This is a true relic of old-fashioned eloquence in that it comes from the eulogy of L. Caecilius Metellus which was delivered by his son Quintus in the year 221 B.C., three years before the outbreak of the Second Punic War. Pliny the Elder, to whom we owe our knowledge of the passage, incorporated in his *Natural History*[48] quotation of a consecutive context to which we shall later refer. Just before the quotation Pliny lists formally the higher offices held by Metellus and adds a further distinction, namely, that in the triumph celebrated by that general elephants were for the first time in Roman history a feature of the procession.[49] The kinship of this matter with the epitomized *cursus honorum* and *res gestae* of the two oldest Scipionic

[47] Tacitus *Ann.* xiii. 3.

[48] vii. 43. 139. I agree with H. Graff, *De Romanorum laudationibus commentatio* (Dorpat, E. J. Karow, 1862), 78, that the epitomized *cursus honorum* as given by Pliny derives from the *laudatio*; Vollmer, 480, was too conservative in excluding from the *laudatio* all but the passage actually quoted directly by Pliny.

[49] A statement that conflicts with other evidence and is doubtless inaccurate—further proof of its provenience from the *laudatio*; *see* Graff, *op. cit.* 81.

epitaphs is obvious. The *laudatio* of course could expand these various items with regard to chronology and circumstance as the *elogium* could not.

The *laudatio* also found space for a narrative treatment of salient incidents in a man's career. The circumstances attending the death of Claudius Marcellus, the conqueror of Syracuse, who was killed in 208 B.C. while leading a reconnaissance against the troops of Hannibal, were set forth in the *laudatio* delivered by the son, Marcus. To do justice to the fame of his father, who had laid himself open to the charge of rashness, the younger Marcellus had to give an account of the incidents connected with the tragic affair. Other versions, which we learn from Livy (xxvii. 27. 12–14) made the details of the event a bone of contention among historians, had to be anticipated and refuted. Evidently this involved expanded narrative, in which, we may be sure, the son sought to present his father's motives and conduct in a favorable light. The eulogist would also make the most of his authority as an eye-witness; he was in the thick of the fight and received a wound.

Incidents sequent upon the death of Marcellus undoubtedly were narrated in the speech. In Plutarch's *Life of Marcellus* (30) it is related that Hannibal, moved by chivalrous admiration of his great opponent, caused the body to be richly attired and cremated in due form, and then gave orders that the ashes, inclosed in a silver urn, be sent to the son. According to a picturesque story told by Plutarch on the authority of Cornelius Nepos and Valerius Maximus, the ashes were scattered in a struggle between the escort and a band of Numidians, and no pains were taken by Hannibal to have them collected. However, a pleasanter version, vouched for by the Emperor Augustus in a work not named by Plutarch, had it that the remains reached the younger Marcellus safely and were buried with great pomp. Obviously this kinder variant was that current in the family annals and was derived from the son's tribute. For the work of Augustus in question could scarcely have been other than the *laudatio* pronounced by him in honor of the Young Marcellus,[60] immortalized in the sixth book of the *Aeneid.* The emperor, as was customary with funeral eulogists, reverted to the early history of the family whose scion he was praising.

All that we know of the emphasis laid by the Roman on the practical side of life would persuade us to believe that the average *laudatio* must have included the details pertaining to a person's domestic life as well as to his public career. A homely realism would thus be achieved by the natural promptings of the Roman temperament alone. Generalities of appreciation and idealizing declamation there would be in plenty; there would also be no shrinking from blunt recording of the concrete fact. The prudential nature of the Roman and the control that his financial rating exerted over his place in the social structure and hence over his career, would serve to commend the theme of property to any record of a Roman's life. Although the actual evidence coming from the *laudationes* of Republican times is meager, Vollmer was certainly not rash in assuming that the topic was regularly introduced.[61] Mention of a man's worldly

[60] Servius *ad Aen.* i. 712.

[61] *Op. cit.* 477.

goods is not out of place in any biographical treatise. The Suetonian *Life of Vergil* (13, Diehl), the *Atticus* of Nepos (5; 13–14), and the *Agricola* of Tacitus (44) all testify that, irrespective of a biography's character as commemorative or informatory, some general allusion or specific reference to property was expected.

The clearest indication of the extent to which, even in the sophisticated days of the Principate, a Roman eulogist might publish to the world at large the intimate concerns of private life is furnished by those well-known examples of memorial tribute, the *Laudatio Murdiae*[62] and the *Laudatio Turiae*,[63] as the latter inscription was once designated. The old attribution, long since discredited,[64] has never been superseded by another equally definite; since we do not know the name of the wife who, as we are told, did not permit the murder of her parents to be unavenged (i. 3–6 Bruns) and sold her jewels to aid her husband to escape with his life from proscription (ii. 1), and since we can only theorize concerning the husband who so fervently extolled her, we are forced in speaking of the inscription to take refuge in the use of the saving prefix "so-called." On the other hand, if later scholarship does not share Mommsen's faith in the original ascription of the monument, his reluctance to see in the memorial an actual *laudatio* preserved in epigraphical form has not been shared

[62] *C.I.L.* VI 2, 10230; C. G. Bruns, *Fontes iuris Romani antiqui* (ed. 7; Tübingen, I. C. B. Mohr, 1909), no. 127. The date assigned to the inscription is the first century A.D.

[63] *C.I.L.* VI, 1527; 31670; Bruns no. 126. The inscription dates from the principate of Augustus; probably it is not far removed in either direction from the beginning of our era.

[64] For the most recent discussion *see* E. Weiss *in P-W* Halbd. XXIII, 995.

by most critics. Even if the description 'epitaph' be persevered in by the skeptical, it can still be invoked to reconstruct the tone and the subject-matter of the actual *laudatio* with which, in character, it would be closely akin.

The mother and the wife respectively are portrayed by their eulogists not only as good women, endowed with the virtues appropriate to their sex and race; they are delineated as good housewives and fair-minded dispensers of their patrimonies. Murdia's son puts on record his mother's equitable distribution of her inherited wealth among the children of two marriages and her surviving husband, the eulogist's stepfather (4–6). In the other *laudatio* the bereaved husband sets forth the minute processes of litigation faced by his wife because of an attempt by a third party to have her father's will set aside. Tribute is paid to the integrity and sound judgment with which she conducted herself in this difficult situation (i. 13–24). In a *praeteritio* the eulogist takes cognizance of his wife's traits of character and her simple taste in dress (i. 30, 31). The magnanimity of this admirable but infecund matron prompted her even to offer her husband a divorce in the hope that a second marriage might populate a childless home. Crowning touch of self-abnegation: The husband even so was to retain control of her property! A score of lengthy lines unfold this pathetic little drama of intimate domesticity (ii. 41–61).

We must, to be sure, bear in mind that in the *laudatio* of a woman the affairs of private life would loom large. But even with this admission we need not infer that the normal eulogy of a man would eschew analogous details. There never was a time in Roman life at which the conduct of a man as father and householder would have seemed a matter of indifference in the calculations of a kinsman or friend who was seeking in a discourse, uncircumscribed by the obvious limitations restricting the content of *elogium*, to perpetuate a life and to set it up as an example of achievement and behavior. Constant Martha, whose essay on the funeral speech among the Romans Vollmer's classic monograph surpasses in exhaustiveness though not in literary grace, asserted that the Romans who read a *laudatio* "*lisaient l'histoire de toute une vie.*"[55] Emended by the insertion of the adjective *encomiologique* after *l'histoire*, the assertion may stand approved.

"Who read," we may say, because in the time of Cicero there were in circulation published *laudationes* dating from the Second Punic War.[56] The practice of committing them to writing must have originated at a period still earlier. Perpetuation by the written word had had prior to the last quarter of the third century B.C. a history to be reckoned in centuries so far as legal and official documents are concerned, in decades if we think of such specimens of oratory as the famous speech of Appius Claudius against peace with King Pyrrhus. The incentives to secure literary permanence for the funeral speech would be strong even in the ruder days of Rome—quite as strong as were the motives that caused the publication of Claudius' speech.

[55] *Revue des deux mondes*, XXI (1877), 675.

[56] Cicero *De. senec.* 12.

The strictures passed by Cicero[57] and Livy[58] upon the liberties taken with history by the authors of *laudationes* cannot, it is needless to remind the tolerant reader of this book, dislodge the average funeral speech from the ordinary levels of veracity fixed by the easygoing standards of ancient encomiastic biography. Neither have Cicero's somewhat patronizing tone concerning the literary qualities of the old *laudationes*[59] and his feeling that applause of the orator was out of place in the solemn funeral assemblage[60] anything to do with the standing of the eulogy as a biographical document. Son, kinsman, or official associate of the dead man might or might not have been appointed an orator by nature herself; nevertheless the chosen spokesman had to meet the exigencies of the occasion. A close following of copy as represented in the specimens of the funeral speech to which he had access, a mechanical recourse to traditional methods and material must, in the older days especially, have given rise to many a crude stylistic performance by 'prentice hands. Small wonder that Cicero, wedded to Greek theories of technique, could not discern in these casual productions of previous generations the spontaneous vigor and the untutored eloquence that he found in the pioneers of Roman forensic oratory. For our calculations it is a matter of no small moment that, long before the days of book biography, the Romans had molded for themselves a prose form devoted to the history and the appreciation of a person's life. This recording of a personality in isolation was the result

[57] *Brutus* 62.

[58] viii. 40.

[59] *Op. cit.* 61.

[60] *De orat.* ii. 84. 341.

of a folkway and gave scope for portraying and evaluating a human life when the Romans were free literary agents. It must be the task of the next chapter to carry these implications still farther.

CHAPTER VIII

ROMAN TALENTS AND GREEK MODELS

And there are compositions of the same strain to be found in the books of all ages.

—Emerson, *Essay on History*.

The derivative relationship in which most branches of Latin literature stand to the Greek did not prevent the Roman from imparting distinctive character to work modeled on or inspired by Greek prototypes. The conscious efforts of adaptation and selection, it is true, displaced with the Roman craftsman the welling spontaneity that led to the creation by the Greeks of the various literary forms. Yet the deliberative processes of the intellect may win through to originality. This triumph is not alone an achievement of spiritual afflatus. Individual and national traits, controlling Roman pens as they wrote over the fresh pages inscribed by Hellenic creativity, produced literary palimpsests, to be sure, but palimpsests on which the later hands added something beyond a mere retracing. Thanks to the truer standards of criticism that modern scholarship has learned to apply in its study of the several productions of Roman belles-lettres, we have emancipated ourselves from the erroneous notion, especially promulgated by the eighteenth century's access of devotion to the Greek masterpieces, that all Roman literature worthy of the name is only a servile imitation of Greek. That reproach is uttered nowadays only by the half-informed.

In certain instances we comprehend more clearly than did the Romans themselves the full measure of the originality they attained. The Italian Elishas were wont to plume themselves on having donned the mantles of the Greek Elijahs. The garb was often adjusted in a fashion that was essentially new. Vergil's *Ascraeum carmen* has greater spiritual contrasts with the *Works and Days* than likenesses to it. Our appreciation of the native elements in Plautus grows apace. With the exception of Tibullus, the Augustan elegists insisted on voicing their conventional declaration that Callimachus and Philitas were their masters. Nevertheless, the Roman exponents achieved an individuality as regards technique and atmosphere that was tantamount to novelty. Quintilian's comment, "In elegy, too, we challenge the Greeks,"[1] was founded on a basis more solid than chauvinistic prejudice.

The Roman elegist had to cultivate a state of mind that amounted to a revolutionary departure from the old-time attitude. Sentimental gallantry, lovesick surrender, in the city or in the more romantic setting of the country, to triumphant femininity had nothing in common with the robust, heartily physical views of the genuine Roman temperament. The sturdy fathers of the Roman state would have felt nothing but contempt for a program of life that played havoc with the national ideals of *gravitas* and *constantia*, and set the languishing existence of the

[1] *Inst. orat.* x. 1. 93.

carpet-knight above the claims of military and civic service. On the other hand, what the Roman satirist took over from Greek philosophical diatribe, whatever Greek fable, mime, and comedy may have suggested in the way of pungent invective, pithy anecdote, breadth of caricature, and playful parody, merely added wealth and quality to native stores. The Puck of satire knows no barriers of clime or nationality but "puts a girdle round about the earth." The satiric spirit was indigenous to Egypt, Greece, and Italy. As was the case with satire, so is it true that to the type of biographical composition most favored in Rome, namely, the commemorative record of a citizen's life, Greece had nothing to contribute that was out of keeping with native predilections that had spontaneously expressed themselves.

These predilections were deeply rooted in the soil of national prejudices and from the start were at variance with the Greek mode. Nowhere are the differences between the two ethnic temperaments more strikingly illustrated than in the sepulchral art and literature of the two races. The student of biography may with great profit bear these contrasts in mind. Obviously, inference must not be carried to extremes and it must be based upon study of those epochs that represent most faithfully inborn attitude as this existed before cosmopolitanism had modified original Greek ideals and Rome had reacted to Hellenistic methods. It needs but a smattering of Greek art to realize how charged is Greek tomb sculpture with idealism and symbolism. That these tendencies were elemental to the race is clear at once from the sixth century specimens; a spirit of heroization, which saw the dead as gods and hence, so far as technical skill permitted, strove to represent them as greater than reality and more beautiful, dictated the types of these earlier efforts of commemoration.[2] As art advanced, the principle persisted. So the vast majority of grave stelae on into the fourth century portray the type of humanity—athlete, warrior, mother, nurse—to which the dead belonged, not the particular man or woman. The scenes themselves, whether they picture the devoted family group, linked by ties that death cannot sever, vouchsafe a glimpse into the homely routine of daily life, or depict the stirring action of the combat, as on the famous stele of Dexileos[3] and the so-called Alexander Sarcophagus, avoid photographic realism and literal truth.[4] It is emblematic of Greek principles that Dexileos, who was himself the victim of the enemy, should be shown in a moment of triumph, a charging knight in the act of piercing a fallen adversary.[5] The artist must needs depict what might have been, not what actually befell.

Utterly foreign to the spirit that moved the Greek to grasp and express in his commemorative art the typically suggestive and to eschew the specific moment[6] was the mimetic show contrived by the Roman with his wax portrait masks. The rigid

[2] M. Collignon, *Les statues funéraires dans l'art grec* (Paris, Leroux, 1911), 380.

[3] A. Conze, *Die attischen Grabreliefs*, II, 1 no. 1158; II, 2, pl. CCXLVIII; Collignon, *op. cit.* 95.

[4] A. Furtwängler and H. L. Urlichs, *Greek and Roman Sculpture* (trans. by H. Taylor, London, J. M. Dent, 1914), 145.

[5] Percy Gardner, *Sculptured Tombs of Hellas* (London, Macmillan, 1896), 147, 148.

[6] With, of course, such occasional exceptions as the astonishing picture on the stele from Pagasae of the death in childbirth; *Ephem. arch.* 1908, Pl. 1 facing p. 149.

modeling and the dry, prosaic lineaments discernible on certain examples of Roman portraiture seem to perpetuate the bluff realism of the wax image.[7] As M. Galletier[8] has well remarked in his interesting work, the heads sculptured on Roman funerary monuments have always the appearance of true portraits. By a similar instinct the Roman was actuated to introduce into epitaphs those explicit data that would cause the departed subject to stand out as a distinctive personality. Taken by and large, Greek tomb inscriptions do not tend toward the wealth of personal details which, to the sympathetic amusement of the modern reader, are found amassed in the epitaphs of Romans of the humblest classes. In the fourth century, when the individual had acquired a larger place in the Greek scheme of life, the epitaphs begin to elaborate on the simple brevity characteristic of fifth-century monuments. However, they still tend to be tributes rather than records. They relate in a general way a story of death, animadvert upon merit, and voice the survivors' sense of loss. Biographical details such as the statement that Dexileos was one of the "Five Horsemen," whatever the real meaning of this phrase may be, are exceptional.

The concessions that sounder methods of criticism than those formerly in vogue have increasingly made to Roman originality in other fields of literature have not been extended to biography. Rather, the trend of opinion has been away from earlier theories promulgated by scholars minded to be liberal

[7] A. Hekler, *Greek and Roman Portraits* (London, Heinemann, 1912), xxvi.

[8] *Op. cit.* 95, 96.

in their acknowledgment of the presence in certain specimens of Roman biography of elements domestic in origin. Thus Leo's thesis that Suetonius was a conscious adapter of the form in which the learned Alexandrian biography was cast and that this biographer's originality of execution displayed itself only in the application of a method better fitted for the lives of men of letters to the lives of men of action, stands in abrupt contrast with Nissen's[9] view, now forty years old. This eminent scholar sought to show that the scheme characteristic of the *Lives of the Caesars* was inspired by the *Index rerum a se gestarum*, as Suetonius[10] terms it, composed by Augustus and inscribed after the death of the emperor on bronze stelae set up at the door of his mausoleum. For the precedent of this autobiographical memorandum it is unnecessary to point, as some scholars have done, to monumental records of virtues and deeds written by or for the Egyptian kings and couched in the first person. Augustus both in public and private life posed as a Roman of the old school. Hence as the careful housefather of former days kept and handed on to his descendants a record-book of the important concerns of his life in and out of office, so the first *princeps* rendered for all men to see an accounting of his career. Thus, if it could be believed that Suetonius fashioned his biographies after this norm, his inspiration would be satisfactorily Roman.

The more or less fragmentary reproductions of this great autobiographical inscription—in recent years British and American enterprise has added

[9] *R. M.* XLI (1886), 481–99. [10] *Aug.* 101.

another to the copies known[11]—reveal its nature as an organized compilation of the deeds of Augustus both in military and civil life, his measures of administration, the offices held by him, the honors accorded to him, the buildings with which he or others acting on his suggestion adorned the city. Augustus grouped the various entries in this log-book of his long voyage as captain of the Roman ship of state according to categories, *per species*. Herein lies the chief resemblance of the Suetonian biographies to the inscription. Suetonius' knowledge of the *Index rerum gestarum* was not limited to the fact of its composition. Certain data found in the *Life of the Deified Augustus* parallel so closely in content and phraseology contexts of the inscription that the view is generally held that Suetonius drew upon the record, not in its monumental form, but from the documentary version preserved in the imperial archives.

To the detriment of the merit to be attributed to Roman inventiveness in the field of biography, Nissen's theory has not stood the test of scrutiny. It was effectively demolished by W. L. Schmidt[12] in a study that to some degree paved the way for Leo. At least Schmidt anticipated Leo in discoursing upon the resemblance borne by the Suetonian lives of literary men to such products of the Greek grammatical biographers as the *Lives of the Ten Orators*, and in concluding that in this field of biography Suetonius and Nepos before him were imitators of

[11] Sir William Ramsay, *Jour. of Rom. Stud.* VI (1916), 108–29; D. M. Robinson, *Am. Jour. of Philol.* XLVII (1926), 1–54.

[12] *De Romanorum imprimis Suetonii arte biographica* (Marburg, Dumont-Schaub, 1891).

Greek procedure. The attitude taken by Schmidt with respect to the presence in Greek biography of the method of exposition by categories tends, on the whole, to be agnostic, although, because of the constant dependence of Roman men of letters on Greek predecessors, he regards it as a priori plausible that the Greeks had anticipated the Romans in this technical principle of biographical exposition. Great stress is laid by him on the fact that in certain of the *Lives* of Nepos, notably the *Epaminondas* and the *Atticus*, the author followed the topical method. Strangely enough, Schmidt failed to take cognizance of a complication resident in the respective characters of the two examples from the biographies of Nepos and of the normal Suetonian treatment of an emperor. The former are encomiastic, the latter, by intention, informatory. Had Schmidt remembered that from the earliest specimens of prose encomium among the Greeks the topical method of delineating virtues was canonical, he would not have confined himself to searching for analogy to the Suetonian scheme in Plutarch.

Potent though the spell of Leo's presentation of his views has remained, doubts have been harbored as to the entire cogency of his derivation of the Suetonian form of biography from Greek prototypes. The extant lives of Vergil, Horace, and Terence, which in substance at least reproduce the original studies devoted to these poets by Suetonius, are analogous in respect to arrangement of subject-matter to the manifold specimens of Greek learned biography. The unstudied diction of the Roman parallels the concise notebook style of the Alexandrian *vitae*. The topics treated by him belong to the customary rubrics, and his information is often, as with his forerunners in biography, the result of deduction from the writings of the author whose life he records. Suetonius' little biographies of literary men are miniatures of his *Lives of the Caesars*, though in the latter the number of rubrics has, naturally, increased. Emperor's careers are more varied and eventful than are the lives of men of letters, and furthermore both acts and personality are more copiously documented.

There is sometimes a melancholy pleasure, after long years of mulling over a subject, in recalling the unmitigated enthusiasms of dogmatic youth. The present writer likes to dwell in thought upon the thrill with which on his first reading of *Die griechisch-römische Biographie*—more years ago than he cares to remember—he was persuaded by the lucid argumentation of the book and its captivating manner. *Omnia fert aetas*, dogmatism also. The misgivings that assail one as to Leo's theory, the beautiful simplicity of which makes in itself a strong appeal to the orderly minded philologian, ever tempted to subscribe to an attractive literary evolution, are, to be sure, inspired by general considerations. Specific evidence does seem all on Leo's side. As the acquaintance of Suetonius with the work of the Peripatetic biographers is sufficiently attested by his own allusion to them, so his familiarity with the grammatical lives may be taken for granted.

Nevertheless, it is undeniable that the methodical analysis and the formal grouping, according to topics of career and personality, that give the *Lives of the*

Caesars their character might be due to the perpetuation of a mode as natural to the Roman mind as it came to be inherent in the products of Greek formal biography. On a small scale, the *elogia* of Barbatus and his son, which itemize schematically character, offices, military deeds, and building activity, anticipate the essential qualities of the *Index* of Augustus and the biographies of Suetonius. Moreover, the *Lives of the Caesars* reflect perfectly the mental traits and the literary processes of the author himself. He was a compiler extraordinary, a chronic lexicographer; many of his books were organizations of material under head and subhead and were thus the results of the industrious use of the method of the 'card catalogue' or its ancient equivalent. Perhaps the cataloguist's professional devotion to the method of lemma and article was chiefly instrumental in conferring upon his biographies their likeness to repertoria. This was sufficient explanation for A. Macé,[18] writing previous to the appearance of Leo's book and innocent of any necessity for seeking any lineal connection of the Suetonian biographical form with Greek forerunners. According to this scholar, Suetonius classified and listed the data that he had gathered concerning his human subjects "comme il eût catalogué, dans les paragraphes d'une 'ars' [grammatica] i.e. les noms, les verbes, les adjectives." There is food for thought in this.

Knowledge on the part of a given mind of a literary performance antedating its own similar effort does not of necessity inspire or control that mind's

[18] *Essai sur Suétone* in *Bibliothèque des écoles françaises d'Athènes et de Rome*, LXXXII (1900), 54, 239, 322. Schmidt, in spite of his tendencies, emphasized the influence of the literary individuality of Suetonius on the form of his biographies; *op. cit.* 31.

practice. The distinction between the influence of a literary prototype and a writer's own response to the promptings of a natural, independent option are often quite imponderable. Something that is old may be for his purpose tantamount to new, since the old is also the ineluctable formula for his particular design. The book *De vita propria* of Jerome Cardan, scientist and physician, one of the ablest minds of the sixteenth century as his life-sketch is one of the outstanding specimens of self-revelatory literature, possesses a striking likeness in form—or formlessness—to the Suetonian scheme of literary portraiture. Through the great bulk of the treatise the contents are grouped under captions such as personal appearance, health, mode of life, character, friends and patrons, clothing, dwellings, marriage and children, honors and distinctions. We learn from his own statement that Cardan had read his Suetonius; at least, in the fourth chapter of his autobiography, in which he presents for the convenience of his readers an epitome of his career from birth to the time of writing, Suetonius is criticized for his failure to adopt a like plan. Yet the nature of Cardan's book reproduces so faithfully his own intellectual personality that one somehow feels that he would in any case have framed his autobiography as he did. His was a scientist's mind, ever exercised with observation and classification, yet untrammeled by exactions of unity or consistency, and tremendously discursive in its interests. So his autobiography is a disconnected series of diagnoses of his personality and reports rendered concerning himself, a spasmodic and redundant chronicling notwithstanding its outwardly precise scheme.

Biographical composition does not in the very nature of the case permit the variety of procedure attainable in richer and more imaginative fields of literature. Hence between the works of biographers separated in time and environment there are bound to be analogies not due to literary contact. The truth will be that minds confronted with similar tasks and actuated by the same purposes have fallen independently into the use of a common alphabet of expression. Because Goethe's memorial of Philipp Hackert opens with the stereotyped phrases of the average obituary, it does not follow that Goethe was imitating any specific precedents.[14] When, as we have seen was the case, certain Christian biographers utilized the dialogue form, there is no reason to suppose that they were consciously reviving the older literary mode of Satyrus. Is it not possible that this Suetonian scheme, which has been with so many portentous parallels and such solemn verbiage dignified into a seriously ratiocinated device, has been thereby too highly sublimated, too formally divorced from the natural processes of a certain kind of intellect? I am persuaded that the manner of Suetonian biography is as much Roman as Greek, as truly autogenic as mediated.

Among the Romans informatory biography, whether devoted to representatives of learning and literature or applied to emperors' lives in place of history (a substitute, be it said, of such glamor as to thrust historiography permanently into the background after the epoch of Suetonius and Tacitus), responded, of course, to interests acquired in the

[14] I borrow this illustration from Frey, *op. cit.* 4, n. 2.

progress of culture. It was otherwise with purely commemorative biography. This answered to a need indigenous to a race surpassed by no people, ancient or modern, in its appetite for fame and the store set on the various methods of perpetuating individual glory. Political and social conditions at Rome were peculiarly calculated to foster a free production of commemorative life-histories. The circles of friends, henchmen, and protégés of various sorts that formed about the Roman grandee as steel filings cluster about the magnet, were natural nurseries of benevolently intentioned biography. The educated freedman became in more than one instance the 'authorized' biographer of the magnate to whom he was attached. These cliental productions extended to prose the literary exploitation for which, to quote a classic instance, M. Fulvius Nobilior, consul in 189 B.C., had taken with him to his province the poet Ennius. In the next century Cornelius Epicadus, freedman of Sulla, is found completing the dictator's autobiographical treatment of his career;[15] this work, like the work of L. Voltacilius Pitholaus (or Plotus) on the achievements of Pompey the Great and Pompey's father,[16] was actuated by the biographical spirit. Tiro's life of Cicero[17] and the life of Augustus by Julius Marathus, the *princeps*' freedman and keeper of records,[18] are further examples of biography devoted to a great man by a literary retainer. In contrast with the compact sketches of Suetonius, such works

[15] Suetonius *De grammaticis* 12.

[16] Suet. *De rhetoribus* 3.

[17] The fragments are collected in H. Peter, *Historicorum Romanorum fragmenta*, 212.

[18] *Ibid.*, 269.

might run to several books.[19] Their partisan tone, which might be taken for granted, is demonstrated by the information that we have concerning them.[20]

In the last century of the Republic the composition of a biographical tribute to a man who had left his mark on the history of the times was as natural a thought as it is today. The freeborn Roman, moved by the usual incentives to commemorative biography, friendship, political or intellectual sympathy, would treat the lives of his associates or his admirations. Nepos in writing lives of Cicero and Atticus did not stray for a subject outside his social milieu. Cornelius Balbus and C. Oppius, friends of Julius Caesar, commemorated the dictator in books which *testimonia* reveal were biographical.[21] The personality of Cato Uticensis became a veritable cult center of biographical tribute;[22] in the days of terror under Nero, Thrasea Paetus, himself a Stoic and Catonian character, renewed the offering of biographical incense on the old shrine.[23] The Elder Pliny felt that the composition of a biography of his friend Pomponius Secundus, who was praised as a poet and also rose to the consulship, was a duty owed to friendship.[24]

[19] We have a reference to the fourth book of Tiro's biography of Cicero; Asconius *in Mil.* 48. 25–26 Clark.

[20] E.g., Tiro's assertion that Cicero divorced Terentia and married his rich ward not for love but to secure money with which to pay his debts; Plut. *Cic.* 41; Marathus' determination to give Augustus as commanding a stature as possible; Suet. *Aug.* 79.

[21] Peter, *op. cit.* 248, 249.

[22] Munatius Rufus and M. Fadius Gallus composed such works; Plut. *Cato Min.* 37; Cicero *Ad fam.* vii. 24. 2. Cicero's published *laudatio Catonis* called forth counterblasts from Caesar and Hirtius, as is well known, and impelled M. Brutus to write an encomium supplementary of it.

[23] Plut. *op. cit.* 25, 37.

[24] Pliny *Epist.* iii. 5. 3.

It is needless for our purpose to multiply examples here, the more because analogous expressions of the commemorative spirit will have to be mentioned later. There can be no doubt that the growth of commemorative biography at Rome was so copious because the national genius had been receptive to such literature from time immemorial and had made its own experiments before it came into contact with Grecian modes. It did not have to learn from the Greeks the power to appreciate and record a mortal career. The long-established wish had been father to the thought. It would seem, therefore, that scholarship, in its estimate of those specimens of biographical activity that carried on the memorial aim with which *elogium* and *laudatio* were animated, would be minded especially to search for survivals of national mode and capability. Here again the tendency has been in the other direction.

The long debate concerning the literary character and antecedents of the *Agricola* is the most signal instance of the kind. The venerable theory of Hübner,[25] who held that the treatise is a published version of an actually delivered funeral speech, and our only completely surviving specimen, has been left as far below the horizon of criticism as Nissen's explanation of the genesis of the Suetonian form of biography. For the last twenty-five years scholars in general have paid scant courtesy to the thought that the *Agricola* owed anything to the paternity of the *laudatio*, national institution though this was. Most students of the *Agricola* have been willing to concede that the historical interests of Tacitus, later

[25] *Hermes* I (1866), 438–48.

to materialize in his great annalistic works, were already to the fore when he composed his pious tribute to his father-in-law. Hence he was impelled to introduce into the book material properly suited to a history of Britain and of the campaigns carried on under Agricola's leadership. It has been held that this liberty taken within the limits of an ostensible biography—there is by no means unanimity as to the extent of the admixture of historical material—alone imparts to the work a unique character as compared with Greek encomiastic biographies. Owing to this departure only, it is asserted, does the *Agricola* possess an originality attributable not to generically Roman influences but to an individual Roman's impulse.

At the opposite pole from Hübner's theory stands Professor Gudeman's[28] view that the *Agricola* is a perfectly normal specimen of the *basilikos logos* or panegyric of a king, in the composition of which Tacitus followed the recipes formulated by the handbooks of Greek rhetoric. Gudeman's acute thought of measuring the biography by Greek rhetorical principles brought the study of the treatise into new paths. Nevertheless, there is a fatal fascination that nearly always attends such efforts to make Roman productions in literature conform with orthodox Greek models. With deference be it said that the preconceived view tempts one to an optimistic manipulation of data. One must go to extravagant lengths if the *Agricola* is to be reconciled with the normal pattern of encomium. Too many chapters are devoted exclusively to the political history, the

[28] Presented most fully in his German edition of the *Agricola* (Berlin, Weidmann, 1902), 1–13.

geography, and the ethnology of Britain and do not so much as mention the hero's name. On the other hand Leo,[27] in his just protest against Gudeman's determined adjustment of the *Agricola's* manner and content to the norm of encomiastic biography, in his turn overstressed the admixture of historical elements. It remained for Professor Hendrickson[28] to make clear in one of the soundest pieces of criticism ever devoted to this much-discussed treatise that many chapters in which Leo traced merely the technique of the historian contrive to keep Agricola in the foreground. Under the historical manner is disguised subtly that of the encomiast. The aim of eulogy is attained by suggestion, by characterization direct and indirect, as well as by objective appreciation.

In reviewing the possible literary prototypes of the *Agricola* as well as of the whole body of kindred works produced by the Romans, Leo kept his glances fixed on Greek models as unwaveringly as did Gudeman. The *Evagoras* and the *Agesilaus*, marking the beginning of the long series of memorial tributes to which the Roman encomiastic biography belongs, served as models to the Roman craftsman, whether by direct imitation or by adherence to the methods that the two Greek works were foremost in crystallizing. Leo, to be sure, admitted the affinity between Roman memorial biography and the *laudatio* in respect to spirit and aim, but he dismissed firmly the possibility that the *laudatio* affected the organic development of book biography. Hendrickson sug-

[27] *Die griech.-röm. Biog.* 224–33.

[28] *The Proconsulate of Julius Agricola* (The Decennial Publications of the University of Chicago, VI, 1902), 29–59.

gested in passing that the *laudatio funebris* must have influenced the composition of biographies of friends and relatives to the extent of imparting to them a markedly encomiastic character. However, since his paper was chiefly concerned with other ends, he did not seek to carry the analogy farther.

The more one meditates upon the literary character of the *laudatio*, compares it in respect to aim and subject-matter with such extant specimens of memorial book biography as the *Atticus* of Nepos and the *Agricola*, the more righteous seems the conviction that it is myopic criticism to see in these works the continuations of Greek precedent only. The fact that the *laudatio* was primarily a spoken tribute does not disqualify it from contact with the *Agricola*, Leo to the contrary notwithstanding. The *Agricola* has in many contexts a pronounced oratorical ring. When once the *laudatio* passed into permanent documentary form, it fell into the literary bailiwick tenanted by biographical memorials proper, originally written as books or life-sketches. These pious tributes inevitably partook of the aim and the mood of the funeral speech. The word *laudare* was used indifferently to describe the function of an author who wrote a eulogistic life of a dead man and of an orator who made a speech over him[29] which afterwards might have at least a limited circulation in book form.

The book memorial biography was regarded by the Romans themselves as a by-form of the *laudatio*. The written eulogy was the natural substitute when for some reason, such as a death in foreign parts,

[29] E.g., *Agricola* 2; Suet. *Iul.* 6; *Claud.* 1.

the usual speech had to be dispensed with.[30] In the second chapter of the *Agricola* Tacitus refers to two memorial biographies; one was a life of Thrasea Paetus written by that stoic's stout-hearted friend, Rusticus Arulenus; the other was a life of Helvidius Priscus, who died a victim of Vespasian's repressive measures, and at the request of Fannia, the bereaved wife, was honored by a literary eulogy composed by Pliny's friend, Herennius Senecio. These books, written some years after the deaths of their subjects, were belated *laudationes*, we may plausibly assume, intended to compensate for the actual spoken eulogies that would certainly be denied to alleged enemies of the state. It is an enlightening thought that Tacitus cited these works and reprobated Domitian's suppression of them because his *Agricola* was a work identical with them in character and elicited by the same exigent circumstances. It, too, is a substitute for the formal oration. If Tacitus had been present in Rome when Agricola died, the *laudatio funebris* would certainly have been pronounced by him unless Domitian's hostility, of which Tacitus doubtless makes too much, had prevented.

Nepos wrote the major portion of the *Atticus* during the lifetime of the subject. This fact might seem to differentiate the sketch from other specimens of Roman memorial biography. But the addition of four chapters after the death of Atticus renders this life as true an example of the pious memorial as are the *Agricola* and its kind. All alike, let us remember,

[30] The earliest known instance seems to be the eulogy composed by M. Brutus in honor of Appius Claudius, his father-in-law, who died in 49 B.C. *See* Fr. Münzer, *Römische Adelsparteien und Adelsfamilien* (Stuttgart, Metzler, 1920), 341; Vollmer, *op. cit.* 469, 482.

were classed by Leo merely as Roman continuations of Greek biographical encomium, and his opinion has, on the whole, remained canonical.

But, as Homer says of the courses of day and night in the land of the midnight sun, the "paths" of Greek biographical encomium and of the Roman *laudatio* were bound to "run close together." Both alike were works of special pleading, hence were colored by partisanship, real or assumed. Even the comparatively judicial Polybius remarks that his biography of Philopoemen differed from history in that, as was the rule of encomia, it was "a rhetorical amplification of his [subject's] deeds."[31] On the Roman side roseate exaggeration of a man's nobility of lineage and of the honors that had fallen to his lot was a general practice in the funeral speech.[32] The characterization given by Polybius of the *laudatio* as he heard it applies perfectly in substance to the *Evagoras* and the *Agesilaus.* "The eulogist," he says, "tells about the virtues of the deceased and the acts performed by him in his lifetime." Even though the description of Polybius dates from a time subsequent to the first incursions of Greek literary culture into Rome, there is not the slightest reason to assume that his words would not fit any *laudatio* of earlier periods. A continuity of literary practice would inevitably result from the preservation of the *laudationes* in the family archives and their use as models and sources for later efforts.

[31] x. 21 (24). 8.

[32] *See* p. 219, n. 57, 58. Münzer, *op. cit.* 132, 133, warns against the tendency of modern research to accept sweepingly the ancients' disparagement of the credibility of the *laudationes.* Such falsification of history as there was, he contends, would be the work only of prominent plebeian families.

Our résumé in the previous chapter has shown that the topics treated in the funeral speech square, to put it conservatively, quite as fully with the common stuff of biography as do the contents of the Greek biographical encomium. Variations touch detail rather than principle, and, if we are comparing the *basilikos logos* with the typical *laudatio*, are partly inherent in the differences between the places occupied in the world by the respective subjects. Furthermore, the matter-of-fact respect paid by the Roman mind to record of the facts of life and fortune, as well as the contrast between the less systematized Greek official life and the orderly fashion in which the career of the average Roman of position was punctuated by his steps up the ladder of preferment, must have secured to the *laudatio* a precise objectivity which even encomia of a citizen like Gryllus could not have rivaled. Free narrative of historical events was common to both encomium and *laudatio*. On all these counts of subject-matter our surviving specimens of book memorial biography approach the Roman funeral speech as closely as, or more closely than they approach Greek encomium. But there are considerations of greater import yet to be noted: Even in that relatively early period of Latin literature when Rome was at death grips with Hannibal, there were *laudationes* composed that show a talent developed beyond a bare recital of personality and career. Their authors, from whatever source instructed, fell into the devices and responded to the moods of Greek commemorative forms, even though to the ear of a Cicero sentences jolted and cadence was lacking.

After Pliny the Elder has given in the passage before noted[33] the digest of the honors held by L. Metellus (not forgetting the elephants' parade, as Kipling might say), there follows a quotation in consecutive text from the son's eulogy of his father. The opening sentence is: "Metellus achieved the ten greatest and most excellent things in the quest of which men of wisdom spend their lives." These ten desiderata of the perfect life follow; note how thoroughly of the practical Roman world these ambitions are:

> Metellus wished to be a champion warrior, the best orator, the bravest general, to hold command in the greatest undertakings, to meet with highest official preferment, to be a leader in wisdom, to be deemed the leading senator, to gain great wealth by honest methods, to leave many children, and to be the most distinguished man of the state. These things fell to his lot, and to the lot of no other man since the founding of Rome.

The unmistakable analogy borne by this stray leaf from an early Roman biographical tribute to the *macarismi* of the *Evagoras* and the *Agesilaus* has never been pointed out. Neither has it been bracketed with the passage in which, in a precisely similar vein, Tacitus eloquently enumerates the separate articles of Agricola's felicity (44, 45) from both a positive and a negative point of view. These advantages are: A life ended in its prime but rich in glory; attainment of the true blessings of virtue; consular and triumphal honors; wealth sufficient for his desires;[34] the fact that he did not outlive wife and daughter;

[33] *See* p. 213.

[34] One's conception of Agricola's property will, of course, vary with his choice between the variants *speciosae non contigerant* in chap. 44 and *speciosae contigerant*.

integrity of position and reputation; unsevered links of relationship and friendship; immunity from the massacres that followed on his death. It seems to have escaped the notice of most critics and editors of the *Agricola*[35] that the configuration of this stately passage accords with the old Greek rhetorical commonplace. The likeness should have come as grist to the mills of those who have been bent on proving the fidelity of the *Agricola* to Greek models. As it is, however, the parallelism can have no such exclusive value in demonstration now that we are aware that an early Roman eulogist, self-instructed or following Roman mode, drew up a similar inventory of blessings, a summary which, because human wishes, wherever and whenever formed, have their universal objects, coincides in occasional detail with the earlier Greek and later Roman analogues.[36] A recent writer,[37] impressed by the presence of like summaries in the Roman historians' appraisals of careers, has indulged in the conventional hypothesis that the *laudatio* of Metellus set a mode imitated by the historians. The thought seems too human and too Roman to justify this conclusion.

The admonitory and consolatory mood pervading the final chapter of the *Agricola* and even certain conceits of the thought recall the epilogues of the *Evagoras* and the *Agesilaus*.[38] But the mood of con-

[35] The present writer includes himself in this reproach.

[36] As Evagoras is said to have excelled all in intelligence, so Metellus is credited with the possession of consummate wisdom; the felicity of both included many children. Wealth is a topic mentioned both in the *macarismus* of Agricola and in the summing up of Metellus' blessings.

[37] Münzer, *op. cit.* 263, n. 1.

[38] Gudeman's citation of parallels is perhaps the most comprehensive. C. W. Mendell, "Literary Reminiscences in the *Agricola*," *Trans. Am. Philol. Assoc.* LII (1921), 53–68, especially concerned himself with the

solation easily finds a place in all memorial tribute, poetical or prose. Certainly it was not foreign to the *laudatio*. In his essay *On Old Age* (12), when Cicero makes Cato the Elder allude to the speech delivered by Fabius Cunctator in honor of his son Q. Fabius, the censor is represented as saying: "When we read the *laudatio*, what philosopher do we not despise?" In the early days of Roman literature, the funeral orator, untaught by the Greeks, had learned to tap the sources of consolation and to meditate for his own comfort and that of the other mourners on the compensations that temper sorrow. Cicero's characterization points, not to the set consolatory themes of Greek philosophy and rhetoric, but to the home-spun, virile resignation of an old Roman father in the face of bereavement. This conception accords with Plutarch's description[39] of the oratory of Fabius. It is pronounced free from affected elegances; his manner is product and outward expression of a solidly sensible nature. Plutarch's critique, whether the traditional judgment or his own, is partly founded on knowledge of the *laudatio*, expressly referred to in the context of the *Life of Fabius*. Thus we again find the *Agricola* in as close contact with national as with Greek encomiastic utterance.

Every reader of the *Agricola* will recall the attention paid by Tacitus to the phases of his father-in-law's last illness, the pathetic allusions to the death-bed scene, and the reference to the final admonitions

similarities between Tacitus and his Roman predecessors in thought and language. It is difficult to discern how many of these parallels are due to imitation on the part of Tacitus, how many are commonplaces from the anthology, both Greek and Latin, of encomiastic literature.

[39] *Fabius* 1.

which the absence of the biographer and his wife prevented them from receiving from the lips of the dying man. The atmosphere of the concluding scene is there, even though Tacitus' treatment cannot vie with the realism with which Nepos describes, in language so frank as to be worthy of the attendant physicians themselves, the course of Atticus' fatal malady. The words in which the sick man apprised his friends of his resolve to hasten his death by voluntary starvation are directly quoted. Agrippa's demonstrations of sorrow and the gist of his grieved protest against his father-in-law's stoical determination form a part of the story.

Depiction of death scenes is always fraught with possibilities, dramatic and melodramatic, for portraying the character of the departed. "The tongues of dying men enforce attention like deep harmony." So it is that the final moments of personages and their last words have through the centuries been a common motive in biographical composition. Compilers ancient and modern, reckoning on the human interest of this sort of material, have devoted whole books to it,[40] though nowadays biographers tend to be more reticent in these matters than formerly they were.[41] Nepos and Tacitus could certainly have found ample precedent for their descriptions in the *laudationes*. The lips of no Roman eulogist would have been hushed before such an opportunity for

[40] E.g., the work of C. Fannius referred to by Pliny *Ep.* v. 5. 3, as *Exitus occisorum aut relegatorum a Nerone;* F. R. Marvin, *The Last Words (Real and Traditional) of Distinguished Men and Women* (New York, Revell, 1902).

[41] W. L. Cross in his delectable little essay, *An Outline of Biography from Plutarch to Strachey* (New York, Henry Holt, 1924), has some words on this subject.

eloquent magnification of conduct. An instance in point, Marcellus' account of his father's death in action, has previously been referred to. A passage from the Younger Pliny's letters[42] offers corroborative testimony that description of the death scene was a usual member of the funeral oration. Pliny is speaking of a work of Titinius Capito which contained accounts of the deaths of several illustrious friends. Having been unable to be present at their funerals, Pliny, obliging as always, proposes to attend a reading of the work. To hear this book read, is the comment, will be tantamount to listening to the funeral orations pronounced over them.

In our reconstruction of the Roman *laudatio* we have assumed that it attained the dimensions of true memorial biography as completely as it had, even in the days of the earliest examples of which we can form any concrete estimate, not as a result of Greek tutelage but in response to the indigenous qualities of the Roman mind and to universal, human impulse. Rome, of course, had had a foretaste of the finished prose eloquence of the Greeks in the days when the senators listened to Cineas, envoy of King Pyrrhus. It may be that, as Leo has suggested, the Romans by direct contact with Sicily and Greek Italy had gained some familiarity at the fountain-head with the esthetics of formal rhetoric. But at the close of the third century B.C. it was on poetry that the literary culture imported from the subjugated cities of Magna Graecia was exerting its transformative force. In the days of Polybius' sojourn in Rome, when Greek rhetoricians and philosophasters were

[42] viii. 12. 4–5.

becoming ubiquitous, it is difficult to see what acquaintance with the productions of formal rhetoric had to offer to the Roman funeral eulogist besides subtler stylistic elaboration and richer stores of conceits. The essentials of memorial biography had been discovered by the Romans themselves. Centuries of experimentation had solidified its literary attributes.

In the full flush of Roman devotion to Greek models parallelism between the *laudatio* and Greek biographical encomia in respect to aims and themes resulted in a complete synthesis of motives and technique. In such works as the *Atticus* and the *Agricola* it is wrong to see only efforts mechanically studied after the precedents of the Greek encomium. They are products of natural growth as well as of rhetorical virtuosity, literary compounds blended from the universal elements of encomiastic biography as this had developed in both races. It goes without saying that each biography, the *Agricola* especially, bears the stamp of the individual mind following its own bent apart from the conventional exactions of form.

In the case of the *Atticus* it is easy for the type of critic that bows down before the idol of rhetorical form to make much of the resemblance between the treatise and the *Agesilaus* of Xenophon in respect to arrangement of material. Beginning, as any normal biography would, with lineage, boyhood and education, the *Atticus* carries on the narrative from event to event; it sets forth in connection with the times items of the conduct of Atticus as citizen of Athens and Rome. This narrative portion, continued through the twelfth chapter, is followed by a topical exposition of his virtues, *continentia*, *fides*, *humanitas*, and *pietas;* it concludes with a treatment of his intellectual life, his antiquarian interests, that is, and the genealogical works due to this proclivity. The surface resemblance of this scheme to one of the methods of Greek biographical encomium does not prove to the heretical mind that Nepos, who, of course, was familiar with the *Agesilaus*,[43] meditated thus: "I am going to write a life of a good man and my friend; I shall fashion, therefore, an encomium of Atticus after the manner of Xenophon and the Greeks." After all, the likeness between the two treatises is superficial. The division in Nepos is between a characterization of Atticus as a citizen and a description of him as householder, friend, son, and literary man. There is no such distinction in the *Agesilaus* between the virtues displayed in public and in private life. The logical naturalness of the plan makes against any exclusive allocation of it to the Greek mind.

The *Agricola* does not present any such conspectus of virtues apart from the narrative. The portrayal of the several excellencies and abilities of the hero keeps pace with the chronological unfolding of his career. As from youth to manhood Agricola serves his novitiate in arms and in political life, and rises from one post to another, Tacitus weaves into the story his laudatory estimates of the conduct and capabilities of the man as these are revealed at every stage. Generally a sentence or two suffices. Again, a longer context is devoted to appreciation, as in the tribute paid to Agricola's régime in Aquitania (9),

[43] *Ages.* 1. 1.

and to his measures of administration in Britain (19). The atmosphere of this latter passage and its markedly antithetical style vividly recall Isocrates' general appraisal of Evagoras as ruler (42–46).[44] These passages, long or short, are dexterously made integral parts of the narrative. The reader is constantly orientated by references to contemporary history and to the successive periods of Agricola's career. Hence it is that Tacitus so imparted to his work the appearance of a book on Agricola and his times that occasionally critics have been beguiled by what is partly the result of conscious art, partly the result of the author's interests in history, into exaggerating the historical elements in the treatise.

The method in principle is the same as that followed by Nepos in the first twelve chapters of the *Atticus*, though the superior mentality and literary skill of Tacitus are always apparent. Tacitus also marks more definitely the succeeding chronological periods; the changes in the principate and the successive phases of Agricola's official career made for a treatment more clearly outlined than was feasible in the case of Atticus. Atticus was a spectator of the history of his times rather than an active participant in affairs, a man devoted to business and to literature. Hence his career could only be defined in

[44] Editors of the *Agricola* might have cited more numerous parallels between the treatise and the *Evagoras* than appear in their exegetical notes; e.g., the envy that assails the great, *Agr.* 1 and *Evag.* 6; the authors' depreciation of their literary ability, *Agr.* 3 and *Evag.* 73; each hero civilizes and educates a barbarous country, *Agr.* 21 and *Evag.* 47, 49, 50; the conditional assertion of the immortality of the great and good, *Agr.* 46 and *Evag.* 70; the protreptic appeal to surviving family, the disparagement of sculptured likenesses, and the challenge to perpetuate memory rather by imitation of the character of the dead, *Agr.* 46 and *Evag.* 73–76. Such resemblances as these are not surprising in view of the conventional nature of encomiastic tributes in general.

terms of the changing phases of political history. Such chronological signposts Nepos frequently sets up in the course of his life-sketch.

In respect to this lucid chronological development both Roman biographies surpass the broadly chronological presentation of the narrative portion of the *Agesilaus* and of the whole *Evagoras*. It would be especially illuminating to know whether in the funeral speech there was precedent for using the *cursus honorum* as an outline in which to sketch, as Tacitus does, event and conduct. Our knowledge of the *laudatio* fails here; yet, since *cursus honorum* and *res gestae* were essential ingredients of a portrayal of a Roman's life, and the latter were so indissolubly linked to the various offices, it is hard to believe that many a eulogist did not systematize his exposition as his subject's life had been in itself punctuated sequentially.

There is a further contrast between the two Greek works and their Roman analogues that shows a nearer approach by the authors of the latter to modern conceptions of a biographer's responsibility. Isocrates and Xenophon were more completely engrossed in praising a life than in transmitting a personality in all its essential details. Both the *Evagoras* and the *Agesilaus* are, therefore, declamatory in their effect. One seems primarily to be listening to the words of an orator seeking to persuade an audience to adopt his estimate of a person's character, incidentally to be reading a record of a life. Nepos interposes occasionally a challenging appeal after the encomiast's manner. "If the man who saves a ship from storm and from a sea beset with rocks is extolled with especial praise, why should not the sagacity of the man be deemed extraordinary who has won to safety through the many tempestuous blasts of civil life?" (*Att.* 10) recalls Xenophon's interrogatory outbursts to his invisible jury. Tacitus, on the contrary, in the strictly biographical portions of the *Agricola* preserves the tone of declarative record as completely as he does in the historical and ethnological chapters in which he is painting background. He does not break forth, in behalf of his hero, into rhapsodical bids for applause, or ask others to share his opinion. He chronicles the various items of Agricola's conduct, and points its excellence, now by comparison with ordinary standards of behavior exemplified by men confronted by emergencies and responsibilities of the sort that Agricola was called on to meet, now by briefly noting the impression created by Agricola's course of action on those who witnessed it.

Neither Nepos nor Tacitus, eulogistic though the aim of their delineations is, fails to honor biographical material for its own sake. Each assumes that posterity will wish to know, for the sake of knowing, specific things about his hero, will desire to picture him and his environment, not merely to admire him. Certain data owe their presence to the informatory motive only. Thus Nepos gives the amount of the legacy left to Atticus by his crabbed uncle, Q. Caecilius (5); mention of the fact of a large legacy would have been sufficient to illustrate the rewards of respectful piety. Reference to the locations of the city house of Atticus (13), to the grove that was its chief ornament, to the place of Atticus' burial (22), and the digression on the merits of Cicero's letters as a historical source (16) also reflect the informative rather than the encomiastic aim. These topics were introduced for the same reason that Suetonius records in his biographies analogous details. The last context (16) might bring some slight comfort to critics who have been unduly disturbed because Tacitus stepped for a moment aside from biography to relate (*Agr*. 28) the story of the mutinous cohort's voyage around John o'Groat's to the mainland.

Tacitus is less given to presenting small informatory details than is Nepos. However, Tacitus records even to the day the dates of birth and death (44), Nepos the date of death only (22). The description given by Tacitus of Agricola's personal appearance (44) is sketchy enough, but Nepos does not touch on this topic at all. Behind the inclusion of the detail in the *Agricola* was confessedly the informatory purpose: "If succeeding generations should desire to know his appearance also (i.e., as well as when he was born and when he died), he was attractive rather than imposing; his mien did not betoken an intense nature, but he had a most charming expression." This is the judicial tone of real biography. Tacitus had the discernment to realize that the world does not love a man of inhuman perfection. The quotation of Agricola's own confession that his youthful enthusiasm for philosophy threatened to pass the bounds proper for the gentlemanly amateur and the Roman man of affairs (4), our author's admission that his father-in-law had a temper that did not suffer knaves gladly (22), are true touches of discriminative portraiture. How modern are the tribute paid to the formative influence of an excellent mother, whose name, by the way, is given (4), and the consciousness that environment has an effect on tender years! This consciousness stands revealed in the comment of Tacitus on the debt owed by Agricola's probity to his education at Marseilles, "a place where Greek graces and provincial frugality are happily blended." (4)

In all the pother about the literary type and antecedents of the *Agricola* it has come to pass that the book has been grudgingly evaluated in respect to its merits as a biography, idealistic, to be sure, but not intemperately panegyrical. The *Agricola* loses much of its traditionally enigmatic character if interpreters do not exert themselves exclusively in discovering in it the fruits of rhetorical training, the results of deliberate study of Greek precedents and literal adherence to their doctrines, and a lust for literary reminiscence. Into its making went the play of an acute intelligence, independently alive to many of the desiderata of personal portraiture as these through the centuries had impinged on the minds of Roman as well as Greek commemorators—an intelligence bent on handing down, together with the fame of a revered man, some information concerning the times and places in which he had worthily comported himself.

INDEX

ERRATA

Page 113, line 7. *For* Symposim *read* Symposium.
Page 149, line 15. *For* Hanno *read* Hasdrubal.
Page 176, note 41. *For* B. Frey *read* H. Frey.